The Brown Bag, Blue Collar Recovery Planner

First Addiction Edition

Robert L. Hobbs, Jr.

Paduka Press
Atlanta

Disclaimer

The author of this book does not dispense medical advice or prescribe the use of any technique as a form of treatment for physical, emotional, or medical problems without the advice of a physician, directly or indirectly. The intent of the author is only to offer information of a general nature to help in your quest for well-being. In the event you use any of the information in this book, the author and publisher assume no responsibility for your actions.

Published by

 PADLIKA PRESS

Printed in the United States of America
Hardback
ISBN: 978-0-9989008-4-1
Paperback
ISBN: 978-0-9989008-9-6
EBook:
ISBN: 978-0-9989008-2-7

Dedication

To My Dad

Robert L. Hobbs, Sr.

Born December 7th, 1936
Died December 8th, 2019

In life you showed me how to live and now in death you showed me how to die. I am forever grateful for your life and your death.
I miss & love you, Dad!

Endorsements

The lure of drugs and alcohol is capturing today's youth and young adult population in its fatal grip. Ultimately, it may destroy our nation's future generations. The vicious cycle of abuse is one that teachers, parents, counselors, pastors, and other citizens decry on a daily basis. Dr. Robert Hobbs, a proven expert on Alcohol and Other Drug (AOD) use, provides crucial advice regarding recovery from the abuse of all major drugs.

Dr. Hobbs contends that in order to confront the monster that is destroying families and their quality of life, we should better understand the nature of drug and alcohol abusers and the natural progression of the disease. This powerful book also examines solutions for the fatal relationship between drugs and associated problems which create complex lives for addicts.

Finally, Dr. Hobbs presents his material through the eyes of a professional who has seen all sides of this battle including his own family's twists and turns with his son's addiction.

We now live in a society where 12-year-olds are budding alcoholics, and grandmothers, substituting for addicted or deceased parents, have begun regular addiction to prescribed pain medication; with the practical wisdom of this accessible guide we can learn the techniques that will save our next generation from ruining their lives through hopeless addiction.

I highly recommend this book and I salute Dr Hobbs for its honest and intense view of working hand in hand with the addict.

Robert Marchese, Former Deputy Director Northeast Ohio ADAMH/DD Emotional Behavioral Health Services

Bob takes the average (addicted) person and breaks down every aspect of not only getting that person to navigate the journey into recovery but also learning what that means. The education one will learn in this book is priceless and the book is a must read.

Readers will also learn about the conditions underlying the addiction like PTSD, hopelessness, and mental illness.

I would recommend this book for anyone; even if you do not have a loved one in addiction, you might just be able to help that friend in need.

Tim Ryan, A Man in Recovery, @AManInRecovery

The Brown Bag, Blue Collar, Recovery Planner is BRILLIANT. Rev. Dr. Robert L. Hobbs, Jr. has outdone himself this time. He talks about the "The State of American Behavioral Health", and as you probably know it is not good. But he doesn't just state the problem, Robert goes on to offer solutions, he gives us HOPE that recovery is possible. Hope and light and a "Recovery Planner" which gives the reader in depth information about the disease of addiction, and then takes us through a day by day plan to get and STAY clean and sober. From a safe and sane detox plan to mental, physical and spiritual wellness, and everything in between, Hobbs leaves no area untouched.

The daily work sheets and readings give the reader a clear-cut plan for each and every day. With "Healing Treatments" and "Daily Affirmations", everything needed for starting and maintaining recovery is here. Hobbs includes meeting attendance log as well as a reading list that includes some of my all-time favorites and The Big Book of Alcoholics Anonymous. Many times, when people begin recovery, they don't know what to do in between talking to their sponsor and going to meetings. Robert knows first-hand how important those early days in recovery are. Whether you are ready to get clean and sober or have been sober for a bit this book should sit at the top of your daily to dos.

In addition, people who sponsor others, people who are in recovery field, people who have a loved one they want to help, therapist and basically anyone touched by the disease of addiction should read this book. I give this book five stars.

Jeannie Rabb-Marshall, Co-Founder and President of Keys to Recovery Newspaper,
Vice President of Women's Association for Addiction Treatment (WAAT),
and a woman who has "recovered from a seemingly hopeless state of mind and body" for over 33 years.

Foreword

by Ryan Hampton
November 28, 2019

If you want something done, you've got to do it yourself.

That's incredibly clear to those of us who are working to fight this public health crisis. Addiction recovery policy is lagging while families, communities, grassroots organizers, and non-profits are on the cutting edge of saving lives. In this case, change is bubbling from the bottom up, not the top down. But without leadership, innovation, and a new way of thinking—there's only so much we can do. That's why I'm so honored to pen this brief foreword for Robert Hobbs' new book.

People keep dying. Obituary columns are full with articles about wonderful young men and women who had "bright futures." We are brokenhearted and tired. We're also frustrated and fed up. It's time for the government to look at what's working in the grassroots and support the sweeping changes we need.

As the crisis worsens, our families and communities are the ones bearing the burden of these monumental losses. Yet, we haven't given up hope and we haven't stopped pushing for change. If anything, the people who stand up most are actually working the hardest to stop this deadly drug epidemic. Families, churches, local law enforcement, grassroots organizers, philanthropists, and local leaders are the ones in the trenches. We experience the crisis first-hand. We love and care for people with substance use disorder.

The movement to help people with substance use disorder isn't a new one. It's been around for a century or more, functioning under different names, since the Revolutionary War. An early temperance movement started in the 1770s, when farmers in Connecticut, New York, and Virginia formed associations to ban whiskey distilling. In the 1820s, these groups spread and became more radical, calling for total abstinence from alcohol. They called alcohol a "scourge" and distributed pamphlets that showed families torn apart by intoxication. The Oxford Groups, Alcoholics Anonymous, and other spiritual programs have carried the banner of these early movements.

Now, our society is more sophisticated. A century ago, all we had was prayer: now, medicine, psychology, and other treatment modalities have shown that they are also useful tools to fight addiction. Private clinics and hospitals have often spearheaded experimental treatment for people who were considered "doomed" and untreatable. Today, we incorporate those methods into standard treatment for substance use disorder. They have become the "norm," because people on the front lines pushed hard to make this kind of help available. We're still doing this work today, through action networks, committees, and citizens' groups.

And that work must be done: there is no time to waste.

The grassroots recovery movement is innovative, responsive, and progressive. By keeping the focus on our mission, we've been able to accomplish a lot. There is still much more to do. The death toll continues to rise. And yet, the addiction crisis is not acknowledged as what it is: the largest public health crisis we've faced in a generation. It's claimed more American lives in this year alone than the entire Vietnam war.

Advocates and people with lived experience have accomplished so much over the last decade in destigmatizing substance use disorder, finding a place at the bargaining table, and focusing on health care and human rights. While non-profits, families, and communities fill in the massive gaps left by non-effective public policy, we must keep calling on legislators and decision makers to catch up.

We're light years ahead. And yet, for some people and their families, we're already too late. But that won't keep us from trudging forward, together.

One thing that recovery advocates, doctors, and addiction science all agree on is *connection*. Other, healthy people are the key to finding recovery and staying sober for long periods of time. While policy and funding are slow to meet demand, one of the best things we can do is support one another and create meaningful, valuable connections that support recovery. It sounds simple, but self-care, learning more about addiction, and connecting with people in the recovery community are the "prescription" for our illness. Slowly, research is catching up with what grassroots advocates and recovery groups have known for a century. We need help, and for that, we support each other.

We can't wait for someone to rescue us, so we've built our own lifeboats. Our community, out of necessity, has created some innovative ways to deal with the drug crisis. That's why I'm so excited about this book.

Many thanks to the innovative work of Bob Hobbs and the valuable contributions of so many that are pushing back against the drug epidemic. Your work is so valuable, and, in this public health crisis, essential.

You may not always make the front page, but we see you. And your work is not going unnoticed.

> *by Ryan Hampton,*
> *@RyanforRecovery, ryanhampton.org*
> *Son, Activist, Writer, & Person in Recovery from Addiction, Author: American Fix*

Acknowledgements

When I wrote my first book: Heroin-Living and Dying with an Addict You Love, How to Survive when Everyone Dies, I finished the entire project in 90 days; it was easier to remember everyone who had helped me in that case because everything was so fresh.

This project has taken nearly a year and I will definitely forget someone's valuable contribution and for that I both apologize and thank you for your contribution.

This manuscript has been proof-read at least a hundred times and edited five times. Proofreading is tedious work that I cannot do, so my friend Linda Bell did it for me. Her diligence was amazing, and I think you'll agree that the work output is nearly perfect.

The man who penned the foreword for me is one of the most influential persons in the recovery community. Ryan Hampton organizes protests against Big Pharma, fights for us as a Department of Justice appointee, writes for USA Today, consults multiple projects, and founds multiple causes including the Voices Project, while keeping his social media followers up to date with what's going on in the drug and addiction industry. Despite being one of the busiest yet most productive people in recovery, Ryan made time to write the foreword and found the time to fall in love and become engaged. Thank you and Congratulations Ryan.

Jeannie Rabb Marshall has been one of my biggest fans since Heroin Living and Dying and her editorial endorsement is much appreciated. She and her husband founded and operate the Keys to Recovery Newspaper.

Tim Ryan has a very busy schedule he's constantly on the road; he is seemingly always on an airplane, yet he still managed to support this work and I thank you Tim.

Bob Marchese is busier in retirement than he was when he worked with Ohio Mental Health and Addiction Services (OMHAS), but he too was able to read the manuscript and write an endorsement; I appreciate you Bob.

My buddies from Ohio University - my roommate Keith Kaple, and Brock Onat, my spiritual advisor and fellow board member at Stainless Souls, provided great comments and feedback and made the manuscript better than it was when I sent it to them.

Thank you to Don McDonnell for his continuous encouragement to reach higher and higher.

Thanks to Dave Keil for continuing to support me as a mentor and friend.

Special Thanks to Keith Harryhill, a virtual brother, for providing insight from the addicted person's point of view. Keith runs a treatment center in Florida

This work would not be possible without the generous donations to our cause by our benefactors and I'd like to take this time specially to thank Jason Keever whose regular support keeps us going.

Thanks to Helena Trangata for her candid feedback on an earlier version of the manuscript. I will release a simpler version in the future.

My parents continue to support me and my endeavors in my 50s as much as they did in my teens and I am forever grateful. (RIP DAD). I have also been well supported by all five of my brothers: Tommy, Kevin, Billy, Joey, and Ray. Finally, my brothers and sisters in AA, IOP, and in private counselling, as well as my counsellors, teachers, psychologists, and psychiatrists; I am forever in your debt.

Preface

The State of American Behavioral Health:

- 70,000 Accidental Overdose Deaths – mostly due to opioids (not including alcohol)

- 10,000,000 seriously contemplate suicide, 225,000 give suicide a valid try, 45,000 succeed

- 20,000,000 addicted to narcotics

- 20,000,000 active enabler/codependents of narcotic activity

- 2,000,000 sleep on the streets at least once per year

- 8,000,000 suffering with active traumatic stress daily; 45,000,000 annually

Meanwhile,

- 10% of 12-17 year olds suffer from Major Depressive Disorder

- 1 in 6 Americans are taking antipsychotic/antidepressants every day

- There are less than 125,000 doctoral level psychologists and psychiatrists; most over 55 years old

- Theres just 38,000 psychiatric hospital beds

- 60% of US counties are without a psychiatrist

- Opioid Use Disorder recovery rate is <13% following treatment

- Less than half of professional therapists are formally trained in suicidal tendency identification and prevention

What can you conclude?

- Politically, a 60,000 annual overdose rate would be considered a huge success – Think about that! More dead annually than the combined total in Vietnam is what success looks like

- There are too many people suffering from behavioral health issues, and

- Not nearly enough doctors or hospitals to address their needs

- 10% of what should be the most hopeful (the young) of our population, are hopeless

- Opioid Use Disorder recovery rates are a sham! After 30 days and $30,000, 87% relapse! Yet, we keep paying the same people over and over again.

What can we do?

- A complete overhaul of "the system" is in order, but it will take time and thousands more will die

- Innovation is key – if success is measured by beating a 13% success rate – what is there to lose – try everything

- We know that 30 days of treatment is not enough, $1,000/day is too expensive, AA alone is ineffective for OUD, there are not enough therapists, we need to act now – right now

- We can start, by providing those who suffer with tools they can use right now, on their own, to get started toward recovery, these planners are the toolboxes for the tools.

· We can integrate the tools and toolboxes with interactive and multi-media content that engages the suffering where they live – at home

· We can start right now!

· Additional Detail in Appendix 1

Rev. Dr. Robert Hobbs
The Realization of Stainless Souls
www.StainlessSouls.com

Notes and Sketches

Dear Readers

Dear Reader

First and foremost, this is a planner. Use it to organize your day, week, month, quarter. Secondly, it is packed with suggestions, thousands of suggestions, that have helped me immensely. Every suggestion has been carefully thought out to fit in the best possible place in the context of the book. You don't have to complete all the suggestions, but if you want to become clean and sober, you want to do your very best to **complete all the suggestions.**

If you fully commit, the planner that you hold in your hand is going to help you save your life. It is going to intervene in your life and put a halt to your use of illicit drugs and alcohol. (Well, the planner isn't but the contents of the planner and the content of your soul are going to.) The Brown Bag Blue Collar Recovery Systems are 90 days in length and require an average of 4 hours per day complete; that's 360 hours of dedicated recovery activity at your home and office.

Introduction

Too many alcoholics and addicted persons spend too many weeks, months, and years *after deciding* that they would *like to be* clean and sober, figuring out *how to become* clean and sober.

Even after multiple trips to rehabilitation centers, years in and out of recovery meetings, and after being presented with discharge plans, many *still don't know what to do on a daily basis* to become and remain clean and sober.

During this time, *most continue using their drug of choice* - and though committed to quitting once they have a plan - *while waiting for the plan* - **many die**. Their life-saving decisions were made - they just *didn't know where or how to start.*

Their deaths were both unfortunate and unnecessary.

In the AA system of recovery, we attempt to *"keep it simple stupid;"* but, simplicity can mean up to 22 hours per day with nothing to do - many newcomers become bored, and *they end up stupid* - then dead.

*"Don't drink, go to meetings, call your sponso*r," works 100% of the days where all three are practiced, and virtually none of the days where any one of the three are skipped. And of course, there is a delay between the time a newcomer enters the program, and the time when he or she has a sponsor - and then more time before beginning the steps and then finishing them.

How do we limit our losses in the period between the decision and the practice?

Then there are people who very badly want to quit, but they have jobs, families, and responsibilities that stand in the way of *finding a path.* Many of these people could benefit from a 30-day plus inpatient treatment program, but they could not afford the $1,000 per day price even with their insurance. Even if they could - they couldn't afford the time away from work or family. The opportunity cost is just too high.

These people often feel trapped.

They feel trapped both by their addictions and by their life circumstances.

Most never recover.

It just doesn't ever seem practical. Meaningful lives are lost not only to death but sometimes just to the continuous fog of inebriation, which spans an entire lifetime.

This planner is written for those wanting to quit yet have no idea where to begin; or, they have started, but find too many hours left each day following a meeting and call to their sponsor. Twenty-two hours is a long time to be stuck in a body, sharing a mind with an active addiction. This plan and this book fill the other 22 hours of those long, endless days, and it occupies enough *mind-time* and *mind-space* to drown out the cries of active addiction.

Distraction is essential when overcoming addiction. However, eventually, the habit sees through the strategy and begins to cry through whatever the distracting activity might be. This book offers distractions that are not only going to occupy *mind-time* and *mind-space* but will start sowing hardy seeds of *wisdom and knowledge* which will grow into a thick fabric of *defensive thinking* against *addictive thinking.*

It is mulch for your mind.

Another way to think of your mind is as a mop bucket of dirty water. You must always maintain a constant level of water in the bucket. If you simply drain everything out, you have no mind. So, what you have to do is begin adding clean, pure water on top, while draining dirty water from the bottom. This draining and filling have to be done slowly, in a controlled fashion, over a long period. You cannot overstimulate the mind. Keep in mind - the way mop -water works - even after draining out one gallon and adding one gallon there is still a specific concentration of dirt in the water. Even after a hundred gallons in and a hundred gallons out, there are still traces of the dirt.

Meanwhile, as you're going through the process of purifying your mind by draining and filling, draining and filling, everyday life continues to happen. You are still exposed to an endless array of advertisements, conflicts, confrontations, at home, at work, and in the places where you live your daily life. All of this dirt enters the bucket and adds to the concentration of dirt, so the process of draining and filling, draining and filling, can never end, it is a lifelong necessity.

By continuously working to drain out what you don't want, while filling with what you do want, you will purify your mind - of everything unwanted - including your addiction.

As you work the suggestions look at each day as 1 gallon of pure water in - and 1 gallon of dirty water out - at the end of 90 days - you will have a much clearer mind. It will continue to clear up - the clarity at 2 years is substantially better than the clarity at 365 days, which is considerably brighter than the clarity at 90 days.

Also keep in mind Facebook, Fox News, CNN, etc., are not pure water. What you take in at work, on TV, at the movies, etc., is not pure water; so even though in this book you'll focus on pure input - life will continue to fill your mind with dirty, corrupted, and contaminated water.

How the Program Works

Every business in the world operates on an annual basis, divided into four equal 13-week periods or quarters. Therefore, most corporate goals and objectives are measured quarterly. 13 weeks is approximately 90 days or three months.

This duration fits our purposes because it is short enough to keep us engaged, yet long enough to provide sufficient opportunity to make progress toward meaningful goals. Further, it gives adequate time for a person in early recovery to regain a sense of clarity.

Most inpatient programs are 30 days in duration. In my experience, 30 days is not enough time for the person to feel "human" again. It is very tough to develop any recovery skills in 30 days when you feel lousy and can hardly focus on any one particular item. 60 days is better, and 120 days better still. But most people agree on an initial 90-day period of getting back on track. This program is 90 days and is potentially the first of what will be four success programs that will be developed to help guide a recovering person through the first 12 months.

So, you have a 90-day, 3-month, 13-week, 1-quarter program to work with. This program is designed with one week of orientation/detox, followed by two six-week semesters; each week will have a different area of focus. Recovery absolutely must focus on the entire holistic nature of what is likely a very sick human being. Most holistic teachers discuss human nature in three domains - mind, body, and soul.

Sometimes, for simplicity sake, I do too. However, very early in my career, I was introduced to the teachings of Dr. Stephen R. Covey, and in his capstone achievement - a book titled *"The 7 Habits of Highly Effective People,"* Dr. Covey separated *"emotion"* from Mind, Body, Soul so that there were four domains involved in an individual; Mind, Body, Soul, and Emotion - sometimes referred to as *the heart* – and also occasionally combined with the *state of relationships*.

Covey also introduced me to the concept of *"Sharpen the Saw,"* which was his seventh habit. He teaches that once you improve your life across the four domains of mind-body-emotion-soul, you should do daily maintenance in each area to keep them sharp, i.e., *"Sharpen the Saw."*

The Brown Bag, Blue Collar Recovery System's equivalent category to *"Sharpen the Saw,"* is referred to as *Immunity and Defense*. We build a moat around our kingdom of Mind-Body-Soul-Emotion. In treatment circles, you may have heard this category referred to as *"relapse prevention."*

The 6th area we teach is *Lifestyle Wellness*, which consists of two main elements; the first is known as *minimalism*, and the second is *essentialism*. This area is about how to live with less worry and anxiety about the material side of life.

Following **week one**, which is *orientation/detox*, there are two 6-week semesters where each week focuses on one of the following areas.

· Body - Physical
· Mind - Mental
· Heart - Emotional and Relationships
· Soul - Spiritual
· Lifestyle – Minimalism, Essentialism
· Immunity and Defense – Relapse Prevention

The primary objective of the first six weeks is that through reading assignments, self-study, research, and practice, you develop a sound fundamental understanding of each of these areas of living.

The primary objective of the second 6 weeks is that you increase your basic level of knowledge to the point of being comfortable teaching or speaking about a concept or two. And, you develop your own personal growth and development plans for the first 90 days, and the 1, 3, 5 years that will follow this program.

Basically, at the end of 90 days, you will have:

· Learned fundamental knowledge in six critical areas of successful sober living,
· Taught at least one other person parts of what you have learned,
· Developed a plan of holistic living for the next 90 days, 1, 3, and 5 years, and
· Attended 90 meetings,
· You will have a sponsor
· Belong to a homegroup,
· Worked all 12 steps at least once,
· Read parts of at least 12 books,
· Walked or exercised at least 60 hours,
· Learned mindfulness meditation and other meditation, and practiced for nearly 70 hours
· Completed substantial service work,
· and many other achievements.

But most of all you will have been clean and sober for 90 days which by itself is a miracle. So, let's quit talking and start doing, let's get to Week 1.

Sample: Daily Left Hand Page (DLHP)

Enter Date Circle Day

Brown Bag Blue Collar Recovery Systems
Date:_____ Day: M T W Th F S Su

Day 42 Required Activities
Meditation:
Reading:
Aerobic: 40
Flexibility:
Meeting: 60

Required Activities

Today's Study Areas
What must
What is R
How to p
How to be
What is th

Study Topics

Week 6: This Week's Focus
Lifestyle: Minimal &
Minimalism
Essentialism
Wants vs Needs
PMA: Positive Ment

Weekly Focus

Needs, Habits, Healings, Affirmations, & Visualizations
Needs: Personal Growth & Development (Expa
Covey Habit 3: Put First Things First
Healing Treatment Six
Today and every day, I will be presently cons do - differently, better, and with more aware before. I am Universally directed to live up to me. For this, I give thanks, I let it be so, and

Needs, Habits, Healings Affirmations

Meetings and Appointments

00 / 30	
00 / 30	
00 / 30	
00 / 30	
00 / 30	
00 / 30	
00 / 30	
00 / 30	
00 / 30	
00 / 30	
00 / 30	
00 / 30	
00 / 30	
00 / 30	
00 / 30	
00 / 30	
00 / 30	

Step & Service Work
Phase 3: Believe: Step 7

Step and Service Work

Meetings and Appt Scheduler

Prayer & Gratitude List
"My Creator, I am now willing t   od and bad. I pray that you now remo character which stands in the   y fellows. Grant me strength, as   ding. Amen." (AA Big Book).

Prayer and Gratitude List

Notes, Numbers, & Future Appointments

Quick notes and reminders

Sample: Daily Right Hand Page (DRHP)

Brown Bag Blue Collar Recovery Systems

Date:_____ Day M T W Th F S Su

Morning Wellness Check			Evening Wellness Check	
Physical				
Mental				
Emotional				
Relational				
Spiritual				
Lifestyle				
Immunity				

Morning and Evening Wellness Checks Score 1-5

Journaling		
Date:	Sobriety Date:	Number Days Clean & Sober:

Draft 90-day plan for weeks 14-26 (days 91 - 182) Physical, Mental, Emotional/Relational, Spiritual, Lifestyle, & Relapse Prevention

Journaling and extra assignments

What I am Proud of/Happy About Today	What I Want to Improve/Remember

What Did I Learn	Can I Teach Someone Like Me?

Nightly Self Evaluation

To Discuss with Sponsor, Doctor, Therapist, or Other Professional:

Important Items to Discuss with Advisors

Rev. Dr. Robert Hobbs
The Realization of Stainless Souls
www.StainlessSouls.com

Program Syllabus

There are numerous ways to think about how the program is organized

· Detox plus 6 topics,

· Detox plus 2 semesters,

· 13 Weeks,

· or 5 Phases which are closely aligned with the original 6 steps of AA

Below we present 2 tables that represent the contents of the program, the first is organized by phase in columns, the second is organized by week in rows.

Phase	Surrender	Forgive	Believe	Serve	Integrate
Weeks	1, 2, 3	3, 4, 5	5, 6	8, 9	10, 11, 12, 13
AA Steps	1, 2, 3	4, 5	6, 7, 8	9, 10, 11, 12	10, 11, 12
Books	Big Book, Power of Now	Polishing the Mirror	Untethered Soul, Minimalism, Essentialism, Universe has Your Back	Autobiography of a Yogi, Notes from a Friend	Heroin Living and Dying, Surrender Experiement, The Tapping solution, AoY
Meditation	15-30 min/day	45-60 min/day	60 min/day	60 min/day	60 min/day
Exercise	30 min/day	30-35 min/day	35-45 min/day	50-55 min/day	55-60 min/day
Need	Certainty, Love	Love	Growth	Contribution	Variety, Significance
Habit	7, 1, 2	5	4, 3, 6	7	1-7
Healing	1, 2, 8, 3	4, 5	5, 6, 7	8, 9	10-13
Prayer	Basic Step 1, Step 3	Step 3	Step 3, Step 7	Step 3, Step 7, Self-Composed	Step 3, Step 7, St Francis, Self-Composed

Week	Focus Area	Reading	Need	Habit	Healing Treatment	Phase	Step	Prayer	Teach
1	Detox & Orientation	Big Book	Certainty	7	1, 2	Surrender	1	Basic	-
2	Physical	Big Book	Certainty	1	1, 2, 8	Surrender	2, 3	Step 3 Prayer	-
3	Mental	Power of Now	Love	2	3, 9	1, 2	-	Step 3 Prayer	-
4	Emotional	Polishing the Mirror	Love	5	4, 10	Forgive	4	Step 3 Prayer	-
5	Spiritual	Untethered Soul	Growth	3	5, 11	2, 3	5, 6, 7	Step 7 Prayer	-
6	Lifestyle	Minimalism & Essentialism	Growth	4	6, 12	Believe	7	Step 7 Prayer	-
7	Immunity	The Universe has Your Back	Growth	6	7, 13	Believe	8, 9	Step 7 Prayer	-
8	Physical - teach	Autobiography of a Yogi	Contribution	7	8, 2	Serve	9, 10, 11, 12	Step 7 Prayer	Week 1, 2
9	Mental - teach	Notes from a Friend	Variety	1, 2	9, 3	Serve	9, 10, 11, 12	Step 7 or St Francis	Week 3 & Meditate
10	Emotional - teach	Heroin-Living and Dying	Variety	5	10, 4	4, 5	9, 10, 11, 12	Step 7 or St Francis	Week 4
11	Spiritual - teach	Autobiography of a Yogi	Significance	3	11, 5	Integrate	9, 10, 11, 12	Step 7 or St Francis	Week 5
12	Lifestyle - teach	The Surrender Experiment	Significance	4	12, 6	Integrate	9, 10, 11, 12	Step 7 or St Francis	Week 6
13	Immunity - teach	The Tapping Solution	Significance	6	13, 7	Integrate	9, 10, 11, 12	Step 7 or St Francis	Week 7

Rev. Dr. Robert Hobbs
The Realization of Stainless Souls
www.StainlessSouls.com

Basic Program Hours & Achievements

Imagine if you were in treatment. Twenty-four hours of every day would be determined by the clinical director. Whether you enroll for 30 days or 180 days, time is spent in accordance with the agency. If you are not going to treatment, you need to find a balance between working a disciplined recovery program and performing your necessary everyday activities. The below table provides a basic estimate of how much time you must budget toward recovery in the Brown Bag, Blue Collar System. It also demonstrates that some of the most substantial changes you will implement in your daily life. By the time you finish, you will have meditated for 69 hours, walked 68 hours, stretched 15 hours, attended 91 hours of meetings, studied for 45 hours, and read 12 books.

Week	Meditation per Day		Reading Per Day	Aerobic per Day	Flexibility per Day	Study per Day	Meeting per Day	Min. Total Hours/day
1	15	3 min x 5	Big Book	30	10	30	60	3.25
2	20	5 min x 4	Big Book	30	10	30	60	3.25
3	30	10 min x 3	Power of Now	30	10	30	60	3.5
4	45	15 min x 3	Polishing the Mirror	30	10	30	60	3.5
5	60	20 min x 3	Untethered Soul	35	10	30	60	3.75
6	60	30 min x 2	Minimalism/Essentialism	40	10	30	60	3.75
7	60	30 min x 2	Universe has Your Back	45	10	30	60	4
8	60	30 min x 2	Autobiography of Yogi	50	10	30	60	4
9	60	30 min x 2	Notes from a Friend	55	10	30	60	4
10	60	30 min x 2	Heroin-Living&Dying	60	10	30	60	4.5
11	60	30 min x 2	Autobiography of Yogi	60	10	30	60	4.5
12	60	30 min x 2	Surrender Experiment	60	10	30	60	5
13	60	30 min x 2	Tapping Solution	60	10	30	60	5
			12 Books					**AVG**
Total	**Hours**	**69**		**68**	**15**	**45**	**91**	**4**

Week 1: Detox and Orientation

The first week of the 13-week program is designed to allow you to complete detox and withdrawal before beginning the more tedious work of weeks 2 through 13.

It is best if, after receiving this planner, you make the appropriate arrangements to withdraw and detoxify from your drug of choice safely. Then, once the arrangements are made, schedule your arranged detoxification week to coincide with your week 1 of this program.

The time before beginning the first week can be utilized to prepare for and acquire any additional items that you will need to participate fully in the program's activities.

You will likely want a notebook or journal for keeping notes. Many clients opt for two notebooks - one for *private and confidential* note-taking - which will probably be burned or shredded at some point. The second for *general note taking* and keeping, which will be held long-term and will be used for teaching in the 2nd six-week semester. Along with the notebooks, you'll want a pen or pencil that you are comfortable writing with.

There are several books (see list at the end of this chapter, and works cited at end of book) that you will be required to read over the course of the program. You will need a library card, bookstore membership, or online access to the required reading volumes. I personally use **www.scribd.com**, **www.thriftbooks.com**, and the e-catalogues of several local libraries. During the first one and a half weeks, the required reading is the first 164 pages of the *Alcoholics Anonymous* Big Book - More formally titled *"Alcoholics Anonymous."* As you read the Big Book - substitute references to alcohol and alcoholic with your drug of choice and addict as appropriate.

For the next 90 days, you will be doing a lot of walking (or other aerobic activity) in fact 60 hours or more - and 60 more hours meditating. You may want to get a good pair of shoes to walk in and any comfortable clothing that you prefer while exercising.

For meditation, you will want to set aside a place at home that can be quiet and private and equip it with flowers, incense, an altar, and a good chair or cushion.

You are going to do 30 minutes of research on different topics every night. Therefore, an internet connection and an understanding of Google search would be ideal; otherwise, a library card will be necessary.

You'll also be attending 90 meetings in 90 days - so you will need your local meeting schedule and arrange for transportation to the meetings you plan to attend.

This Week's Focus

Each day of the planner has two planning pages that will always be presented together when you view that day. One page will be on your left (the daily left-hand page, DLHP), the other on the right (the daily right-hand page, DRHP). The Week's Focus Areas are provided daily on the top-right hand corner of each day's left-hand page.

1. Become oriented with the *Brown Bag Blue Collar Recovery Planner* and begin acquiring the necessary items to complete the program successfully
2. Learn through self-study and from your medical professional about Medication-Assisted Treatment (MAT) especially for opioid addicts and alcoholics.
3. Become familiar with goal setting
4. Learn the difference between addiction and dependence
5. Form a working definition for *recovery*

Study Areas

Rev. Dr. Robert Hobbs
The Realization of Stainless Souls
www.StainlessSouls.com

The weekly focus and study areas are subjects that you will research and study either at the local library or online using a search tool such as Google. Many of the topics are well presented on YouTube. You should not have difficulty finding educational content.

Each week, there are seven topics; you are expected to research and study all seven items, one topic per day. The Week's Study Areas are presented in the Top Center Box of the daily left-hand page.

Spend at least 15 minutes searching on relevant terms and then 15 more minutes reading and taking notes. The idea is that you will get a basic knowledge of each topic and be able to share (teach) that knowledge from memory and your notes in the second semester of the program.

The self-study part of the program is specifically designed for you to seek and find answers that *you can best relate to*. This method is often better than the alternative where you would be forced to learn what is pre-printed in this or another curriculum.

Your curiosity and intuition will guide you, but please do not use *"street sources"* for your research. Nor should you believe you already *"know"* what you need to. These exercises are designed to deepen and enhance the knowledge you have so that when sharing (teaching) it later, you are providing useful, accurate, and educational information and knowledge to your student.

Day 1: Medicine Assisted Treatment, Dope Sickness, and Delirium Tremens

This is pretty self-explanatory and is especially crucial for opioid addicts and alcoholics. Medicines can and should be used following your doctor's instructions to help keep you alive and comfortable during withdrawal. It is possible if there are some related mental or emotional disorders, that medication is dispensed to help you with these issues while you work on your sobriety. Once you gain some stability in your recovery, it may make sense to look at reducing your medications again following the doctor's instructions. Sometimes addiction specialists will recommend some longer-term medicine for you. It is not unusual for this treatment to last for the first full 12 months after detoxification.

Day 2: Suboxone, Methadone, Benzos, Vivitrol, Narcan

Depending on the severity of your physical dependence and strength of your cravings, physicians can prescribe meds that will reduce your symptoms over a predefined duration. Ideally, the dosage of these meds will be systematically reduced until you no longer suffer from symptoms. These meds have various side effects and can become just as much a nuisance as your drug of choice. Take your time learning all you can about these medications and ask your doctor plenty of questions. Keep an open mind, take good notes, and always have a long-term goal to be free of as many drugs (legal or not) as is possible.

Benzos - avoid these if possible; if avoidance is not reasonable, limit any usage. Over time, these can be more addictive and equally as deadly as heroin.

Narcan - you should always, always have Narcan with you. Not just for you or your loved ones but for any public emergency.

Vivitrol - after a few weeks of good sobriety and after all opioids are out of your system, it might be a good idea for you to become a patient using Vivitrol. It can help keep you clean - find out how.

Day 3: Opioid Receptors

These are an essential part of your nervous system, and you should find out how they were designed to serve you and how they promote drug abuse; especially consider how heroin, Narcan, Vivitrol, compete for attachments, etc.

Day 4: Endorphins and Dopamine

These are two neurotransmitters that naturally occur in your body. Study their purpose and how they relate to opioid receptors and thus the drugs you are studying this week. Compare the feelings that endorphins and dopamine are designed to give you with the feelings that heroin or your drug of choice gives you.

Day 5: Heroin >>> to >>> MAT >>> to >>> Abstinence

Your long-term goal should be freedom from all drugs. It is not an easy path, but it is a necessary one to undertake even if you never make it. So, study the transition from heroin (or your drug of choice) addiction to medication-assisted treatment to abstinence.

Day 6: The Power of Goal Setting

Read articles and watch YouTube videos on the power and advantage of goal setting. Find out how written goals not only enhance performance but also throughout a lifetime result in higher salaries, more achievements, and more life fulfillment. Begin today by writing down three to five short, medium, and long-term goals for yourself.

Day 7: Covey Habit 7 Sharpen the Saw

I guess I am beginning with the end in mind by requiring you to learn Dr. Covey's last habit first. The part of Habit 7 that I'd like to impress upon you the most is that there are as many as four dimensions to your being:

· Physical,
· Mental,
· Emotional, and
· Spiritual

We are going to build the entire program around these four parts of "you," along with two other major sections.

Required Activities

Required Activities are presented on the Top Left Corner of the daily left-hand page.

There are far more than *five required activities* each day; each week you must strive to complete all of your tasks with as much effort, intensity, and ingenuity that you used to score dope and booze. You must fight for your recovery; everyday fight to complete all of your tasks; but at the barest of minimums, you must complete the *five required activities* every single day. These items must become habits. If you forget to do something on this list, you should feel empty - as if you skipped a meal or a good night's sleep. This is your commitment to yourself, to your future self. It is that important.

There are *five required activities* each week, and they are always the same; they are:

1. Meditation
2. Reading
3. Aerobic exercise
4. Flexibility/Mobility exercise
5. Daily AA, NA, recovery meeting

These five activities are foundational in your recovery. If you cannot or will not do these five activities, it is unlikely that you will gain any long-term improvement. Beyond recovery, these activities are an essential daily component of any healthy, prosperous life.

Meditation

This week sit for 3 minutes, five times each day. Usually, when:

1. You wake up and before doing anything else, and
2. The last thing you do before sleeping, and
3. Once before lunch,
4. Once Before dinner, and
5. After your required recovery meeting.

This week practice very simple mindfulness meditation; find a quiet place to sit privately, then with a straight spine and closed eyes (if possible), calm and center yourself while becoming fully aware of your breathing.

Focus intentionally on your breath, while sitting-up straight and while calm. Your thoughts will wander - when they do simply notice your thoughts, without judgment of any kind, release that thought, and return your attention to your breath. Stay on it for 3 minutes.

Focus on the breath, if you have a thought - notice without judgment - release it - return to the breath.

The goal is not to become free of thought - that is unlikely. The goal is to take notice of your mind's activity and gently with intention, return your attention to your breath.

Please note that if you have anxiety or PTSD, it is a good idea to have another responsible person nearby to help you if you get stuck.

Reading

Consider your mind to be a mop bucket - filled to the brim with grimy water. The ground rule is the bucket must always be full. It cannot have less water in it than it does now. If the bucket overflows - it's a waste of time and water.

So, the idea here is to drain water out of the bottom while adding pure, clean water at the top. Ideally, the bucket will always stay precisely full at the brim without too much pure water being lost due to overflow.

The work you are doing in this program is draining the cruddy water from your addicted mind. The reading you are doing is pure water being added to the top keeping the bucket full. It would be great, wouldn't it, if we just dumped the cruddy water, rinsed the bucket, and then refilled it with pure crystal-clear water? But your mind doesn't work that way - not while you are alive anyway. Therefore, we take a measured approach draining a little and adding a little each day. Slowly, the mind begins to clear; eventually – say in 90 days - you have a relatively clear mind to work with.

Also, don't forget that outside of this program, life is still happening - Facebook, pornography, work issues, video games, etc., are always available to you. If you partake in anything less pure then crystal-clear water, it will take longer to achieve a crystal-clear mind. Is it possible that you could avoid anything that might contaminate your bucket of water for 90 days?

If you were in a treatment center, they would limit your exposure to only sources of pure water. In this case, you are at home. So, it is up to you - how clear would you like your mind to be?

For 90 days, limit your exposure to anything unrelated to your recovery, in the end, you'll be happy you did.

> *A Zen master once received a university professor who came to inquire about Zen.*
>
> *The master served tea. He poured the professor's cup full and then kept pouring. The professor watched the overflow until he no longer could restrain himself. "It is overfull. No more will go in!"*
>
> *"Like this cup," the master said, "you are full of your own opinions. How can I teach you Zen unless you first empty your cup!"*

This week's readings are the first 7 chapters of the Big Book, or more formally *Alcoholics Anonymous*, read one chapter each day. As you read each chapter, try to concentrate on how the message relates to your situation, past behavior, and experiences.

It is recognized that you are in detox this week and that this activity might be challenging.

Do your best, forget the rest.

Aerobic Exercise

The ideal activity here is walking. Walking in daylight, either in the early morning or late afternoon, is best because you will benefit from the sunlight. Walk for the designated amount of time at a comfortable pace for you. During this time, you can repeat your affirmations, or try to focus on your breathing.

Do not allow your mind to run away from you. Start taming it. Recognize that you are the owner of your mind - and therefore you are its boss. It is not you or your boss - it is a tool gifted to you for success in this world.

While you walk - make sure you remain relaxed, that none of your joints, especially your knees lockout or overextend. Maintain a stable and firm posture with an erect spine and without bending at the waist.

For your first few walks - simply head out from your starting point in one direction for 15 minutes - then turn around and retrace your course back to the starting point.

Some of you may wish to jog, run, swim, or do aerobics or Pilates. I'd rather you not substitute - but if you must - go for it. But remember there is a lot to be said for a brisk walk in nature!

> ### *Who is the boss?*
>
> *A horse suddenly came galloping quickly down the road. It seemed as though the man had somewhere important to go.*
>
> *Another man, who was standing alongside the road, shouted, "Where are you going?" and the man on the horse replied,*
>
> *"I don't know! Ask the horse!"*

Flexibility

The activity here doesn't change for the whole of the 90 days. It is merely a 10-minute effort to increase your flexibility and mobility.

I have a rule that you should never stretch a cold muscle - so the best time to do this activity is just after your aerobic exercise.

The movements I'd like you to work on are forward and backward bends with feet together and then with feet spread apart. 5 minutes while standing or sitting, followed by 5 minutes while sitting or prone. There is plenty of variety and progress available in these simple movements.

If you are familiar with *Hatha Yoga asanas*, you can alternate between *downward-facing dog* and *upward facing dog* or *cobra* and blend in some *plank*. Otherwise, just stand with your feet about hip-width apart - take a breath in, and then while letting it out - with your knees slightly bent - bend forward toward your toes. Keep your knees bent and your core strong as your chest approaches your knees. Stick your butt up and just hang there enjoying the sensations along your spine.

Then, when you're ready, using your hands on your knees to support you, flex your core slightly and inhale deeply; come to straight up and down, and once you have your balance, put your hands over your head and bend backward without straining. Exhale and come to vertical or into another forward bend if appropriate.

You can perform the same basic bends with your feet spread apart; while seated, you can bend forward and hang between your legs and then reach over your head and bend back toward the back of your chair.

As you gain proficiency in elongating both sides of your spine, you can add variety with side bends, and straight leg stretches. Always remember to protect your back when changing position.

Meetings

Most discharge plans suggest that clients attend 90 meetings in the first 90 days after discharge. We can debate whether AA, NA, Smart Recovery, or other programs are right or wrong for you. We would just be wasting time. The point of 90 meetings in 90 days is not to teach you some dogma or some religion or to teach you something that you don't want to learn. The point of 90 meetings in 90 days is many-fold - here are the highlights:

AA is everywhere.

On any given night there are meetings available almost everywhere. So, you must do your very best to find out where all the meetings are and then write the one you will attend each day into your schedule in this planner. Then go and meet people in recovery. It is free, it is ubiquitous, and it is filled with people just like you.

You do not have to agree with anything, believe in anything, or accept anything; just go with the idea that you are becoming an expert in the AA program of recovery and you're going to meet as many people as you can.

As a part of the BBBC program, you will do the 12 Steps quickly the old-fashioned way. It will be useful to have an hour each day to go and focus solely on your recovery and the recovery of others you meet.

Needs, Habits, Healings, Affirmations, and Visualizations

Not that life preserver!

If you were drowning in a pool, I would undoubtedly toss you the first flotation device I could find;

You would not look at the life preserver and decide, "This life preserver is not the right one for me, I need to look for one better suited to my preferences."

"Take what floats and survive; you can figure out how to thrive later."

Each week the program will focus on:

· A particular set of human needs as taught by Tony Robbins in many of his courses,
· One of Stephen Covey's 7 Habits of Highly Effective People,
· A Healing Treatment for the area of living that the week is focused on, and
· The development of a daily affirmation and visualization (Advanced Prayer) practice.

Needs: Certainty, Security, Safety, Stability

Whether it is Tony Robbins, Wayne Dyer, or Abraham Maslow, all teachers of human needs build their foundation on a feeling of certainty or security. Without any certainty - your life would be chaotic. Not knowing, for example where you live, where you belong, who your friends are, where you work from day-to-day, where your next meal is coming from, etc., would make it impossible to find contentment. There must be a sense of certainty of your physical security and well-being. From that foundational level of confidence, you can build more of the exciting things into your life.

For purposes of this week's work on needs, the first thing to do is to evaluate:

1. What can you be sure of in your life? Food, shelter, clothing, income, relationship?
2. How certain are you of your security in the above areas? Can you keep them? Are they at risk?
3. What parts of your life are too uncertain or unstable? Kids, parents, job situation, home, relationships
4. What would you like to be more certain about?
5. What can you do this week to gain a little more certainty in your life?

How much better would your life be if you were more certain about the things that matter most to you? What can you do to become even more certain?

Covey Habit Seven: Sharpen the Saw

Rev. Dr. Robert Hobbs
The Realization of Stainless Souls
www.StainlessSouls.com

The 7th habit is based on the idea of production and production capability. One way to look at it is if you drive your car continuously at high speeds and never stopped to maintain it - it will wear out before it should. The same is true about your body, your mind, your soul, and your emotions/relationships. If you don't invest in the maintenance of these parts of life, eventually, they will wear down and not be able to serve you or your interests.

This week consider these four areas of your life and how you think about them.

1. How do you treat yourself concerning your body, mind, soul, and heart?
2. Do you take them for granted?
3. Are you overly demanding?
4. Do you ignore any of these elements of life?

Take time this week to establish a baseline of health for each area and then make a *written commitment* to improve each one in a balanced way each week for the next 13 weeks.

Healing Treatment

Each week for 13 weeks, you will practice a *spiritual healing treatment* on yourself using the methods located in the back of the planner. These treatments are based on my study and understanding of the works of my professor Dr. Paul Leon Masters, my guru Paramahansa Yogananda in *Scientific Healing Affirmations*, Evelyn Monahan in *The Miracle of Metaphysical Healing*, and Joel Goldsmith in *The Infinite Way*.

Healing treatments are much like mini-meditations or detailed affirmations. Simply follow the instructions for the healing as outlined and take into account the affirmation and visualization process outlined below. It will be cumbersome at first; that's why we practice. Stay with it, and in a few days, it will be much smoother.

Affirmations and Visualizations (or Advanced Prayer)

An affirmation is simply the verbal acknowledgment that something you want or need has already been provided. Usually, it begins with *a thought* - a thought is a certain kind of energy. By verbalizing your thinking, you put the energy of your voice, which is physical *vibrational energy,* into the Universe as sound in the audible range.

Additionally, because you verbalize words by passing the air of your breath across your vocal cords, you not only feel the vibration in your body, but you breathe *"your life"* into the affirmation. You started with *a thought* - you spoke it out loud - *hearing it* and *transmitting its vibration* into the Universe and also throughout every cell of your body. In essence, you have given physical existence to your thought!

What exists that did not first start as a thought?

In the story of creation, God spoke light into existence by saying, *"Let there be light,"* we can assume God *thought*, God *spoke*, and then *his thought came to be.*

Visualization

Similarly, we want to give *light energy* to our thoughts. Light is another form of vibrational energy and is an essential part of the creating of our future. As you state your affirmation aloud, *visualize* that it has already occurred in your mind's eye (the point between your eyebrows), *see it* as if it were already in existence, just the way you want it, in the physical world where you exist.

Here's the basic affirmation process.

1. Read the daily affirmation (each day has its own affirmation) and think it through - what does it mean to you?

2. Say it out loud with firm *intention and inflection*. Basically, *command it*. Use *emotional energy* during each step. Begin to *form a picture* of it taking place in your mind's eye. *Feel what it feels like* to have it already.

3. Repeat it, this time *in a whisper* feeling the air pass over your vocal cords, mouth, tongue, and lips - form an even more clear, brilliant *picture of it* in your mind's eye.

4. Say it a third time *mentally*, with no sound, and really concentrate on the words as you imagine it in your mind's eye.

5. Keep the *thought* and the *image* in your mind and consider it as something that has already taken place.

6. Acknowledge it has already taken place and *feel what it feels like* to have this as a part of your reality.

7. Be grateful. Say out loud if possible, quietly if necessary, I am thankful <for whatever this affirmation provides> is taking place, I let it be so, and so it is.

8. Go about your normal activities.

Note that every day for 90 days there is a new affirmation provided. You are encouraged to practice the above affirmation steps three times each day, preferably as a part of your daily meditations and healing treatments.

In the back of the book, there are 90 additional short-form affirmations that you can use while walking, or exercising, or at other times when you might need a lift or a boost.

Affirmations are a Form of <u>Advanced Prayer</u>.

Step and Service Work

Each week you will focus and work on at least one of the 12 steps of recovery as published by Alcoholics Anonymous. We don't want to undermine your sponsor by providing a suggested course of completion for you, but we don't want you to die either.

In the early days of AA, all steps were completed in a weekend, and the new AA would then be the recovery leader in the city or town where he lived. We consider the working of these steps a matter of your life and death; we strongly urge you to courageously study them and work through them with another person in recovery; typically, this person is referred to as your sponsor.

In reading the *Twelve Steps and Twelve Traditions*, you'll find that *Step One* is the only perfect step or the single step that must be completed perfectly. If you approached Step One with perfection in mind, the probability of long-term recovery is significantly increased. All other steps can be completed again and again once step one is done the right way.

From the *Brown Bag, Blue Collar* perspective, *Week 1* and *Step 1* are in the *"Surrender Phase,"* of recovery. Literally, *surrender*. You should be at a place where you admit that you cannot be victorious in the life you desire unless you overcome your addiction. The only way to overcome addiction is to surrender; surrender the idea that you alone can beat it.

Think this way: addiction is an illness of the mind, and therefore, my current state of mind, being part of the sick mind, is too ill to overcome the addiction by itself. My sick mind needs help overcoming my sick mind, and therefore, I will seek help from a higher power (than my sick mind) and from others who have learned how to overcome addiction.

The two most essential items you can complete concerning recovery programming this week are

1. Find a *temporary sponsor* to help you with Steps 1 through 3, and

Rev. Dr. Robert Hobbs
The Realization of Stainless Souls
www.StainlessSouls.com

2. Find a *home group* where you will become a member - participating fully following the group's guidelines.

In early recovery, only spirituality and sobriety are necessary.

You can't have one without the other;

without both, you will have nothing else.

If you don't know what this means, ask someone at the seven meetings you attend this week. The reason for meetings every day is to establish a stable foundation of people, places, times, where you can count on recovery happening. New habits are necessary to break old ones. Form good habits early in AA by:

1. Come a little early to every meeting, and
2. Stay a little late and learn to place names with faces

It is the people you will meet now who will get you through 90 days - and if you make 90 days, you'll make a year, and if you make a year, you'll make a lifetime.

Service Work

Start by making your bed. There's a YouTube video by a military guy where he explains the importance of making your bed every day. Find that video and watch it. Then each day, do just a little bit more than you did the day before until you are living a life full of accomplishment, contentment, and satisfaction.

At the beginning of each week, *preferably on Sunday* - sit down with your planner and the printed or online schedule for AA, NA, and any other recovery meetings you are interested in.

Choose the meetings you plan to attend each day for the coming week and write them in on the meeting and appointment schedule for the appropriate time. Make sure to allow time to arrive early and stay a bit late, and for travel time to and from the meeting and make any arrangements you might need for transportation. If you're picking people up in a carpool - make sure you account for that as well.

It is during this time (on Sunday) that you should write in any medical appointments, court appointments, therapy appointments, and meetings with your sponsor for recovery group into the meeting an appointment section of the planner. Once these are written in, write in your meditation time, and the time that you plan to use for reading. Also, write in the time where you will do your aerobic and flexibility exercises.

Finally, schedule your study time - the time where you will research and study the topics that are focused on that day and that week.

Your meditations will be short initially; your healing treatment will be at least 15 minutes of practice periods three times each day. These must be scheduled, or you will not do them - write them in your planner!!

There are 24 hours in a day. If you are working, subtract your work and commute time from 24. What is left is the time you have for recovery. This first week will require up to five hours of your time EACH DAY, leaving you 19 hours for whatever else is necessary.

No! Television is not necessary; video games are not needed; social media is not required!

Wellness Checks (Top DRHP)

Every morning when you wake up, do a quick wellness check on the seven areas listed. Grade each field as a one for low wellness, up to a five for perfect wellness, for that area. Use the space provided to make a quick note for anything that stands out as you evaluate the area.

Just before bedtime make another quick wellness check for how you feel in each of the seven areas. At the end of the day or week or both, plot your responses on the bubble grid page at the back of the book. Use this graph to compare your responses over several days and also to evaluate if there is any correlation or inverse correlation across the different areas. For example, one common trend is that emotional responses track with relationship responses. Get an idea of how you respond holistically to different stimuli in your life.

Journaling

Every day write down your sobriety date and the number of clean, sober days you have accumulated. Take a moment when you write them down to consider how far you have come. Be grateful. Say to your higher power, *"Thank You."*

Throughout the day, specific ideas, thoughts, and inspirations may arise. The journaling section is a place for you to capture those. It is also space for you to track - or for us to remind you of - the critical things you need to do. Essays and detailed step work should be done in your notebook - use this journaling section to capture what's on your mind.

When you complete Step 1, write down what Step 1 means to you.

At the end of each day, take a moment of gratitude. Tony Robbins says, *"When you are grateful - you are rich!"*

Be grateful;
Be Rich.

Write down at least one thing that made you proud or happy, and one thing you'd like to improve. Also, write down at least one thing you learned, and - this is important - *one thing you think you could teach another person.*

In the second semester of the program, you will be required to prepare and teach a person like you something from the first-semester curriculum. Usually, we teach something we are interested in learning - so make sure you are curious about the topics you will teach.

Prayer and Gratitude List

Every day write down what you are grateful for and remember to pray every morning and evening. Keep prayers simple for now. God knows what you want!

Notes for Advisors

Always write down your questions. It never fails that when we are with our doctor or sponsor - we forget what we want to discuss. Write the questions down and take your planner with you wherever you go.

The Realization of Stainless Souls:

A Come-as-You-are Church of Recovery, Discovery, and All Religions

Recovery | Discovery | Restoration | Realization

#StainlessSouls

Reading List with Amazon Affiliate Links

Required Reading:

Alcoholics Anonymous. *The Big Book of Alcoholics Anonymous.*

--- *Twelve Steps and Twelve Traditions.*

Bernstein, Gabrielle. *The Universe Has Your Back: Transform Fear to Faith.*

Dass, Ram. *Polishing the Mirror: How to Live from Your Spiritual Heart.*

Milburn, Joshua Fields and Nicodemus, Ryan. *Minimalism: Live a Meaningful Life*

Hobbs, Jr. Robert L. *Heroin Living and Dying with an Addict You Love, How to Survive When Everyone Dies.*

McKeon, Greg. *Essentialism: The Disciplined Pursuit of Less.*

Ortner, Nick. *The Tapping Solution: A Revolutionary System for Stress-Free Living.*

Robbins, Anthony. *Notes from a Friend.* A Quick and Simple Guide for Taking Charge of Your Life

Singer, Michael. *The Surrender Experiment: My Journey into Life's Perfection.*

----*The Untethered Soul: A Journey Beyond Yourself.*

Tolle, Eckhart *The Power of Now: A Guide to Spiritual Enlightenment.*

Yogananda, Paramahansa. *Autobiography of a Yogi.*

Optional Reading:

Chapman, Gary. *The 5 Love Languages: The Secret to Love that Lasts.*

Covey, Stephen. *The Seven Habits of Highly Effective People.*

Dyer, Wayne. *Change Your Thoughts, Change Your Life: Living the Wisdom of the Tao.*

Goldsmith, Joel, S. *The Infinite Way.*

Hill, Napoleon. *Think and Grow Rich.*

Hill, Napoleon, and Stone, W. Clement. *Success Through a Positive Mental Attitude.*

Rath, Tom. *Strengths Finder 2.0.*

Monahan, Evelyn, M. *The Miracle of Metaphysical Healing.*

Stanley, Charles. *The Gift of Forgiveness: Put the Past Behind You and Give...*

Notes and Sketches

Day 1 Required Activities	Today's Study Areas	Week 1: This Week's Focus
Meditation: 3 Minutes five times	MAT – Dope Sick - DTs	Orientation & Detox
Reading: Big Book Dr.'s Opinion		Medication Assisted Treatment
Aerobic: 30 minutes once		Goal Setting
Flexibility: 10 minutes once		Addiction vs Dependence
Meeting: 60 minutes		What Is Recovery?

Needs, Habits, Healings, Affirmations, & Visualizations

Needs: Certainty/Security/Safety/Stability

Habit 7: Sharpen the Saw

Healing Treatment One

Coupled with the knowledge of the Higher Power that emerges from the center of my mind and as a result of what I have overcome and I am overcoming now, I have complete belief that my future will be better than anything I could have previously imagined.

Step & Service Work

Phase 1: Step 1 & Surrender – The Only Perfect Step

Get a Temporary Sponsor/Find an Initial Home Group

Make Bed

Prayer & Gratitude List

Please keep me sober today

Thank YOU for keeping me sober today

Meetings and Appointments

Time	
__00 __30	
__00 __30	
__00 __30	
__00 __30	
__00 __30	
__00 __30	
__00 __30	
__00 __30	
__00 __30	
__00 __30	
__00 __30	
__00 __30	
__00 __30	
__00 __30	
__00 __30	
__00 __30	
__00 __30	

Notes, Numbers, & Future Appointments

Rev. Dr. Robert Hobbs
The Realization of Stainless Souls
www.StainlessSouls.com

Morning Wellness Check		
Physical		
Mental		
Emotional		
Relational		
Spiritual		
Lifestyle		
Immunity		

Evening Wellness Check		
Physical		
Mental		
Emotional		
Relational		
Spiritual		
Lifestyle		
Immunity		

Journaling		
Date:	Sobriety Date:	Number Days Clean & Sober:

What I am Proud of/Happy About Today

What I Want to Improve/Remember

What Did I Learn

What Can I Teach Someone Like Me?

To Discuss with Sponsor, Doctor, Therapist, or Other Professional:

Day 2 Required Activities	Today's Study Areas	Week 1: This Week's Focus
Meditation: 3 Minutes five times	MAT – Dope Sick - DTs	Orientation & Detox
Reading: Big Book Bill's Story	Suboxone/Methadone/Vivitrol	Medication Assisted Treatment
Aerobic: 30 minutes once		Goal Setting
Flexibility: 10 minutes once		Addiction vs Dependence
Meeting: 60 minutes		What Is Recovery?

Needs, Habits, Healings, Affirmations, & Visualizations

Needs: Certainty/Security/Safety/Stability

Habit 7: Sharpen the Saw

Healing Treatment One

In the Presence of the Healing Power of the Universal Mind within me, I surrender all causes and feelings of stress and anxiety from my mind and body.

Step & Service Work

Phase 1: Step 1 & Surrender – The Only Perfect Step

Get a Temporary Sponsor/Find an Initial Home Group

Make Bed, Make Coffee

Prayer & Gratitude List

Please keep me sober today

Thank YOU for keeping me sober today

Meetings & Appointments

Time	
__00 __30	
__00 __30	
__00 __30	
__00 __30	
__00 __30	
__00 __30	
__00 __30	
__00 __30	
__00 __30	
__00 __30	
__00 __30	
__00 __30	
__00 __30	
__00 __30	
__00 __30	
__00 __30	

Notes, Numbers, & Future Appointments

Rev. Dr. Robert Hobbs
The Realization of Stainless Souls
www.StainlessSouls.com

Morning Wellness Check		
Physical		
Mental		
Emotional		
Relational		
Spiritual		
Lifestyle		
Immunity		

Evening Wellness Check		
Physical		
Mental		
Emotional		
Relational		
Spiritual		
Lifestyle		
Immunity		

Journaling		
Date:	Sobriety Date:	Number Days Clean & Sober:

What I am Proud of/Happy About Today

What I Want to Improve/Remember

What Did I Learn

What Can I Teach Someone Like Me?

To Discuss with Sponsor, Doctor, Therapist, or Other Professional:

Day 3 Required Activities
Meditation: 3 Minutes five times
Reading: BB: There is a Solution
Aerobic: 30 minutes once
Flexibility: 10 minutes once
Meeting: 60 minutes

Today's Study Areas
MAT – Dope Sick - DTs
Suboxone/Methadone/Vivitrol
Opioid Receptors

Week 1: This Week's Focus
Orientation & Detox
Medication Assisted Treatment
Goal Setting
Addiction vs Dependence
What Is Recovery?

Needs, Habits, Healings, Affirmations, & Visualizations

Needs: Certainty/Security/Safety/Stability

Habit 7: Sharpen the Saw

Healing Treatment One

I know that positive trends are coming in my life because my conscious mind is open to receive Divine Guidance from my Higher Mind.

Step & Service Work

Phase 1: Step 1 & Surrender – The Only Perfect Step

Get a Temporary Sponsor/Find an Initial Home Group

Make Bed, Make Coffee, Make Breakfast

Prayer & Gratitude List

Please keep me sober today

Thank YOU for keeping me sober today

Meetings and Appointments

Time	
__00 __30	
__00 __30	
__00 __30	
__00 __30	
__00 __30	
__00 __30	
__00 __30	
__00 __30	
__00 __30	
__00 __30	
__00 __30	
__00 __30	
__00 __30	
__00 __30	
__00 __30	
__00 __30	
__00 __30	
__00 __30	

Notes, Numbers, & Future Appointments

Rev. Dr. Robert Hobbs
The Realization of Stainless Souls
www.StainlessSouls.com

Morning Wellness Check		
Physical		
Mental		
Emotional		
Relational		
Spiritual		
Lifestyle		
Immunity		

Evening Wellness Check		
Physical		
Mental		
Emotional		
Relational		
Spiritual		
Lifestyle		
Immunity		

Journaling		
Date:	Sobriety Date:	Number Days Clean & Sober:

What I am Proud of/Happy About Today

What I Want to Improve/Remember

What Did I Learn

What Can I Teach Someone Like Me?

To Discuss with Sponsor, Doctor, Therapist, or Other Professional:

Day 4 Required Activities	Today's Study Areas	Week 1: This Week's Focus
Meditation: 3 Minutes five times	MAT – Dope Sick - DTs	Orientation & Detox
Reading: BB: More About Alcohol	Suboxone/Methadone/Vivitrol	Medication Assisted Treatment
Aerobic: 30 minutes once	Opioid Receptors	Goal Setting
Flexibility: 10 minutes once	Endorphins and Dopamine	Addiction vs Dependence
Meeting: 60 minutes		What Is Recovery?

Needs, Habits, Healings, Affirmations, & Visualizations

Needs: Certainty/Security/Safety/Stability

Habit 7: Sharpen the Saw

Healing Treatment One

Knowing that my life is protected and guided to success and happiness by the Higher Power of my Universally Attuned Mind, I release all fear, anger, and doubt about my life.

Step & Service Work

Phase 1: Step 1 & Surrender – The Only Perfect Step

Get a Temporary Sponsor/Find an Initial Home Group

Make Bed, Make Coffee, Make Breakfast, Hold the Door

Prayer & Gratitude List

Please keep me sober today

Thank YOU for keeping me sober today

Meetings and Appointments

Time	
__00 __30	
__00 __30	
__00 __30	
__00 __30	
__00 __30	
__00 __30	
__00 __30	
__00 __30	
__00 __30	
__00 __30	
__00 __30	
__00 __30	
__00 __30	
__00 __30	
__00 __30	
__00 __30	
__00 __30	
__00 __30	

Notes, Numbers, & Future Appointments

Rev. Dr. Robert Hobbs
The Realization of Stainless Souls
www.StainlessSouls.com

Morning Wellness Check		
Physical		
Mental		
Emotional		
Relational		
Spiritual		
Lifestyle		
Immunity		

Evening Wellness Check		
Physical		
Mental		
Emotional		
Relational		
Spiritual		
Lifestyle		
Immunity		

Journaling		
Date:	Sobriety Date:	Number Days Clean & Sober:

What I am Proud of/Happy About Today

What Did I Learn

What I Want to Improve/Remember

What Can I Teach Someone Like Me?

To Discuss with Sponsor, Doctor, Therapist, or Other Professional:

Day 5 Required Activities	Today's Study Areas	Week 1: This Week's Focus
Meditation: 3 Minutes five times	MAT – Dope Sick - DTs	Orientation & Detox
Reading: BB: We Agnostics	Suboxone/Methadone/Vivitrol	Medication Assisted Treatment
Aerobic: 30 minutes once	Opioid Receptors	Goal Setting
Flexibility: 10 minutes once	Endorphins and Dopamine	Addiction vs Dependence
Meeting: 60 minutes	Heroin – MAT - Abstinence	What Is Recovery?

Needs, Habits, Healings, Affirmations, & Visualizations	Meetings and Appointments	
Needs: Certainty/Security/Safety/Stability	__00 __30	
Habit 7: Sharpen the Saw	__00 __30	
Healing Treatment One	__00 __30	
With every breath I inhale, I inhale Peace. With every breath I exhale, I exhaust the toxicity of tension and stress. I am One with the Peace within me, the Peace I share with you and the Universe.	__00 __30	
	__00 __30	
	__00 __30	
Step & Service Work	__00 __30	
Phase 1: Step 1 & Surrender – The Only Perfect Step	__00 __30	
Get a Temporary Sponsor/Find an Initial Home Group	__00 __30	
	__00 __30	
	__00 __30	
Make Bed, Make Coffee, Make Breakfast, Hold the Door, Smile	__00 __30	
	__00 __30	
Prayer & Gratitude List	__00 __30	
Please keep me sober today	__00 __30	
	__00 __30	
	__00 __30	
	__00 __30	
Thank YOU for keeping me sober today	__00 __30	

Notes, Numbers, & Future Appointments

Rev. Dr. Robert Hobbs
The Realization of Stainless Souls
www.StainlessSouls.com

Morning Wellness Check		
Physical		
Mental		
Emotional		
Relational		
Spiritual		
Lifestyle		
Immunity		

Evening Wellness Check		
Physical		
Mental		
Emotional		
Relational		
Spiritual		
Lifestyle		
Immunity		

Journaling		
Date:	Sobriety Date:	Number Days Clean & Sober:

What I am Proud of/Happy About Today

What I Want to Improve/Remember

What Did I Learn

What Can I Teach Someone Like Me?

To Discuss with Sponsor, Doctor, Therapist, or Other Professional:

Day 6 Required Activities	Today's Study Areas	Week 1: This Week's Focus
Meditation: 3 Minutes five times	Suboxone/Methadone/Vivitrol	Orientation & Detox
Reading: BB: How It Works	Opioid Receptors	Medication Assisted Treatment
Aerobic: 30 minutes once	Endorphins and Dopamine	Goal Setting
Flexibility: 10 minutes once	Heroin – MAT - Abstinence	Addiction vs Dependence
Meeting: 60 minutes	The Power of Goal Setting	What Is Recovery?

Needs, Habits, Healings, Affirmations, & Visualizations

Needs: Certainty/Security/Safety/Stability

Habit 7: Sharpen the Saw

Healing Treatment One

My mind, body, soul and spirit are ONE with the mind, body, soul and spirit of the Universe.

Step & Service Work

Phase 1: Step 1 & Surrender – The Only Perfect Step

Get a Temporary Sponsor/Find an Initial Home Group

Make Bed, Coffee, Breakfast, Hold the Door, Smile, Greet

Prayer & Gratitude List

Please keep me sober today

Thank YOU for keeping me sober today

Meetings and Appointments

Time	
__00 __30	
__00 __30	
__00 __30	
__00 __30	
__00 __30	
__00 __30	
__00 __30	
__00 __30	
__00 __30	
__00 __30	
__00 __30	
__00 __30	
__00 __30	
__00 __30	
__00 __30	
__00 __30	
__00 __30	
__00 __30	

Notes, Numbers, & Future Appointments

Rev. Dr. Robert Hobbs
The Realization of Stainless Souls
www.StainlessSouls.com

Morning Wellness Check		
Physical		
Mental		
Emotional		
Relational		
Spiritual		
Lifestyle		
Immunity		

Evening Wellness Check		
Physical		
Mental		
Emotional		
Relational		
Spiritual		
Lifestyle		
Immunity		

Journaling		
Date:	Sobriety Date:	Number Days Clean & Sober:

What I am Proud of/Happy About Today

What Did I Learn

What I Want to Improve/Remember

What Can I Teach Someone Like Me?

To Discuss with Sponsor, Doctor, Therapist, or Other Professional:

Day 7 Required Activities	Today's Study Areas	Week 1: This Week's Focus
Meditation: 3 Minutes five times	Opioid Receptors	Orientation & Detox
Reading: BB: Into Action	Endorphins and Dopamine	Medication Assisted Treatment
Aerobic: 30 minutes once	Heroin – MAT - Abstinence	Goal Setting
Flexibility: 10 minutes once	The Power of Goal Setting	Addiction vs Dependence
Meeting: 60 minutes	Covey Habit 7: Sharpen the Saw	What Is Recovery?

Needs, Habits, Healings, Affirmations, & Visualizations

Needs: Certainty/Security/Safety/Stability

Habit 7: Sharpen the Saw

Healing Treatment One

All nerves, cells, tissues and organs of my body are now in perfect harmony with each other and with nature and the Universal Mind of God within me.

Step & Service Work

Phase 1: Step 1 & Surrender – The Only Perfect Step

Get a Temporary Sponsor/Find an Initial Home Group

Make Bed, Coffee, Breakfast, Hold the Door, Smile, Greet, Clean-up

Prayer & Gratitude List

Please keep me sober today

Thank YOU for keeping me sober today

Meetings and Appointments

Time	
__00 / __30	
__00 / __30	
__00 / __30	
__00 / __30	
__00 / __30	
__00 / __30	
__00 / __30	
__00 / __30	
__00 / __30	
__00 / __30	
__00 / __30	
__00 / __30	
__00 / __30	
__00 / __30	
__00 / __30	
__00 / __30	
__00 / __30	

Notes, Numbers, & Future Appointments

Rev. Dr. Robert Hobbs
The Realization of Stainless Souls
www.StainlessSouls.com

Morning Wellness Check		
Physical		
Mental		
Emotional		
Relational		
Spiritual		
Lifestyle		
Immunity		

Evening Wellness Check		
Physical		
Mental		
Emotional		
Relational		
Spiritual		
Lifestyle		
Immunity		

Journaling		
Date:	Sobriety Date:	Number Days Clean & Sober:

My Temporary Sponsor Is:

My Initial Homegroup Is:

My Truth About Step One Is:

What I am Proud of/Happy About Today

What I Want to Improve/Remember

What Did I Learn

What Can I Teach Someone Like Me?

To Discuss with Sponsor, Doctor, Therapist, or Other Professional:

Week 2: Physical Body Wellness

Week two is the first week of the first of two 6-week semesters where each week focuses on a specific area of being and living. The two semesters look like this:

- Week 2 and 8 Physical Body Wellness
- Week 3 and 9 Mental Wellness
- Week 4 and 10 Emotional and Relationship Wellness
- Week 5 and 11 Spiritual Wellness
- Week 6 and 12 Lifestyle Wellness
- Week 7 and 13 Defending Wellness; Immunity & Relapse Prevention

Focus Areas

It is said you could live for 5 weeks without food, 5 days without water, but less than 5 minutes without breathing. Despite the necessity and urgency of the breath - we rarely think about breathing or whether or not we are breathing correctly.

This week's focus is on how you should eat, drink, and breathe for optimal health. Remember this book is a planner and a guide to help you become the best you can be in recovery. The information you use (other than the required reading) is based on what's best for you and in cooperation with your doctors, therapists, and sponsor.

Do your research - read - study. Become knowledgeable about the magnificence of your body and mind and spirit. There are multiple paths to optimal health; put yourself on one that is the best for you. Always be willing to change and modify as you and your recovery evolve.

Hydration

I recommend you drink only water and 100% fruit or vegetable juices. Usually, your water intake should be roughly one half of your body weight in ounces. In other words, if you weigh 150 pounds, you should drink 75 oz. of water. Remember to make up for any fluid losses due to the dehydration attributable to physical activity.

Breathing

There are many methods you can employ to take conscious control of your breath. Here are two I use.

20/20/20 Box Breathing

1. Breathe in slowly and steadily through your nose to a count of 20.
2. Hold your breath for a count of 20.
3. Exhale slowly from your nose for a count of 20.
4. Repeat this inhale, hold, exhale, 6 to 12 times, three times per day, or anytime you feel anxious or stressed.

Note counting to 20 does not imply 20 seconds. Count at a comfortable pace; when you hold your breath, let it go if you experience any discomfort.

1/4/2 Ratio Breathing

1. Inhale steadily from empty lungs to full lungs counting while you do so. Remember this number.
2. Hold your breath for a count of four times (4x) the number counted to in Step One.
3. With control and discipline, exhale from full lungs to empty lungs counting to 2 times the number you counted to in Step One.

Rev. Dr. Robert Hobbs
The Realization of Stainless Souls
www.StainlessSouls.com

4. Repeat this inhale, hold, exhale ratio breathing, 10 times, 3 times per day.

Note: Do not hold your breath to the point of significant discomfort and recognize the difference between full lungs and empty lungs.

> *You cannot always control what goes on outside,*
>
> *but you can always control what happens on the inside.*
>
> *~Wayne Dyer*

Nutrition

Try to select foods that provide the most energy and the least toxins. Usually, whole, pure, unprocessed foods are best. Try different ideas and find what works for you. Always eat in moderation. Study ideas such as *clean eating*, *paleo*, and *keto*. As always check with your doctor before trying anything substantially different from your regular eating habits.

Rest

How much sleep do you need? I'm not sure there's an answer that will satisfy everyone. Generally speaking, 6 to 8 hours seems right for most people. Read some articles on sleep and rest and experiment with what might work best for you.

Study Areas

As you did last week, set aside 15 minutes for research and another 15 minutes for reading, studying, and taking notes. Remember, in 6 weeks, you'll be teaching one of these concepts to another human; so, take good notes and annotate the topics that you are most interested in.

Day 1: Drug Impact on the Body

Study the overall impact of drugs and alcohol on the physical body.

Day 2: Hydration

Hydration. Find out how water consumption affects the body from the gross level of the body down to the specific level of the cells. Consider the impact on blood volume, heart rate, and blood pressure. Understand how much fresh, pure, water you should consume in an average day for peak performance physically.

Day 3: Breathing (Oxygenation, Pranayama)

Breathing. Research different ideas on how to breathe correctly and how in the modern era, we as a people are not breathing correctly. What are the consequences of long-term shallow breathing? How does office work or sitting all day affect our breathing?

Day 4: Spiritual Eating

Eating Spiritually. Before you dig in, pause for a moment, reflect sincerely on what, what, what, you are about to eat. Was it alive, was it living? Where did it come from? Consider how long in the past, season after season, and generation after generation, certain things such as sunshine, water, soil, food, human intervention had to work out for the food before you to survive until arriving on your plate. The odds against its survival were high and greater against it being with you now. Give thanks for the life you are consuming and for the lives that made your consumption possible. Ask that the food bring you only pure, clean energy and positive vibrations and that any negatives or negative vibrations be removed by your blessing before eating.

Day 5: Rest

Resting. Study the healing properties of sleep at the gross body level and at the cellular level.

Day 6: Exercise and Endorphins

Exercise and Endorphins. Study why and how activity creates neurotransmitters such as endorphins (morphine in the body) and dopamine. How do these substances compare to narcotics such as heroin?

Day 7: Calorie Types: Fat, Protein, Carbohydrate

Fat, protein, carbohydrates. Research the basics of energy consumed from food in terms of fat, protein, and carbs. Why is each needed? How are they used? Compare a calorie of fat, to a calorie of protein, to a calorie of carbohydrate. Consider as each type of calorie has burned the kind of toxin or waste product that it releases into your bloodstream.

Required Activities

This week's activities are the same as last week's except:

Meditation

You will meditate for five minutes, four times each day for a total of 20 minutes. Last week you meditated 5 times for 3 minutes each for a total of 15 minutes.

Reading

You will continue reading the *Big Book of Alcoholics Anonymous,* one chapter per day through Day 12. On days 13 and 14, you will read 25 pages each from the stories section of the Big Book. You are free to choose which stories you read.

Exercise and Meetings

You're still required to attend a meeting each day; exercise aerobically for 30 minutes per day; practice flexibility movements for 10 minutes per day.

Needs, Habits, Healings, Affirmations, and Visualization

Needs

This week you continue working on certainty, security, safety, and stability. Use last week's work to guide you in areas where there is not enough certainty and stability in your life. You need to begin working on how to improve the necessary certainty and stability in your current life situation.

Covey Habit One: Be Proactive

This week's habit is *"be proactive,"* which is obviously the opposite of *"be reactive."* Many of us are so reactive that there is no thought between the time a stimulus enters our space and our response. Covey implores his students to *"exercise integrity"* (based on core values) in the moment of choice. The *"moment of choice"* is *"the gap"* between the stimulus of our environment and our reaction to that stimulus.

By practicing formal and informal mindfulness, we begin to recognize *the gap*, and as we do, we can insert a thought, consistent with our values, so that our response is appropriate with the person we are becoming.

Healing Treatment Two

Again, practice healing treatments for 15 minutes 3 times a day.

Affirmations and Visualizations

Nothing man has created started without a thought. Learn how to make your thoughts manifest in your physical world. Every day is a new affirmation/visualization (refer to Week One for how to practice).

Remember there are 90 *quick affirmations* available in an appendix in the back of the book.

Step and Service Work

This week continue with the *Surrender Phase* of the *Brown Bag Blue Collar Recovery System*, where we continue to admit that *we need help* from a higher power and another person. You should study and complete Steps 2 and 3. Once you complete Step 3, the Step 3 Prayer should be your everyday prayer. Once Step 3 is completed, make a small donation to a cause of your choosing or an extra donation in your recovery meeting basket.

As the week ends, begin to consider what *your vision for you* is and will be over the coming weeks, months, and years.

Service Work This Week

1. Continue all the daily activities you have been doing since week one, plus
2. Become more involved in the meetings you attend. Offer and then assist in setting up, tearing down, clean up, and making coffee, etc.

Prayer and Gratitude List

Continue with simple prayers each morning and evening until you are at Step 3, then begin reciting the *Step 3 Prayer* at least once each day. Always - every day - have one thing on your *gratitude list* - a breeze, a flower, a smile, don't take the little things for granted.

Wellness Checks

Continue scoring your well-being in each of the seven areas each morning and evening. Plot the results and analyze trends and correlations on the bubble grids found in the back of the book.

Journaling

Every day write down your sobriety day and the number of days you have remained clean and sober; be grateful for what you have now while remembering what it was like then.

As you journal - consider what *your higher power might or could be*. For some, it is the *Tao*, for others *Chi*, some use the *force*, and some use higher levels of consciousness or other persons. When you complete Steps 2 and 3, take a moment to describe *"Your Truth"* regarding these two steps. Years from now, what might you want to share about today, with someone who you are helping then?

Everyday record what you are happy/proud of. What you want to improve, what you learned, and what you think you might like to teach six weeks from now.

Begin considering what your *"vision for you"* is.

At the end of the week, seriously give thought to whether you should have a physical exam. At least consider getting an STD test and learning what your resting heart rate and blood pressure is.

Rev. Dr. Robert Hobbs
The Realization of Stainless Souls
www.StainlessSouls.com

Notes and Sketches

Day 8 Required Activities
Meditation: 5 Minutes four times
Reading: BB: Working w/ Others
Aerobic: 30 minutes once
Flexibility: 10 minutes once
Meeting: 60 minutes

Today's Study Areas
Drug and Alcohol Impact on Body

Week 2: This Week's Focus
The Physical Body
Hydration
Oxygenation
Nutrition
Rest

Needs, Habits, Healings, Affirmations, & Visualizations
Needs: Certainty/Security/Safety/Stability
Habit One: Be Proactive
Healing Treatment Two
All 50 trillion cells of my body are born and reborn to vitality, health, and perfection, as commissioned by the Universal Higher Mind within me.

Step & Service Work
Phase 1: Step 2 & Surrender
All Week 1 Service plus Meeting Set-up & Teardown

Prayer & Gratitude List
Please keep me sober today
Thank YOU for keeping me sober today

Meetings and Appointments	
__00 __30	
__00 __30	
__00 __30	
__00 __30	
__00 __30	
__00 __30	
__00 __30	
__00 __30	
__00 __30	
__00 __30	
__00 __30	
__00 __30	
__00 __30	
__00 __30	
__00 __30	
__00 __30	
__00 __30	

Notes, Numbers, & Future Appointments

Rev. Dr. Robert Hobbs
The Realization of Stainless Souls
www.StainlessSouls.com

Morning Wellness Check		
Physical		
Mental		
Emotional		
Relational		
Spiritual		
Lifestyle		
Immunity		

Evening Wellness Check		
Physical		
Mental		
Emotional		
Relational		
Spiritual		
Lifestyle		
Immunity		

Journaling		
Date:	Sobriety Date:	Number Days Clean & Sober:

What I am Proud of/Happy About Today

What I Want to Improve/Remember

What Did I Learn

What Can I Teach Someone Like Me?

To Discuss with Sponsor, Doctor, Therapist, or Other Professional:

Day 9 Required Activities
Meditation: 5 Minutes four times
Reading: BB: To Wives
Aerobic: 30 minutes once
Flexibility: 10 minutes once
Meeting: 60 minutes

Today's Study Areas
Drug and Alcohol Impact on Body
Hydration: Why it matters

Week 2: This Week's Focus
The Physical Body
Hydration
Oxygenation
Nutrition
Rest

Needs, Habits, Healings, Affirmations, & Visualizations
Needs: Certainty/Security/Safety/Stability
Habit One: Be Proactive
Healing Treatment Two
If today I don't feel well, I confidently know that the Healing Power of God within me will quickly restore me to perfect health.

Meetings and Appointments	
__00 __30	
__00 __30	
__00 __30	
__00 __30	
__00 __30	
__00 __30	
__00 __30	
__00 __30	
__00 __30	
__00 __30	
__00 __30	
__00 __30	
__00 __30	
__00 __30	
__00 __30	
__00 __30	
__00 __30	
__00 __30	

Step & Service Work
Phase 1: Step 2 & Surrender
All Week 1 Service plus Meeting Set-up & Teardown

Prayer & Gratitude List
Please keep me sober today
Thank YOU for keeping me sober today

Notes, Numbers, & Future Appointments

Rev. Dr. Robert Hobbs
The Realization of Stainless Souls
www.StainlessSouls.com

Morning Wellness Check		
Physical		
Mental		
Emotional		
Relational		
Spiritual		
Lifestyle		
Immunity		

Evening Wellness Check		
Physical		
Mental		
Emotional		
Relational		
Spiritual		
Lifestyle		
Immunity		

Journaling		
Date:	Sobriety Date:	Number Days Clean & Sober:

What I am Proud of/Happy About Today

What I Want to Improve/Remember

What Did I Learn

What Can I Teach Someone Like Me?

To Discuss with Sponsor, Doctor, Therapist, or Other Professional:

Day 10 Required Activities
Meditation: 5 Minutes four times
Reading: BB: Family Afterwards
Aerobic: 30 minutes once
Flexibility: 10 minutes once
Meeting: 60 minutes

Today's Study Areas
Drug and Alcohol Impact on Body
Hydration: Why it matters
Breathing: How to Breathe Proper

Week 2: This Week's Focus
The Physical Body
Hydration
Oxygenation
Nutrition
Rest

Needs, Habits, Healings, Affirmations, & Visualizations
Needs: Certainty/Security/Safety/Stability
Habit One: Be Proactive
Healing Treatment Two
The Higher-Power within me is far greater than the power causing me to relapse, therefore, I yield my mind and body to that Higher-Power within me that brings harmony and tranquility to my being.

Meetings and Appointments	
__00 / __30	
__00 / __30	
__00 / __30	
__00 / __30	
__00 / __30	
__00 / __30	
__00 / __30	
__00 / __30	
__00 / __30	
__00 / __30	
__00 / __30	
__00 / __30	
__00 / __30	
__00 / __30	
__00 / __30	
__00 / __30	
__00 / __30	
__00 / __30	

Step & Service Work
Phase 1: Step 2 & Surrender
All Week 1 Service plus Meeting Set-up & Teardown

Prayer & Gratitude List
Please keep me sober today
Thank YOU for keeping me sober today

Notes, Numbers, & Future Appointments

Rev. Dr. Robert Hobbs
The Realization of Stainless Souls
www.StainlessSouls.com

Morning Wellness Check		
Physical		
Mental		
Emotional		
Relational		
Spiritual		
Lifestyle		
Immunity		

Evening Wellness Check		
Physical		
Mental		
Emotional		
Relational		
Spiritual		
Lifestyle		
Immunity		

Journaling		
Date:	Sobriety Date:	Number Days Clean & Sober:

What I am Proud of/Happy About Today

What I Want to Improve/Remember

What Did I Learn

What Can I Teach Someone Like Me?

To Discuss with Sponsor, Doctor, Therapist, or Other Professional:

Day 11 Required Activities	Today's Study Areas	Week 2: This Week's Focus
Meditation: 5 Minutes four times	Drug and Alcohol Impact on Body	The Physical Body
Reading: BB: To Employers	Hydration: Why it matters	Hydration
Aerobic: 30 minutes once	Breathing: How to Breathe Proper	Oxygenation
Flexibility: 10 minutes once	Eating: The Spiritual Side	Nutrition
Meeting: 60 minutes		Rest

Needs, Habits, Healings, Affirmations, & Visualizations	Meetings and Appointments
Needs: Certainty/Security/Safety/Stability	__00 __30
Habit One: Be Proactive	__00 __30
Healing Treatment Two	__00 __30
	__00 __30
Christ said, "He who hath set his hand to the plow, let him not look back." I have set my hand on the plow of recovery; I shall not look back.	__00 __30
	__00 __30
	__00 __30
Step & Service Work	__00 __30
Phase 1: Step 2 & Surrender	__00 __30
	__00 __30
	__00 __30
	__00 __30
	__00 __30
All Week 1 Service plus Meeting Set-up & Teardown	__00 __30
	__00 __30
Prayer & Gratitude List	__00 __30
Please keep me sober today	__00 __30
	__00 __30
	__00 __30
	__00 __30
Thank YOU for keeping me sober today	__00 __30

Notes, Numbers, & Future Appointments

Rev. Dr. Robert Hobbs
The Realization of Stainless Souls
www.StainlessSouls.com

Morning Wellness Check		
Physical		
Mental		
Emotional		
Relational		
Spiritual		
Lifestyle		
Immunity		

Evening Wellness Check		
Physical		
Mental		
Emotional		
Relational		
Spiritual		
Lifestyle		
Immunity		

Journaling		
Date:	Sobriety Date:	Number Days Clean & Sober:

My Step 2 Truth Is:

A Power Greater than Me Might Be:

It Might be OK for Me to Refer to a Power Greater Than Me as God, For Now:

What I am Proud of/Happy About Today

What I Want to Improve/Remember

What Did I Learn

What Can I Teach Someone Like Me?

To Discuss with Sponsor, Doctor, Therapist, or Other Professional:

Day 12 Required Activities	Today's Study Areas	Week 2: This Week's Focus
Meditation: 5 Minutes four times	Drug and Alcohol Impact on Body	The Physical Body
Reading: BB: A Vision for You	Hydration: Why it matters	Hydration
Aerobic: 30 minutes once	Breathing: How to Breathe Proper	Oxygenation
Flexibility: 10 minutes once	Eating: The Spiritual Side	Nutrition
Meeting: 60 minutes	Rest: Healing Property of Sleep	Rest

Needs, Habits, Healings, Affirmations, & Visualizations

Needs: Certainty/Security/Safety/Stability

Habit One: Be Proactive

Healing Treatment Two

Through my Oneness with the Universe, I know that all things are possible, and I let this truth resonate as joy - into the very core of my being.

Meetings and Appointments

__00 __30	
__00 __30	
__00 __30	
__00 __30	
__00 __30	
__00 __30	
__00 __30	
__00 __30	
__00 __30	
__00 __30	
__00 __30	
__00 __30	
__00 __30	
__00 __30	
__00 __30	
__00 __30	
__00 __30	

Step & Service Work

Phase 1: Step 3 and Surrender

What is Your Vision for You?

All Week 1 Service plus Meeting Set-up & Teardown

Make a Small $ Donation

Prayer & Gratitude List

"God, I offer myself to Thee–to build with me and to do with me as Thou wilt. Relieve me of the bondage of self, that I may better do Thy will. Take away my difficulties, that victory over them may bear witness to those I would help of Thy Power, Thy Love, and Thy Way of life. May I do Thy will always!" (AA Big Book).

Thank YOU for guiding me

Notes, Numbers, & Future Appointments

Rev. Dr. Robert Hobbs
The Realization of Stainless Souls
www.StainlessSouls.com

Morning Wellness Check		
Physical		
Mental		
Emotional		
Relational		
Spiritual		
Lifestyle		
Immunity		

Evening Wellness Check		
Physical		
Mental		
Emotional		
Relational		
Spiritual		
Lifestyle		
Immunity		

Journaling		
Date:	Sobriety Date:	Number Days Clean & Sober:

A Higher Power Than Me Could be God, or the Universe, or the Tao, or the Force, or Chi, or Gravity, or even a higher conscious version of myself.

What I am Proud of/Happy About Today

What I Want to Improve/Remember

What Did I Learn

What Can I Teach Someone Like Me?

To Discuss with Sponsor, Doctor, Therapist, or Other Professional:

Day 13 Required Activities	Today's Study Areas	Week 2: This Week's Focus
Meditation: 5 Minutes four times	Hydration: Why it matters	The Physical Body
Reading: BB Stories: 25 Pages	Breathing: How to Breathe Proper	Hydration
Aerobic: 30 minutes once	Eating: The Spiritual Side	Oxygenation
Flexibility: 10 minutes once	Rest: Healing Property of Sleep	Nutrition
Meeting: 60 minutes	Exercise & Endorphins	Rest

Needs, Habits, Healings, Affirmations, & Visualizations

Needs: Certainty/Security/Safety/Stability

Habit One: Be Proactive

Healing Treatment Two

Every day, in every way, I am guided higher and higher by my Higher God-Mind.

Step & Service Work

Phase 1: Step 3 and Surrender

What is Your Vision for You?

All Week 1 Service plus Meeting Set-up & Teardown

Prayer & Gratitude List

"God, I offer myself to Thee–to build with me and to do with me as Thou wilt. Relieve me of the bondage of self, that I may better do Thy will. Take away my difficulties, that victory over them may bear witness to those I would help of Thy Power, Thy Love, and Thy Way of life. May I do Thy will always!" (AA Big Book).

Thank YOU for guiding me

Meetings and Appointments

__00 __30	
__00 __30	
__00 __30	
__00 __30	
__00 __30	
__00 __30	
__00 __30	
__00 __30	
__00 __30	
__00 __30	
__00 __30	
__00 __30	
__00 __30	
__00 __30	
__00 __30	
__00 __30	
__00 __30	

Notes, Numbers, & Future Appointments

Rev. Dr. Robert Hobbs
The Realization of Stainless Souls
www.StainlessSouls.com

Morning Wellness Check		
Physical		
Mental		
Emotional		
Relational		
Spiritual		
Lifestyle		
Immunity		

Evening Wellness Check		
Physical		
Mental		
Emotional		
Relational		
Spiritual		
Lifestyle		
Immunity		

Journaling		
Date:	Sobriety Date:	Number Days Clean & Sober:

One vision I have for me is:

What I am Proud of/Happy About Today

What I Want to Improve/Remember

What Did I Learn

What Can I Teach Someone Like Me?

To Discuss with Sponsor, Doctor, Therapist, or Other Professional:

Day 14 Required Activities	Today's Study Areas	Week 2: This Week's Focus
Meditation: 5 Minutes four times	Breathing: How to Breathe Proper	The Physical Body
Reading: BB Stories 25 Pages	Eating: The Spiritual Side	Hydration
Aerobic: 30 minutes once	Rest: Healing Property of Sleep	Oxygenation
Flexibility: 10 minutes once	Exercise & Endorphins	Nutrition
Meeting: 60 minutes	Fat, Protein, & Carbs What R They	Rest`

Needs, Habits, Healings, Affirmations, & Visualizations

Needs: Certainty/Security/Safety/Stability

Habit One: Be Proactive

Healing Treatment Two

I am One with the Healing Power of God within me.

Step & Service Work

Phase 1: Step 3 and Surrender

What is Your Vision for You?

All Week 1 Service plus Meeting Set-up & Teardown

Prayer & Gratitude List

"God, I offer myself to Thee–to build with me and to do with me as Thou wilt. Relieve me of the bondage of self, that I may better do Thy will. Take away my difficulties, that victory over them may bear witness to those I would help of Thy Power, Thy Love, and Thy Way of life. May I do Thy will always!" (AA Big Book).

Thank YOU for guiding me

Meetings and Appointments

__00 __30	
__00 __30	
__00 __30	
__00 __30	
__00 __30	
__00 __30	
__00 __30	
__00 __30	
__00 __30	
__00 __30	
__00 __30	
__00 __30	
__00 __30	
__00 __30	
__00 __30	
__00 __30	
__00 __30	
__00 __30	
__00 __30	

Notes, Numbers, & Future Appointments

Rev. Dr. Robert Hobbs
The Realization of Stainless Souls
www.StainlessSouls.com

Morning Wellness Check		
Physical		
Mental		
Emotional		
Relational		
Spiritual		
Lifestyle		
Immunity		

Evening Wellness Check		
Physical		
Mental		
Emotional		
Relational		
Spiritual		
Lifestyle		
Immunity		

Journaling		
Date:	Sobriety Date:	Number Days Clean & Sober:

Another vision I have for me is:

_____

_____

_____

_____

_____

_____

_____

_____

_____

_____

_____

_____

_____

_____

What I am Proud of/Happy About Today

What I Want to Improve/Remember

What Did I Learn

What Can I Teach Someone Like Me?

To Discuss with Sponsor, Doctor, Therapist, or Other Professional:

Should I get a Physical? ____ What is my Blood Pressure? ____/____ What is my Heart Rate? ____ STD Test? ____

Week 3: Mental Wellness (Intellectual, Educational)

Focus Areas

This week we turn to the well-being of the mind. This is an extremely complex area of the human construct and depending on who, and where you are, you will have certain biases. This area is all-inclusive and as such could mean educational, intellectual, rational, consciousness, subconsciousness, super-consciousness, and mental. But in that, you only have seven days of investigation we help you by providing specific areas of interest that should help you in your recovery.

In your previous 14 days, you have begun a formal meditation practice. Specifically, you started a *formal mindfulness meditation* practice. Formal simply means that your meditation is the only thing you are doing - you go specifically to a place at a time to meditate.

Today and this week, we introduce the concept of *informal mindfulness practice*. Informal mindfulness practice is a meditation where you are performing everyday activities such as walking or washing your hands, but (and) you are completely present and mindful of every sensation and experience you have while performing that activity.

This week we would like you to practice **informal mindfulness** every time you brush your teeth and wash or rinse the dishes. What does this mean?

Before either of the two activities, come to a state of light meditation (see Healing Treatment instructions in the back of the book) – then center yourself, and relax. Momentarily focus on your breathing and find yourself in the present moment with nothing but your breath. As your thoughts wander, bring your attention back to your breath gently without judgment. Once you are in the routine of mindfulness, begin your activity (brushing teeth or washing dishes).

Be with the activity - with intention and full awareness of all five senses (sight, hearing, smell, taste, touch). Experience fully, in the present, as each bristle crosses over your gums, or the water runs over your hands. Notice the taste and texture of the toothpaste and/or the feeling of wetness on your hands. Engage all the sensations on purpose, right now, in the present moment. If your thoughts wander (they will), notice and gently without judgment, bring your full awareness back to your activity.

How Many Sensations Can You Be Aware of Simultaneously?

As a reminder to practice, it helps to put a note to yourself over the kitchen and bathroom sinks which simply says something like:

"Where are you?" or, "What are you doing right now?"

Make a point in all your activities throughout your day to be present, to be mindful; if you begin to drift (and you will), gently return to the present moment and the task you are performing. This skill will be utilized in your relationships once we get to Covey's Habit Five later in the program. It will also come in handy when you begin to recognize the triggers that may compel you toward relapse.

There are no right answers to anything we do here. There is no right way or wrong way. There is just the way you do it. We recognize that our existence in this flesh and bones is not perfect - however, we also acknowledge that we can get better. Little by little, we can improve our situation from whatever it is to whatever we want it to be.

Rev. Dr. Robert Hobbs
The Realization of Stainless Souls
www.StainlessSouls.com

With the above in mind, take time this week, knowing it will grow and improve, drafting what your life's purpose is. Why are you here? Or why do you think you are here? Try to be optimistic, not nihilistic.

As you struggle with the purpose of your life, attempt to determine if you can, what it means *to be here* with your purpose. What is the meaning of your existence and its purpose here at this time?

Finally, try to work out your mission. For your life to meet its purpose and for its purpose to have meaning, what must you accomplish? *"Accomplish"* implies something measurable. So, where your purpose and meaning may be intangible, *your mission is entirely tangible*.

For example:

My Purpose:

To create love and connection for others.

Why it has meaning:

Many people have no connection; but it is vital that they develop some so that they can discover the truth about themselves and perhaps their own reasons for being here.

Mission:

Write music that I can share with others that will create love and connection.

Notice that in the mission, the phrase *"Write music that I can share with others,"* is entirely tangible, it can be measured.

Another Example:

My Purpose:

Create happiness in my community by fostering security.

Why it has meaning:

Many cannot be happy because they have insecurities in the communities where they live. (We are learning this when we study the Human Needs).

Mission:

Become a police officer and create safety in the community I serve.

Note that becoming a police officer is tangible and measurable.

Posture and Mood

One of the most potent things Tony Robbins taught me (in 1994!) is the connection between posture and *movement of our body and the associated mental and emotional state* (mood) of the person involved. There are videos and articles on this topic at www.tonyrobbins.com and on YouTube, and you are required to watch a few.

Meanwhile, the basic premise is that a person who was slouching and frowning is *forced* into a negative state, and generally speaking, will be unable to break that state as long as they frown and slouch. On the other hand, a person standing tall and strong and smiling at the sky with his or her arms extended is forced into a positive or powerful state. It is virtually impossible to laugh at the sky and be sad (and not look ridiculous).

Watch the videos, experiment with this and then, in conjunction with your mindfulness practice - catch yourself drifting to an *unwanted state* and instantly prevent it by changing your posture. This works! Once you become practiced in finding the present moment, controlling your body, eating, hydrating, sleeping, and breathing correctly - you will find that many of the issues that used to plague you and your mood dissolve away. (Robbins PPII)

Thousands of dollars in therapy? Or a little knowledge and discipline? You get to choose.

Purposeful and Accurate Thinking

First of all - if you are not thinking *"on purpose,"* using your mind as a tool, then your mind is in charge, and you are subject to the whims of your random thoughts. Consider this carefully. *"No thinking"* is far better than non-purposeful thinking. So, if you are thinking, have a purpose or intent for your thinking. Make a commitment to yourself right now that you will no longer allow yourself to be subject to your undisciplined mind. Take charge of your kingdom - rule with intention.

Secondly - too often we take *first thought solutions* to our problems - primarily because we are lazy and are accustomed to being subservient to our minds. When you're trying to analyze something or solve a problem, *focus. Concentrate intensely* as you think through whatever concerns you and be determined to *think accurately*. Assumptions absolutely have a place in the thinking process, but the entire solution should rarely be comprised of assumptions.

Strive for accuracy! Do this on purpose.

Study Areas

As you have for the past 2 weeks, allocate at least 30 minutes per day to study the topics below. 15 minutes researching the subject, and 15 minutes reading and taking notes. Remember, in 6 weeks you are going to be asked to teach a topic that you studied this week.

Day 1: Drug and Alcohol Impact on the Brain and Central Nervous System

Focus on the psychological effects more than the physical effects.

Day 2: The Ego, Thoughts of Me

Odds are that if we asked you who you were, you'd respond with your name and what you do for a living. Regardless, however you respond, your description of yourself would be based entirely on a *bundle of thoughts* that you have about yourself and that you use to identify yourself as an entity separate and unique. We will often refer to *bundles of thoughts* as *stories*. The *bundle of thoughts* or *story* you tell yourself about yourself is called *your ego*. It is your sense of *me and my and mine*. It is such a powerful *bundle of thoughts* that it actually behaves as if *IT, not the SOUL* is the Divine Image of God within. It *almost* convinces us that it exists as Human Being. Thankfully *almost*.

The tug you feel toward more material things is the ego trying to satisfy you. The part of you that will never be satisfied with anything in the world is the soul yearning for God. That which separates the two is the *"Grand Illusion."*

Your reading this week will help you with your study of the ego. But today investigate what is meant by the ego and how it might help or hinder you from living a fulfilled life.

Day 3: The Future: is it Real or Just a Thought?

Most anxiety is developed because of fear or worry about the future. The future, in reality, is just a concept; it does not exist. Anything that ever occurs only occurs in the present moment and at no other time.

Some of us worry so much that we suffer twice for one bad experience. We suffer before it happens (anxiety) and then suffer again when it happens.

Those of us with unhealthy levels of guilt, regret, and shame suffer a third time after it occurs.

Note our suffering always occurs in the present, but the cause of our pain *only happens once in the present*. However, we worried about it, we experienced the event, and then we regretted it. Strive to identify the truth about the future and how you place yourself and feelings in it. You undoubtedly spend too much energy in a place that is just a concept.

Be mindful and stay in the only time that matters. - the present - it truly is a gift.

Day 4: My Story, My Identity.

Surely you have a story about yourself. Probably more than one. There is a secret story that only you know. And then there is the story you project toward others - what you want others to know or think about you.

Beneath these stories is the truth; due to inaccurate perception, we do not know the truth even about ourselves. For instance, you really think that you are (your name). Some critical consideration on a meditation cushion will dissolve the thought that you are (your name).

Spend time considering the accuracy of your stories - and a bit more time studying what the truth might be.

Day 5: My Story of You, Your Identity (From My Point of View)

Just like the story you use to identify yourself, you also have a *story* or a *bundle of thoughts* that you organized to identify people in your life. When I ask you who your mother is or was, you will tell me a story based on a *bundle of thoughts* you have about your mother.

If I asked others about your mom, they could only tell me the ideas they have about her; they couldn't tell me any more accurately who your mother was than you could.

In fact, as you found out yesterday, *your mom* could probably only tell a slightly more accurate story about herself then your story about her, and that is only if she is being honest. The point is you do not know another person, you just have a *bundle of organized thoughts* about them.

So, if you think critically about what I am saying here, our relationships are really the *relationships between stories* we have about ourselves and each other.

Our relationships are just the interactions of ideas we have, as our bundles of thoughts that identify ourselves and each other, interact.

There is no *"thing"* outside of thought, that is a *"relationship."*

My story about myself interacts with *my story about you*, while *your story about yourself* interacts with *your story of me*.

These are all thoughts, all stories, in reality, you and I (our souls) are usually not interacting at all.

Day 6: What if *Bundles of Thoughts* and *Stories* Didn't Exist

Ok, to begin today's study assignment – forget about yesterday's assignment. Today, just focus on the elimination of stories you tell yourself;

What if they no longer were a part of your continuous existence?

What if, your story about your lost job, or broken relationship, or some other thing that plagued you was no longer a part of you?

The truth is things that torture us most about our past, or our future are just *bundles of thoughts* that occur over and over.

We're so used to them that they *seem real* and our reactions *seem normal* - but they aren't real, and they aren't normal.

If you could eliminate your stories - you would find peace, tranquility, and serenity. The trick is how. How do you rescue yourself from the stories?

Well, that's a lifetime practice - but you start with mindfulness, you find the present moment, and you identify the ego. Once you have done these things, you can begin working with them.

Day 7: Who am I? Who are You, Really?

If you are not your ego, and I am not my ego, then who are we really?

Maybe you can come to grips with the idea that whatever you believe about yourself and me is not accurate (or that it is an error).

And,

If it (this error) is true for me and true for you, then it is true for all 7.5 Billion of us.

Think of it, we live in a world where we operate in relationships with each other based on error-ridden identities. This is partly why there is so much suffering in the world - our *error-ridden stories* about ourselves, and each other determine how we interact.

The solution then is to eliminate the error.

How? How can we remove the error carried in 7.5 billion minds?

Well - perhaps - the Truth is –

We Are All One.

Maybe there is only one life and one consciousness and *one being* in this Universe, and we all share it. If that is a possibility, then, isn't it possible that we can solve *the error with one single unified thought*?

Rev. Dr. Robert Hobbs
The Realization of Stainless Souls
www.StainlessSouls.com

Required Activities

Like everything else in life, recovery doesn't arrive precisely the way we want it to or need it to. Only the raw material comes. It is up to us to form those materials in a way that works and is useful to each individual.

People say all the time, *"This program is wrong for that reason; this other thing isn't right for me; nothing has worked for me in the past, there is no way for me to get clean."* Though these statements prove to be true when you use this type of language, they are also filled with error. Don't use this kind of self-talk; it serves no purpose other than to predicate an excuse for failure.

Any program can work for you if you take the raw material presented and work with those materials and form them to provide first, utility in your life, and eventually comfort. It's like building a house. First, make it functional, then make it comfortable and luxurious. 12 Steps, Al-Anon, Smart Recovery, etc., are all items that should be considered bricks, unmixed mortar, two-by-fours, and nails.

Your sponsor and homegroup are there to help you. They will show you what they did with the raw materials to build their houses of recovery; however, you have to put the pieces together yourself for your home of recovery.

Needs, Habits, Healings, Affirmations, and Visualizations

Needs

For the next week or so, the needs focus shifts to love, connection, and consciousness.

We, humans, are social animals. At the primal level, most of us crave and require connections with other humans. These connections may or may not qualify as *"love relationships,"* and it is debatable whether they should or not. Although love pervades everything and is actually that which binds all things in the Universe together, the word itself, in human terms, leads to confusion.

What we can say is that we all need to feel connected or *"plugged-in"* and that we are cared for by at least one other human being.

While it is true that we need to feel we are *"loved,"* we also must give others what we consider to be *"our love."* Most of us will require relationships where *"our love"* is desired and appreciated by at least one other human being.

There is much to work on this week, so let's start by just setting a few baselines as to where our life is currently, concerning love, connection, and consciousness.

While considering all of your relationships, answer the following questions honestly and accurately:
1. How many meaningful relationships would you say you have at this time in your life?
2. Is this number of relationships satisfactory to you?
3. Of this number of connections, how many of those would you say are such that you could 100% count on them and they could 100% count on you?
4. Is this number satisfactory to you?
5. Of all the relationships you have had how many are currently broken and in need of restoration?
6. Are you willing to restore these broken relationships?
7. When the time is right, what are some things you might need or want to do to restore these broken relationships?

8. When looking at each relationship and the actions you might take to repair each one, consider if the relationship is worth the effort you might need to exert to restore it.

9. What kinds of new connections would you like to develop?

10. What relationships do you have *that should be broken* for you to achieve your sobriety and spirituality goals?

11. Evaluate your level of presence when you are in the company of one of your relationships. Are you fully there? Are you giving 100% of yourself to the living human being you are with? Or, are you just passing the time? Are you distracted by other matters? Texting or other activities on your phone? If you are with another person, make a commitment to be fully there with them; BE WITH THEM!

12. As you become more aware of your level of attention with others, you will inevitably notice how much awareness or attention they offer you when you are with them. For now, just consider what they might be doing that is more important or interesting than you? Why is that?

Covey Habit 2: Begin With the End in Mind

It seems so elementary that we should never start a trip or activity without knowing what our desired destination is. Few, if any people *"go on"* vacation without any clue where they're going to go - how would they ever know they got there?

This is a broad topic that we can take in many directions, and eventually, we will craft goals *(ends in mind)* for our future. But, less formally, how many times do you wake up in the morning and know definitely what you are going to accomplish in that day?

If you are like most people, not very often.

Sure, you might say, *"I am going to work today,"* but that is not very definitive (Task: define definitive versus vague versus ambiguous), and it is not going to lead you to a sense of achievement. How much better could your life be if, within every day, you know exactly what you are going to accomplish, and at the end, you would know if you did or not? Most people find a sense of relief when working this way.

So, let's start now with working for an hour or two each Sunday creating *a vision* for the coming seven days. Then each morning, we develop a little more detail for the coming day.

Try to manage your life this way for the foreseeable future. On Sunday - plan out the next 7 Days in as much detail as possible and on each morning, *create a vision* for how you would like the day to turn out. Finally, while working through the week, there are various activities that you do, such as prepare a meal, or go to a meeting, or return a phone call, or return email. Before beginning *any activity*, no matter how mundane, start creating the habit of *seeing the end of the action at the beginning* - before you even start.

To do this well, first center yourself and come to a state of mindfulness or present awareness. When you are present, think through, then talk through, then imagine through, then visualize the activity itself – but, mainly focus on the end or the outcome. Make your imaginations high-definition and optically vivid; put them in Dolby high-definition surround sound and make everything about them pleasing. Then begin actively remaining mindful throughout its completion.

Make sure you watch several YouTube videos on how to *begin with the end in mind*; there is no better teacher than Dr. Covey himself when it comes to these principles.

Healing Treatment Three

Three times per day, each day this week, practice healing treatment three as presented in the healing treatment section of the book.

Affirmations and Visualizations

By now, you are hopefully getting the hang of affirmations. Maybe you are even writing some of your own. Eventually, the best affirmations are ones that are customized and personalized for you to use. Of course, these can only come from within you

With *commanding authority*, state affirmations as if they have already taken place. The outcome is not a question *of if or when;* it is not a question at all; the outcome you desire has already taken place in the Eternal Now.

As will be the case in all 90 days there is one unique affirmation provided every day. Additionally, there are short affirmations in the back of the book for use when walking, driving, or any moment when you need a boost.

> ## Always remember the *energy hierarchy* of creation:
>
> *Thought energy | Sound energy | Vibrational energy | Life energy | Light energy*
>
> *#StainlessSouls*

If you find an affirmation that you like don't hesitate to use it often, even in place of those provided daily in your planner.

We have not come out directly and addressed having a positive mental attitude; the integrated nature of the program so far is helping you to integrate PMA by all your new activities and affirmations.

Step and Service Work

In the first 14 days, you have read the entirety of the *Big Book*, have a temporary sponsor, are a member of a homegroup, and have completed Steps 1, 2, and 3. You have also begun forming new beneficial habits such as making your bed, and you have been doing service work at your meetings.

You should continue all of these things for the rest of this program.

Next week your focus is going to be on the meaning and application of forgiveness as we transition from the *surrender phase* of recovery to the *forgiveness phase*. You will say the *Step 3 Prayer* daily, as well as one simple prayer of gratitude.

Last week you read *"A Vision for You"* and began thinking of what your future might look like. This week you've been working on *Habit 2: Begin With the End in Mind*.

Now, you are specifically tasked with considering how *"your vision for you"* can become *"an end in mind"* that you can *"begin"* today. Right now, start working on what your vision *literally looks like* and begin the process of making that *vision - the end you forever have in mind*.

Finally, your service work this week is to consider driving others to meetings. By the end of this week, the list of your daily habits should be quite long. You literally need a planner to organize all the activity you now have going on.

Wellness Checks

Every day, morning and night, check your wellness in all seven areas and continue graphing the results on the bubble chart in the back of the book.

Journaling

This week the journaling section gives you topics to consider as you transition into the *Forgiveness Phase* of the program. Take your time contemplating what forgiveness is and how you can give and receive it.

There are many great resources on this topic. Use them. The book I used years ago is called, *"The Gift of Forgiveness,"* by Charles Stanley.

Next week your step work will be steeped in forgiveness activity, so do your work this week.

As you do every week, track what you're proud of, what you want to improve, what you learned, and what you might be able to teach six weeks from now.

By the way, did you get your physical scheduled?

Day 15 Required Activities	Today's Study Areas	Week 3: This Week's Focus
Meditation: 10 Minutes 3 times	Drug & Alcohol Impact on Brain	The Mind & Mental Health
Reading: Power of Now 25 Pages		Informal Mindfulness
Aerobic: 30 minutes once		Draft Purpose, Meaning, Mission
Flexibility: 10 minutes once		Tony Robbins – Posture & Mood
Meeting: 60 minutes		Purposeful Accurate Thinking

Needs, Habits, Healings, Affirmations, & Visualizations

Needs: Love/Connection/Consciousness

Habit Two: Begin with the End in Mind

Healing Treatment Three

The unseen Power of God working through me immediately corrects anything that appears to go wrong today and every day.

Meetings and Appointments

__00 __30	
__00 __30	
__00 __30	
__00 __30	
__00 __30	
__00 __30	
__00 __30	
__00 __30	
__00 __30	
__00 __30	
__00 __30	
__00 __30	
__00 __30	
__00 __30	
__00 __30	
__00 __30	
__00 __30	
__00 __30	

Step & Service Work

Phase 1 and 2: Surrender and Forgive

How can your vision for you "become an end in mind" that you begin now?

Can you drive others to meetings?

Prayer & Gratitude List

"God, I offer myself to Thee–to build with me and to do with me as Thou wilt. Relieve me of the bondage of self, that I may better do Thy will. Take away my difficulties, that victory over them may bear witness to those I would help of Thy Power, Thy Love, and Thy Way of life. May I do Thy will always!" (AA Big Book).

Thank YOU for guiding me

Notes, Numbers, & Future Appointments

Rev. Dr. Robert Hobbs
The Realization of Stainless Souls
www.StainlessSouls.com

Morning Wellness Check		
Physical		
Mental		
Emotional		
Relational		
Spiritual		
Lifestyle		
Immunity		

Evening Wellness Check		
Physical		
Mental		
Emotional		
Relational		
Spiritual		
Lifestyle		
Immunity		

Journaling		
Date:	Sobriety Date:	Number Days Clean & Sober:

Can You Forgive Yourself?

What I am Proud of/Happy About Today

What I Want to Improve/Remember

What Did I Learn

What Can I Teach Someone Like Me?

To Discuss with Sponsor, Doctor, Therapist, or Other Professional:

Day 16 Required Activities	Today's Study Areas	Week 3: This Week's Focus
Meditation: 10 Minutes 3 times	Drug & Alcohol Impact on Brain	The Mind & Mental Health
Reading: Power of Now 25 Pages	The Ego: The Thought of Me	Informal Mindfulness
Aerobic: 30 minutes once		Draft Purpose, Meaning, Mission
Flexibility: 10 minutes once		Tony Robbins – Posture & Mood
Meeting: 60 minutes		Purposeful Accurate Thinking

Needs, Habits, Healings, Affirmations, & Visualizations

Needs: Love/Connection/Consciousness

Habit Two: Begin with the End in Mind

Healing Treatment Three

I am poised, composed, and confident today and every day because I permit the positive power of my Universal Mind to govern my affairs.

Step & Service Work

Phase 1 and 2: Surrender and Forgive

How can your vision for you "become an end in mind" that you begin now?

Can you drive others to meetings?

Prayer & Gratitude List

"God, I offer myself to Thee–to build with me and to do with me as Thou wilt. Relieve me of the bondage of self, that I may better do Thy will. Take away my difficulties, that victory over them may bear witness to those I would help of Thy Power, Thy Love, and Thy Way of life. May I do Thy will always!" (AA Big Book).

Thank YOU for guiding me

Meetings and Appointments

__00 __30	
__00 __30	
__00 __30	
__00 __30	
__00 __30	
__00 __30	
__00 __30	
__00 __30	
__00 __30	
__00 __30	
__00 __30	
__00 __30	
__00 __30	
__00 __30	
__00 __30	
__00 __30	
__00 __30	
__00 __30	

Notes, Numbers, & Future Appointments

Rev. Dr. Robert Hobbs
The Realization of Stainless Souls
www.StainlessSouls.com

Morning Wellness Check		
Physical		
Mental		
Emotional		
Relational		
Spiritual		
Lifestyle		
Immunity		

Evening Wellness Check		
Physical		
Mental		
Emotional		
Relational		
Spiritual		
Lifestyle		
Immunity		

Journaling		
Date:	Sobriety Date:	Number Days Clean & Sober:

What does forgiveness mean?

_____
_____
_____
_____
_____
_____
_____
_____
_____
_____
_____
_____
_____
_____
_____
_____

What I am Proud of/Happy About Today

What I Want to Improve/Remember

What Did I Learn

What Can I Teach Someone Like Me?

To Discuss with Sponsor, Doctor, Therapist, or Other Professional:

Day 17 Required Activities
Meditation: 10 Minutes 3 times
Reading: Power of Now 25 Pages
Aerobic: 30 minutes once
Flexibility: 10 minutes once
Meeting: 60 minutes

Today's Study Areas
Drug & Alcohol Impact on Brain
The Ego: The Thought of Me
The Future: Real or just a thought

Week 3: This Week's Focus
The Mind & Mental Health
Informal Mindfulness
Draft Purpose, Meaning, Mission
Tony Robbins – Posture & Mood
Purposeful Accurate Thinking

Needs, Habits, Healings, Affirmations, & Visualizations

Needs: Love/Connection/Consciousness

Habit Two: Begin with the End in Mind

Healing Treatment Three

Today and everyday my conscious mind is at peace because the Eternal Peace of God is Present within me.

Step & Service Work

Phase 1 and 2: Surrender and Forgive

How can your vision for you "become an end in mind" that you begin now?

Can you drive others to meetings?

Prayer & Gratitude List

"God, I offer myself to Thee–to build with me and to do with me as Thou wilt. Relieve me of the bondage of self, that I may better do Thy will. Take away my difficulties, that victory over them may bear witness to those I would help of Thy Power, Thy Love, and Thy Way of life. May I do Thy will always!" (AA Big Book).

Thank YOU for guiding me

Meetings and Appointments

__00 __30	
__00 __30	
__00 __30	
__00 __30	
__00 __30	
__00 __30	
__00 __30	
__00 __30	
__00 __30	
__00 __30	
__00 __30	
__00 __30	
__00 __30	
__00 __30	
__00 __30	
__00 __30	
__00 __30	
__00 __30	
__00 __30	

Notes, Numbers, & Future Appointments

Rev. Dr. Robert Hobbs
The Realization of Stainless Souls
www.StainlessSouls.com

Morning Wellness Check		
Physical		
Mental		
Emotional		
Relational		
Spiritual		
Lifestyle		
Immunity		

Evening Wellness Check		
Physical		
Mental		
Emotional		
Relational		
Spiritual		
Lifestyle		
Immunity		

Journaling		
Date:	Sobriety Date:	Number Days Clean & Sober:

If I forgive someone – is it on my terms or theirs if it is really forgiveness?

What I am Proud of/Happy About Today

What I Want to Improve/Remember

What Did I Learn

What Can I Teach Someone Like Me?

To Discuss with Sponsor, Doctor, Therapist, or Other Professional:

Day 18 Required Activities	Today's Study Areas	Week 3: This Week's Focus
Meditation: 10 Minutes 3 times	Drug & Alcohol Impact on Brain	The Mind & Mental Health
Reading: Power of Now 25 Pages	The Ego: The Thought of Me	Informal Mindfulness
Aerobic: 30 minutes once	The Future: Real or just a thought	Draft Purpose, Meaning, Mission
Flexibility: 10 minutes once	My Story = My Identity?	Tony Robbins – Posture & Mood
Meeting: 60 minutes		Purposeful Accurate Thinking

Needs, Habits, Healings, Affirmations, & Visualizations

Needs: Love/Connection/Consciousness

Habit Two: Begin with the End in Mind

Healing Treatment Three

My failures are things of the past and were opportunities to learn how to win; winning is the reality of now and my future, and by God's Presence in my mind, it is so.

Step & Service Work

Phase 1 and 2: Surrender and Forgive

How can your vision for you "become an end in mind" that you begin now?

Can you drive others to meetings?

Prayer & Gratitude List

"God, I offer myself to Thee–to build with me and to do with me as Thou wilt. Relieve me of the bondage of self, that I may better do Thy will. Take away my difficulties, that victory over them may bear witness to those I would help of Thy Power, Thy Love, and Thy Way of life. May I do Thy will always!" (AA Big Book).

Thank YOU for guiding me

Meetings and Appointments

__00 __30	
__00 __30	
__00 __30	
__00 __30	
__00 __30	
__00 __30	
__00 __30	
__00 __30	
__00 __30	
__00 __30	
__00 __30	
__00 __30	
__00 __30	
__00 __30	
__00 __30	
__00 __30	
__00 __30	
__00 __30	

Notes, Numbers, & Future Appointments

Rev. Dr. Robert Hobbs
The Realization of Stainless Souls
www.StainlessSouls.com

Date:_____ Day: M T W Th F S Su

Morning Wellness Check		
Physical		
Mental		
Emotional		
Relational		
Spiritual		
Lifestyle		
Immunity		

Evening Wellness Check		
Physical		
Mental		
Emotional		
Relational		
Spiritual		
Lifestyle		
Immunity		

Journaling		
Date:	Sobriety Date:	Number Days Clean & Sober:

When asking for forgiveness is it given to me on my terms or theirs?

What I am Proud of/Happy About Today

What I Want to Improve/Remember

What Did I Learn

What Can I Teach Someone Like Me?

To Discuss with Sponsor, Doctor, Therapist, or Other Professional:

Day 19 Required Activities	Today's Study Areas	Week 3: This Week's Focus
Meditation: 10 Minutes 3 times	Drug & Alcohol Impact on Brain	The Mind & Mental Health
Reading: Power of Now 25 Pages	The Ego: The Thought of Me	Informal Mindfulness
Aerobic: 30 minutes once	The Future: Real or just a thought	Draft Purpose, Meaning, Mission
Flexibility: 10 minutes once	My Story = My Identity?	Tony Robbins – Posture & Mood
Meeting: 60 minutes	My Story of You = Your Identity?	Purposeful Accurate Thinking

Needs, Habits, Healings, Affirmations, & Visualizations

Needs: Love/Connection/Consciousness

Habit Two: Begin with the End in Mind

Healing Treatment Three

God created me with a winning purpose; He will also create the winning conditions necessary for success in my life as I confidently pursue that purpose.

Step & Service Work

Phase 1 and 2: Surrender and Forgive

How can your vision for you "become an end in mind" that you begin now?

Can you drive others to meetings?

Prayer & Gratitude List

"God, I offer myself to Thee–to build with me and to do with me as Thou wilt. Relieve me of the bondage of self, that I may better do Thy will. Take away my difficulties, that victory over them may bear witness to those I would help of Thy Power, Thy Love, and Thy Way of life. May I do Thy will always!" (AA Big Book).

Thank YOU for guiding me

Meetings and Appointments

__00 / 30	
__00 / 30	
__00 / 30	
__00 / 30	
__00 / 30	
__00 / 30	
__00 / 30	
__00 / 30	
__00 / 30	
__00 / 30	
__00 / 30	
__00 / 30	
__00 / 30	
__00 / 30	
__00 / 30	
__00 / 30	
__00 / 30	

Notes, Numbers, & Future Appointments

Rev. Dr. Robert Hobbs
The Realization of Stainless Souls
www.StainlessSouls.com

Morning Wellness Check		
Physical		
Mental		
Emotional		
Relational		
Spiritual		
Lifestyle		
Immunity		

Evening Wellness Check		
Physical		
Mental		
Emotional		
Relational		
Spiritual		
Lifestyle		
Immunity		

Journaling		
Date:	Sobriety Date:	Number Days Clean & Sober:

Self-Forgiveness:

Societal Forgiveness:

Divine/Universal Forgiveness:

Inner-personal Forgiveness:

What I am Proud of/Happy About Today

What I Want to Improve/Remember

What Did I Learn

What Can I Teach Someone Like Me?

To Discuss with Sponsor, Doctor, Therapist, or Other Professional:

Day 20 Required Activities	Today's Study Areas	Week 3: This Week's Focus
Meditation: 10 Minutes 3 times	The Ego: The Thought of Me	The Mind & Mental Health
Reading: Power of Now 25 Pages	The Future: Real or just a thought	Informal Mindfulness
Aerobic: 30 minutes once	My Story = My Identity?	Draft Purpose, Meaning, Mission
Flexibility: 10 minutes once	My Story of You = Your Identity?	Tony Robbins – Posture & Mood
Meeting: 60 minutes	If stories & thoughts don't exist?	Purposeful Accurate Thinking

Needs, Habits, Healings, Affirmations, & Visualizations

Needs: Love/Connection/Consciousness

Habit Two: Begin with the End in Mind

Healing Treatment Three

Each day, my every thought is under the influence of my Higher God-Mind.

Step & Service Work

Phase 1 and 2: Surrender and Forgive

Before Beginning Step 4 – Schedule Step 5! Do not linger with the feelings of Step 4 longer than necessary – dump it!

How can your vision for you "become an end in mind" that you begin now?

Can you drive others to meetings?

Prayer & Gratitude List

"God, I offer myself to Thee–to build with me and to do with me as Thou wilt. Relieve me of the bondage of self, that I may better do Thy will. Take away my difficulties, that victory over them may bear witness to those I would help of Thy Power, Thy Love, and Thy Way of life. May I do Thy will always!" (AA Big Book).

Thank YOU for guiding me

Meetings and Appointments

Time	
__00 __30	
__00 __30	
__00 __30	
__00 __30	
__00 __30	
__00 __30	
__00 __30	
__00 __30	
__00 __30	
__00 __30	
__00 __30	
__00 __30	
__00 __30	
__00 __30	
__00 __30	
__00 __30	
__00 __30	
__00 __30	

Notes, Numbers, & Future Appointments

Rev. Dr. Robert Hobbs
The Realization of Stainless Souls
www.StainlessSouls.com

Morning Wellness Check		
Physical		
Mental		
Emotional		
Relational		
Spiritual		
Lifestyle		
Immunity		

Evening Wellness Check		
Physical		
Mental		
Emotional		
Relational		
Spiritual		
Lifestyle		
Immunity		

Journaling		
Date:	Sobriety Date:	Number Days Clean & Sober:

What I am Proud of/Happy About Today

What I Want to Improve/Remember

What Did I Learn

What Can I Teach Someone Like Me?

To Discuss with Sponsor, Doctor, Therapist, or Other Professional:

Day 21 Required Activities	Today's Study Areas	Week 3: This Week's Focus
Meditation: 10 Minutes 3 times	The Future: Real or just a thought	The Mind & Mental Health
Reading: Power of Now 25 Pages	My Story = My Identity?	Informal Mindfulness
Aerobic: 30 minutes once	My Story of You = Your Identity?	Draft Purpose, Meaning, Mission
Flexibility: 10 minutes once	If stories & thoughts don't exist?	Tony Robbins – Posture & Mood
Meeting: 60 minutes	Who Am I? Who Are You? Really?	Purposeful Accurate Thinking

Needs, Habits, Healings, Affirmations, & Visualizations

Needs: Love/Connection/Consciousness

Habit Two: Begin with the End in Mind

Healing Treatment Three

From within me, the Higher Wisdom of the Universe guides me now and eternally.

Meetings and Appointments

Time	
__00 __30	
__00 __30	
__00 __30	
__00 __30	
__00 __30	
__00 __30	
__00 __30	
__00 __30	
__00 __30	
__00 __30	
__00 __30	
__00 __30	
__00 __30	
__00 __30	
__00 __30	
__00 __30	
__00 __30	

Step & Service Work

Phase 1 and 2: Surrender and Forgive

Before Beginning Step 4 – Schedule Step 5! Do not linger with the feelings of Step 4 longer than necessary – dump it!

How can your vision for you "become an end in mind" that you begin now?

Can you drive others to meetings?

Prayer & Gratitude List

"God, I offer myself to Thee—to build with me and to do with me as Thou wilt. Relieve me of the bondage of self, that I may better do Thy will. Take away my difficulties, that victory over them may bear witness to those I would help of Thy Power, Thy Love, and Thy Way of life. May I do Thy will always!" (AA Big Book).

Thank YOU for guiding me

Notes, Numbers, & Future Appointments

Rev. Dr. Robert Hobbs
The Realization of Stainless Souls
www.StainlessSouls.com

Morning Wellness Check		
Physical		
Mental		
Emotional		
Relational		
Spiritual		
Lifestyle		
Immunity		

Evening Wellness Check		
Physical		
Mental		
Emotional		
Relational		
Spiritual		
Lifestyle		
Immunity		

Journaling		
Date:	Sobriety Date:	Number Days Clean & Sober:

What I am Proud of/Happy About Today

What I Want to Improve/Remember

What Did I Learn

What Can I Teach Someone Like Me?

To Discuss with Sponsor, Doctor, Therapist, or Other Professional:

Week 4: Relational and Emotional Well-being

Of all the things that become messed up in the wake of active addiction, perhaps the most complex is our emotions and our relationships. Legal problems, financial problems, employment issues, and safety and security issues can become quite intensive - but - once a path is set to correct these items, progress is generally favorable.

Our emotions, on the other hand, are not straightforward - and without professional help, we cannot be confident as to whether we are on the right path or not. It is scary to question whether or not something you are considering, or feeling is relational or sane. However, to become well, we must begin the tedious process of straightening out our emotional lives.

Fear and Anger

Fear and anger are both designed to protect your survival - they trigger the survival responses of fight, flight, or freeze. The important thing for you to know - or begin to learn - is that if you experience fear and anger in situations where your survival is not at risk - then your emotions *are in error* and you are being misled.

It is crucial that you acknowledge and recognize this error this week and before you begin to consider the potentiality that your emotions can serve as your inner guide.

The *ego (bundle of thoughts) may feel threatened* and that *its survival* is at risk, but the ego is not a being; it is not you, and it is not alive. Fear and anger *are not designed to protect the ego* - it is an error to use them for such a reason.

However, most people don't realize that many of their reactions of fear and anger, fight-flight-freeze, are in response to *an ego* that *feels threatened, not a living <u>human being</u>* that *is threatened,* learning the difference is a vital part to your long-term healing.

You must deal with all your shame, guilt, anger, and fear this week and in perpetuity. Steps 4 and 5 will give you a good start on cleaning up some of your messes and a ton of relief emotionally.

Relationships are even trickier than emotions. As discussed last week, you know that your perception of yourself is in error - so is your impression of people you have relationships with. Likewise, the person who has a relationship with you has an error-riddled idea of you and his or herself.

> *How someone treats you is their karma;*
>
> *how you react is yours.*
>
> *~Wayne Dyer*

These ideas alone make relationships complicated - but then - add in emotional error, such as *unnecessary fear and anger* experienced when survival is not at risk or, injured feelings or, guilt and shame, beliefs about right and wrong, fair and unfair, deserve and don't deserve, all are riddled in error and result in damage and then steep paths to forgiveness and reconciliation.

Rev. Dr. Robert Hobbs
The Realization of Stainless Souls
www.StainlessSouls.com

It is possible, likely even, that some of your relationships will be impossible to fix. Take this in stride. Do your best to fix what you can, but don't become too attached to what may have become irreparable. Do your best, forget the rest.

Again - the big picture:

- · Mindfulness - being present - awareness of the ego, and
- · a willingness to forgive and be forgiven –
- · will all weave together this week, and
- · the structure of this program might begin to make a little more sense

This week's Covey Habit is Habit 5: Seek first to understand, before seeking to be understood, or listen empathetically.

I have always told people that God gave them two ears and one mouth and that they should use them proportionally. In other words, they should listen twice as much as they talk! Habit 5 takes this concept further by requiring that you do not express your ideas or position until you understand the other person's opinion fully.

Focus Areas

Empathetic Listening

Listen to all of your company with the attitude of an empath. Listen with the commitment to them that whatever they are saying is the most important thing you could be hearing. Do not make the most common mistake of thinking about what you were going to say next while your company is still talking.

Be present. Be non-critical. Be non-judgmental.

Feelings and Love

Most of us, whether as a response to our addiction or as a result of a life circumstance that led to our addiction, have likely entered a phase of not wanting or not knowing feelings.

We are prone to drown anger, fear, regret, guilt, shame, with the firehose of our drug of choice.

Happiness, joy, pride, and other, more positive emotions are things we have not genuinely felt for a long, long time.

Love is something, in all forms, that seems to confuse and baffle us. Rather than working to figure it all out - we learn to drown it all out.

Sobriety was scary for this reason more than any other.

If we are patient and approach our problems with optimism and forgiveness, we will smooth out all of the bumpy tracks left in the wake of our addiction.

Your Inner Guide

Correctly recognized and interpreted, your emotions serve as your *inner guide* - like a gyroscope if you will. Fear and anger are designed to inform you to defend your survival urgently. Many other emotions intend to serve you and your well-being; with practice, you can learn how to use your *woman's intuition*, *gut feelings*, and *gut-instinct* to better your decision-making.

Learn to trust your gut

Energy and Vibrations: The Vibe

Have you ever gotten *good vibes* from a person you have just met? Or *bad vibes*? If not, have you at least heard others say, *I got a bad vibe from that person?* These are not metaphorical descriptors - they are *real feelings* that people have. You can learn to pick up on these phenomena, by tuning in with your feelings.

Study Areas

Study at least one of these topics at least once every day for seven days.

Day 1: Drug and Alcohol Abuse Impact on Relationships and Emotional Well-being

Study the impact on both of these crucial parts of your life.

Day 2: Covey Habit 5: Seek First to Understand Before Seeking to be Understood

Though my favorite habit is Habit 3: Put First Things First, the one I needed to work on most was Habit 5. I didn't like listening to others. I was always thinking of what I could say next that would make me look smarter or more informed than I actually was. My life changed for the better when I started practicing empathetic listening. There are dozens of videos and articles available online (for free) on this topic. Do yourself (and your loved ones) a favor and study as many of them as you can.

Day 3: Will You Go the Extra Mile?

Will you go the extra mile? For yourself? For your relationships?

By this point, you have probably been through hell, and you've possibly dragged your loved ones with you. Now, you are starting to recognize the damage done and maybe thinking about how hard it is going to be. *IT IS HARD!* You are not the only person who doubts your resolve to build a better life - everyone doubts you - and for that, they will test you.

Will you quit? Or will you persist until you have reconciled and restored all that can be repaired? You must not shy away at the interpersonal gusts of wind that used to blow you asunder. Instead, you must stand firm! You must go the extra mile! For yourself, and your loved ones, don't give up!

Day 4: Pleasing Personality, Smile

Sure, you can make friends without a magnetic personality and without even smiling. But why make it harder than it has to be? Make it easy! Project a pleasing personality that is attractive and magnetic. You can demonstrate this pleasant personality with a sincere, authentic, and genuine smile. Share this smile with everyone you meet.

Day 5: Emotional Triggers, Mine.

All of us have specific triggers that cause us unwanted reactions when interacting with our most important relationships - unfortunately - we don't recognize this fact until we have broken many relationships.

With mindfulness, you can learn to *capture or apprehend* the trigger that puts you into a situation that you might regret. Learn *what* triggers specific unwanted reactions and practice new responses to that trigger and never again deal with the aftermath of a valueless confrontation with your loved ones.

Day 6: Emotional Triggers, Significant Other

Do you know how to "*push his buttons?*" then you already know *his triggers*. In a loving relationship - you should not desire to cause confrontations by pushing buttons - so, break the habit of pushing them.

Now - go back to *your triggers*; if you *know his* - isn't it likely that *he knows yours*? Take a shortcut and ask him what your emotional triggers are, because if he knows what buttons to push, and your buttons are your triggers, then *he can tell you* what your triggers are.

Day 7: Can (should) I Be Trusted?

What is trust? What is mutual trust? Without trust, is there a real authentic relationship? It is likely that through the course of your difficulties you destroyed any confidence you had with your loved ones. It is also likely that you destroyed any trust you had in yourself. It's time to begin rebuilding - from the ground up one brick at a time - a strong foundation of trustworthiness upon which all relationships can be built.

Required Activities

By now, you should have the routine quite habituated. This week we bump all three **Meditations** to 15 minutes each for a total of 45 minutes.

We also begin **Reading** *Polishing the Mirror*, by Ram Dass. Keep an open mind with Ram Dass, he is quite the character, and he can help you in many ways.

Next week, you will gain some flexibility in how you meditate, and your initial exploration should be based on *Polishing the Mirror* and the teachings of Ram Dass.

Needs, Habits, Healings, Affirmations, and Visualizations

Needs

Love and Connection. Consider love! To give something, you have to have it; And if you have it, you must have received it.

Most people respond affirmatively when asked *if they can love someone*, meaning give their love to someone. So, start there; start by giving away what you have - love.

You will find that you never run out of love, no matter how much you give away. Where does this Infinite Source come from?

You'll also find that by giving away what you have, more of what you give will find its way to you. So, give love freely, unconditionally, and you will receive all the love you ever wanted.

Covey Habit 5: Seek to Understand, before Seeking to be Understood

We've covered this topic study it thoroughly.

Healing Treatment Four

Three times per day for 15 minutes each day this week.

Affirmation and Visualization

Focus on the hierarchy of energies this week:

Thought - Sound - Vibration - Life - Light

"See Your Future"

Step and Service Work

This week and next week are the two most important weeks in this program. You must pay attention, follow instructions, and follow through. You are in Phase 2 of the Brown Bag, Blue Collar Recovery System: *Forgiveness*.

The recovery step this week is Step 4.

Two weeks ago, we started to prepare for this week by learning about forgiveness. Last week, we learned about emotions - guilt, shame, anger, and fear and their role in relationships.

This week you will begin and complete Step 4 - exactly as instructed in the chapter, *"How it Works,"* in the *Big Book of Alcoholics Anonymous*. However, *you will not start Step 4 until you have a solidly confirmed appointment with another addict, your sponsor, priest, therapist, or minister, to complete Step 5.*

Here is the underlying philosophy.

First of all, the guilt, shame, fear, and anger you are carrying around is going to cause a relapse and kill you. You must get rid of them as soon as possible. This is a life-and-death week. You are best to deal with these issues completely and quickly.

Secondly, no one should dig around in their sordid pasts for very long without having a time and a place to bury it. So, having Step 5 scheduled provides the burial ground.

Note: We won't study tapping or the Emotional Freedom Technique (EFT) until week 13. It may be a good idea for you to get a head start his week and watch some videos and begin tapping. It will drop your stress levels as you begin to dig up your past and stress over sharing it with another human.

Be courageous - Be honest - Be thorough

Once you deal with what has been casting its long shadow over your life, the sooner you can once more walk in the light.

Listening. Practice listening fully when conversing with others. Especially when the others are our brothers and sisters in recovery.

Prayer and Gratitude List

You can continue to say the *Step 3 Prayer* as your daily prayer. You can also consider your affirmations and healing treatments as your daily prayers. This week use the space provided to list people, causes, and social concerns that you would like to pray for healing. Don't forget to include the people, things, and events that you are grateful for in your daily prayers. *It is also a good idea to begin praying for your enemies.*

Wellness Checks

Continue scoring your wellness in the seven categories and graphing the results on the appropriate page in the back of the book.

Rev. Dr. Robert Hobbs
The Realization of Stainless Souls
www.StainlessSouls.com

As your **journaling** activity this week, take a stab each day at brainstorming on what your personal values and beliefs are. What kind of person would you like to be? What type of character traits would you like to have? Honesty? Integrity? Compassion? Empathy? Courage? Resolve? Resilience? Spend some serious time on this and make sure you summarize the results on day seven.

Also, make sure that you continue to populate the daily summary sections each day on the bottom of the journaling page.

- What are you proud or happy about?
- What do you want to improve?
- What did you learn?
- What would you like to teach?

This is a convenient place where we can remind you to establish a time and a location each week to do your planning for the coming week. Usually, this is done on Sunday for one or two hours. You as the planner will take all of your professional appointments, court dates, probation, doctor's appointments, therapy appointments, work hours, and so forth and populate those first in the appropriate time slots. Generally, those appointments can't change.

Then you as the planner, will start writing, in the available time slots, all of the *priority items* that you want to accomplish for the week; in this case, it might be all of the *Required Activities* that you have to do: meditation, reading, aerobic exercise, flexibility practice, your daily recovery meeting, your study time, etc.; then any remaining time, once all of the required meetings and all of the priority events are taken care of, you as the planner may put in time for rest and relaxation.

Ideally, by using this planning system and this program, you will be kept so busy, and your attention will be kept by your curiosity of the topics that you're studying, you won't have any time for the brain-wasting relapse producing activities such as: arguing on social media, playing video games, or watching filth and violence on television.

Hopefully, all of the water that you're putting into your bucket will be pure, clean water.

So, Sunday's - once a week, plan out the entire coming week, and then you stick to the plan.

Two Frogs

Lesson: Live Another Day; Fight Another Day; Just Today, Fight On!

There were once two frogs, and many of you probably heard this story. These were two dairy farm frogs hopping around. They jumped into the barn, onto a table, and without looking, they leaped from the table, into a bucket of milk. The bucket was half-full, and the sides were smooth, so the frogs were stuck; they couldn't leap out because of the milk, and they couldn't climb out because the sides of the pale were smooth. So, they're in there swimming; and for quite some time they were swimming.

One of the frogs was a lumpy fellow, quite the pessimist, and a little bit older. He was complaining while the two frogs were swimming and he said, "I don't know how much longer I can swim. I don't know if I can keep this up."

The younger frog tried to encourage him to continue, "We don't know what's going to happen; just keep swimming; it's going to be fine."

Eventually, the older lumpy frog gave up and sank to the bottom of the bucket and died. He died as just a frog.

The younger frog, the more optimistic frog, continued to swim. He made a commitment to himself to keep swimming, no matter what! The only way he was perishing in that pail was if his muscles failed to respond to the commands of his mind. He continued to swim and swim and swim.

Just at the point when he thought that his muscles were going to begin to fail him, and he would sink and perish, he felt a firmness under his belly. What happened was he swam in that milk so hard, he had churned that milk so much, that he turned it into butter. Once it turned to butter, he hopped from the pail a much different frog than the frog that hopped in; and a much different frog than the one that perished.

This was a frog of resilience and resolve. He was a butter maker; he was a swimmer; he was courageous!

Now those two frogs in the afterlife, or the next life, depending on how you view immortality, will have two very different outcomes. The one who died just a frog will probably be a frog again; but, the one who hopped out of that bucket as a butter maker, as a survivor, he may be a prince in the next life.

So, it is vital for us, no matter what our plight, no matter what our task, and no matter what our predicament, or ordeal, or dilemma is - that we carry on the fight. It's not just this single lifetime that we are fighting for. We are fighting for the immortal salvation and the redemption of our souls.

For a variety of reasons and circumstances, you have forgotten Your Divine heritage. For you to remember, you came here, to this planet, to overcome some mortal problems, some human predicaments, ordeals, and dilemmas. Eventually, prompted by the difficulties of your life and by successfully overcoming the dilemmas of your life, you will realize once again that you are a child of the Divine.

Rev. Dr. Robert Hobbs
The Realization of Stainless Souls
www.StainlessSouls.com

Notes and Sketches

Day 22 Required Activities
Meditation: 15 Minutes 3 times
Read: Polishing the Mirror 25 Pg
Aerobic: 30 minutes once
Flexibility: 10 minutes once
Meeting: 60 minutes

Today's Study Areas
Drug and Alcohol Impact on
Relationships and Emotions

Week 4: This Week's Focus
Relational/Emotional Health
Empathetic Listening
Feelings & Love
Emotions: Your Inner Guide
Energy and Vibrations: The Vibe

Needs, Habits, Healings, Affirmations, & Visualizations

Need: Love/Connection/Consciousness

Covey Habit 5: Seek to Understand Before Seeking to be Understood

Healing Treatment Four

My conscious mind sends love to the Higher Mind within me and my Higher Mind drenches me in Universal Love.

Step & Service Work

Phase 2: Forgiveness and Step 4

Before Beginning Step 4 – Schedule Step 5! Do not linger with the feelings of Step 4 longer than necessary – dump it!

Listening: Are you fully attentive when others are sharing with you?

Prayer & Gratitude List

Meetings and Appointments

__00 __30	
__00 __30	
__00 __30	
__00 __30	
__00 __30	
__00 __30	
__00 __30	
__00 __30	
__00 __30	
__00 __30	
__00 __30	
__00 __30	
__00 __30	
__00 __30	
__00 __30	
__00 __30	
__00 __30	
__00 __30	

Notes, Numbers, & Future Appointments

Rev. Dr. Robert Hobbs
The Realization of Stainless Souls
www.StainlessSouls.com

Morning Wellness Check		
Physical		
Mental		
Emotional		
Relational		
Spiritual		
Lifestyle		
Immunity		

Evening Wellness Check		
Physical		
Mental		
Emotional		
Relational		
Spiritual		
Lifestyle		
Immunity		

Journaling		
Date:	Sobriety Date:	Number Days Clean & Sober:

My Values and Beliefs

What I am Proud of/Happy About Today

What I Want to Improve/Remember

What Did I Learn

What Can I Teach Someone Like Me?

To Discuss with Sponsor, Doctor, Therapist, or Other Professional:

Day 23 Required Activities	Today's Study Areas	Week 4: This Week's Focus
Meditation: 15 Minutes 3 times	Drug and Alcohol Impact on	Relational/Emotional Health
Read: Polishing the Mirror 25 Pg	Relationships and Emotions	Empathetic Listening
Aerobic: 30 minutes once	Covey Habit 5	Feelings & Love
Flexibility: 10 minutes once		Emotions: Your Inner Guide
Meeting: 60 minutes		Energy and Vibrations: The Vibe

Needs, Habits, Healings, Affirmations, & Visualizations

Needs: Love/Connection/Consciousness

Covey Habit 5: Seek to Understand Before Seeking to be Understood

Healing Treatment Four

As God has already forgiven me for all the errors of my past, I now forgive anyone who has wronged me.

Step & Service Work

Phase 2: Forgiveness and Step 4

Before Beginning Step 4 – Schedule Step 5! Do not linger with the feelings of Step 4 longer than necessary – dump it!

Listening: Are you fully attentive when others are sharing with you?

Prayer & Gratitude List

Meetings and Appointments

__00 __30	
__00 __30	
__00 __30	
__00 __30	
__00 __30	
__00 __30	
__00 __30	
__00 __30	
__00 __30	
__00 __30	
__00 __30	
__00 __30	
__00 __30	
__00 __30	
__00 __30	
__00 __30	
__00 __30	

Notes, Numbers, & Future Appointments

Rev. Dr. Robert Hobbs
The Realization of Stainless Souls
www.StainlessSouls.com

Morning Wellness Check		
Physical		
Mental		
Emotional		
Relational		
Spiritual		
Lifestyle		
Immunity		

Evening Wellness Check		
Physical		
Mental		
Emotional		
Relational		
Spiritual		
Lifestyle		
Immunity		

Journaling		
Date:	Sobriety Date:	Number Days Clean & Sober:

My Values and Beliefs

What I am Proud of/Happy About Today

What I Want to Improve/Remember

What Did I Learn

What Can I Teach Someone Like Me?

To Discuss with Sponsor, Doctor, Therapist, or Other Professional:

Day 24 Required Activities	Today's Study Areas	Week 4: This Week's Focus
Meditation: 15 Minutes 3 times	Drug and Alcohol Impact on	Relational/Emotional Health
Read: Polishing the Mirror 25 Pg	Relationships and Emotions	Empathetic Listening
Aerobic: 30 minutes once	Covey Habit 5	Feelings & Love
Flexibility: 10 minutes once	Will I Go the Extra Mile?	Emotions: Your Inner Guide
Meeting: 60 minutes		Energy and Vibrations: The Vibe

Needs, Habits, Healings, Affirmations, & Visualizations

Needs: Love/Connection/Consciousness

Covey Habit 5: Seek to Understand Before Seeking to be Understood

Healing Treatment Four

The Healing Power of the Universe within me has already forgiven me for my error-filled ways, just as parents forgive children as they grow.

Step & Service Work

Phase 2: Forgiveness and Step 4

Before Beginning Step 4 – Schedule Step 5! Do not linger with the feelings of Step 4 longer than necessary – dump it!

Listening: Are you fully attentive when others are sharing with you?

Prayer & Gratitude List

Meetings and Appointments

Time	
__00 __30	
__00 __30	
__00 __30	
__00 __30	
__00 __30	
__00 __30	
__00 __30	
__00 __30	
__00 __30	
__00 __30	
__00 __30	
__00 __30	
__00 __30	
__00 __30	
__00 __30	
__00 __30	
__00 __30	
__00 __30	

Notes, Numbers, & Future Appointments

Rev. Dr. Robert Hobbs
The Realization of Stainless Souls
www.StainlessSouls.com

Morning Wellness Check		
Physical		
Mental		
Emotional		
Relational		
Spiritual		
Lifestyle		
Immunity		

Evening Wellness Check		
Physical		
Mental		
Emotional		
Relational		
Spiritual		
Lifestyle		
Immunity		

Journaling		
Date:	Sobriety Date:	Number Days Clean & Sober:

My Values and Beliefs

What I am Proud of/Happy About Today

What I Want to Improve/Remember

What Did I Learn

What Can I Teach Someone Like Me?

To Discuss with Sponsor, Doctor, Therapist, or Other Professional:

Day 25 Required Activities	Today's Study Areas	Week 4: This Week's Focus
Meditation: 15 Minutes 3 times	Drug and Alcohol Impact on	Relational/Emotional Health
Read: Polishing the Mirror 25 Pg	Relationships and Emotions	Empathetic Listening
Aerobic: 30 minutes once	Covey Habit 5	Feelings & Love
Flexibility: 10 minutes once	Will I Go the Extra Mile?	Emotions: Your Inner Guide
Meeting: 60 minutes	Pleasing Personality: Smile	Energy and Vibrations: The Vibe

Needs, Habits, Healings, Affirmations, & Visualizations

Needs: Love/Connection/Consciousness

Covey Habit 5: Seek to Understand Before Seeking to be Understood

Healing Treatment Four

As a parent forgives a child, God has already forgiven me for all the errors of my past.

Step & Service Work

Phase 2: Forgiveness and Step 4

Before Beginning Step 4 – Schedule Step 5! Do not linger with the feelings of Step 4 longer than necessary – dump it!

Listening: Are you fully attentive when others are sharing with you?

Prayer & Gratitude List

Meetings and Appointments

__00 __30	
__00 __30	
__00 __30	
__00 __30	
__00 __30	
__00 __30	
__00 __30	
__00 __30	
__00 __30	
__00 __30	
__00 __30	
__00 __30	
__00 __30	
__00 __30	
__00 __30	
__00 __30	
__00 __30	

Notes, Numbers, & Future Appointments

Rev. Dr. Robert Hobbs
The Realization of Stainless Souls
www.StainlessSouls.com

Morning Wellness Check		
Physical		
Mental		
Emotional		
Relational		
Spiritual		
Lifestyle		
Immunity		

Evening Wellness Check		
Physical		
Mental		
Emotional		
Relational		
Spiritual		
Lifestyle		
Immunity		

Journaling		
Date:	Sobriety Date:	Number Days Clean & Sober:

My Values and Beliefs

_____
_____
_____
_____
_____
_____
_____
_____
_____
_____
_____
_____
_____
_____
_____
_____

What I am Proud of/Happy About Today

What I Want to Improve/Remember

What Did I Learn

What Can I Teach Someone Like Me?

To Discuss with Sponsor, Doctor, Therapist, or Other Professional:

Day 26 Required Activities	Today's Study Areas	Week 4: This Week's Focus
Meditation: 15 Minutes 3 times	Covey Habit 5	Relational/Emotional Health
Read: Polishing the Mirror 25 Pg	Will I Go the Extra Mile?	Empathetic Listening
Aerobic: 30 minutes once	Pleasing Personality: Smile	Feelings & Love
Flexibility: 10 minutes once	Emotional Triggers: Mine	Emotions: Your Inner Guide
Meeting: 60 minutes		Energy and Vibrations: The Vibe

Needs, Habits, Healings, Affirmations, & Visualizations

Needs: Love/Connection/Consciousness

Covey Habit 5: Seek to Understand Before Seeking to be Understood

Healing Treatment Four

There is but One Life in this Universe, and I share in that life with God and all sentient beings, and so, by treating others with love, I am treating extensions of myself and the embodiment of God with love.

Step & Service Work

Phase 2: Forgiveness and Step 4

Before Beginning Step 4 – Schedule Step 5! Do not linger with the feelings of Step 4 longer than necessary – dump it!

Listening: Are you fully attentive when others are sharing with you?

Prayer & Gratitude List

Meetings and Appointments

__00 __30	
__00 __30	
__00 __30	
__00 __30	
__00 __30	
__00 __30	
__00 __30	
__00 __30	
__00 __30	
__00 __30	
__00 __30	
__00 __30	
__00 __30	
__00 __30	
__00 __30	
__00 __30	
__00 __30	
__00 __30	

Notes, Numbers, & Future Appointments

Rev. Dr. Robert Hobbs
The Realization of Stainless Souls
www.StainlessSouls.com

Morning Wellness Check		
Physical		
Mental		
Emotional		
Relational		
Spiritual		
Lifestyle		
Immunity		

Evening Wellness Check		
Physical		
Mental		
Emotional		
Relational		
Spiritual		
Lifestyle		
Immunity		

Journaling		
Date:	Sobriety Date:	Number Days Clean & Sober:

My Values and Beliefs

_____
_____
_____
_____
_____
_____
_____
_____
_____
_____
_____
_____
_____
_____
_____
_____

What I am Proud of/Happy About Today

What I Want to Improve/Remember

What Did I Learn

What Can I Teach Someone Like Me?

To Discuss with Sponsor, Doctor, Therapist, or Other Professional:

Day 27 Required Activities	Today's Study Areas	Week 4: This Week's Focus
Meditation: 15 Minutes 3 times	Covey Habit 5	Relational/Emotional Health
Read: Polishing the Mirror 25 Pg	Will I Go the Extra Mile?	Empathetic Listening
Aerobic: 30 minutes once	Pleasing Personality: Smile	Feelings & Love
Flexibility: 10 minutes once	Emotional Triggers: Mine	Emotions: Your Inner Guide
Meeting: 60 minutes	Emotional Triggers: Signif other	Energy and Vibrations: The Vibe

Needs, Habits, Healings, Affirmations, & Visualizations

Needs: Love/Connection/Consciousness

Covey Habit 5: Seek to Understand Before Seeking to be Understood

Healing Treatment Four

I now summon and demand that Transforming Power of the Universe, which eternally resides at the nucleus of my mind, transform my historic and habitual mental and emotional patterns to positive new ones. For this, I give thanks, I let it be so, and so it is!

Step & Service Work

Phase 2: Forgiveness and Step 4

Before Beginning Step 4 – Schedule Step 5! Do not linger with the feelings of Step 4 longer than necessary – dump it!

Listening: Are you fully attentive when others are sharing with you?

Prayer & Gratitude List

Meetings and Appointments

Time	
__00 __30	
__00 __30	
__00 __30	
__00 __30	
__00 __30	
__00 __30	
__00 __30	
__00 __30	
__00 __30	
__00 __30	
__00 __30	
__00 __30	
__00 __30	
__00 __30	
__00 __30	
__00 __30	
__00 __30	
__00 __30	

Notes, Numbers, & Future Appointments

Rev. Dr. Robert Hobbs
The Realization of Stainless Souls
www.StainlessSouls.com

Morning Wellness Check		
Physical		
Mental		
Emotional		
Relational		
Spiritual		
Lifestyle		
Immunity		

Evening Wellness Check		
Physical		
Mental		
Emotional		
Relational		
Spiritual		
Lifestyle		
Immunity		

Journaling		
Date:	Sobriety Date:	Number Days Clean & Sober:

My Values and Beliefs

What I am Proud of/Happy About Today

What I Want to Improve/Remember

What Did I Learn

What Can I Teach Someone Like Me?

To Discuss with Sponsor, Doctor, Therapist, or Other Professional:

Day 28 Required Activities	Today's Study Areas	Week 4: This Week's Focus
Meditation: 15 Minutes 3 times	Will I Go the Extra Mile?	Relational/Emotional Health
Read: Polishing the Mirror 25 Pg	Pleasing Personality: Smile	Empathetic Listening
Aerobic: 30 minutes once	Emotional Triggers: Mine	Feelings & Love
Flexibility: 10 minutes once	Emotional Triggers: Signif other	Emotions: Your Inner Guide
Meeting: 60 minutes	Can I be Trusted?	Energy and Vibrations: The Vibe

Needs, Habits, Healings, Affirmations, & Visualizations

Needs: Love/Connection/Consciousness

Covey Habit 5: Seek to Understand Before Seeking to be Understood

Healing Treatment Four

I release all feelings of resentment toward everyone and enter into the Presence of Eternal Peace within my Universal Higher Mind.

Step & Service Work

Phase 2: Forgiveness and Step 4

Before Beginning Step 4 – Schedule Step 5! Do not linger with the feelings of Step 4 longer than necessary – dump it!

Listening: Are you fully attentive when others are sharing with you?

Prayer & Gratitude List

Meetings and Appointments

__00 __30	
__00 __30	
__00 __30	
__00 __30	
__00 __30	
__00 __30	
__00 __30	
__00 __30	
__00 __30	
__00 __30	
__00 __30	
__00 __30	
__00 __30	
__00 __30	
__00 __30	
__00 __30	
__00 __30	
__00 __30	

Notes, Numbers, & Future Appointments

Rev. Dr. Robert Hobbs
The Realization of Stainless Souls
www.StainlessSouls.com

Morning Wellness Check		
Physical		
Mental		
Emotional		
Relational		
Spiritual		
Lifestyle		
Immunity		

Evening Wellness Check		
Physical		
Mental		
Emotional		
Relational		
Spiritual		
Lifestyle		
Immunity		

Journaling		
Date:	Sobriety Date:	Number Days Clean & Sober:

My Values and Beliefs

What I am Proud of/Happy About Today

What I Want to Improve/Remember

What Did I Learn

What Can I Teach Someone Like Me?

To Discuss with Sponsor, Doctor, Therapist, or Other Professional:

Week 5: Spiritual Wellness

We think about healing and recovery like exercise. After years of eating poorly and abusing our bodies - we decide one day that we have had enough. We commit to ourselves that we will "*get back in shape*," and then after a few days of working out, we feel terrible and convince ourselves that we will never be able to get in shape.

Exercise isn't for me; We quit and get fat.

So, it is with addiction, after years of living badly, we make a decision to get clean, but because it takes longer than a week or so to restore our sanity, we become frustrated, and we give up. We might as well just stay addicted.

Recovery is not for me. We relapse and die.

Brown Bag, Blue Collar Recovery Systems are different because we don't focus so much on what you have done or what you may want to return to. By focusing on spiritual practices that you learn over ninety days and then many years - your sanity will be restored by the growing *realization* of the Soul within you. You will ultimately *Rise Above* addiction and every other problem that plagues you. It's not what *you did or didn't do* that saves you – it is not what you abstain from - it is *the realization* of the presence of God's reflection - *your Soul* - within you that restores your sanity.

The good news is that it never left. It's just been buried in the mud of your mind; the mud covers your mind like silt and sand cover an ancient gold brick in a shipwreck - it's still there - and it as pure and valuable as the day it was buried - you just have to dig it up, rinse it off, polish it, and put it on the altar of your heart.

There is a part of you that is incorruptible, invulnerable, immortal, and stainless!

Stainless Souls, each and every one of us!

Your Soul is Stainless!

There is much to learn and unlearn spiritually that I often wish that you didn't know anything. The attachments to old teachings from our childhoods are hard to let go of and often stand in the way to progress on this spiritual path.

It doesn't mean that you have to change religions or convert to some weird kind of beliefs. Actually, it is quite the opposite - I'd suggest that you believe nothing unless you experience it yourself. In effect, this is the difference between *religion and spirituality*. Religion generally teaches you to believe something someone else experienced; while spirituality teaches that you believe only what you personally experience.

With that out of the way, we are a working and loving group of all religions. Your experiences and beliefs are welcomed and respected here by everybody. We ask that you respect everyone else's experiences and beliefs and keep an open mind while exploring the Universe and your innermost self.

Meanwhile, if *religion and spirituality* are words or concepts that make you feel uncomfortable - that is acceptable too - *philosophy* is a perfectly acceptable word you can use to describe this part of your life.

Regardless of your upbringing, all men and women eventually ask the primal questions of, *"Who am I and why am I here?"* I think it is critical that you seek information and answers to these questions - because if you find answers - you might find your life a bit more manageable.

Rev. Dr. Robert Hobbs
The Realization of Stainless Souls
www.StainlessSouls.com

The mindfulness and meditation practices you have been doing are actually spiritual practices. In the stillness of a calm and quiet mind, you can discover infinite wisdom and knowledge about yourself and the origins of all things.

This week, now that you have read *Polishing the Mirror*, you can begin to experiment with the deeper transcendental or yogic meditations. You'll do this while reading this week's assignment by fellow Yogi, Mickey Singer called, *"The Untethered Soul."* I hope you find his experiences helpful as you begin your own path to freedom. You should also reflect on your second reading assignment, *The Power of Now*. Learning about and discovering *the ego* is paramount in learning and discovering its opposite - *your Spirit*.

The focus this week is on your *spiritual well-being*. Perfect health of your body, mind, and relationships will wobble and eventually topple if you ignore your spirituality and your Soul.

Spirituality, by my own experiences, contains all things - including physical, mental, and emotional well-being. And while it (Spirituality), includes all things, it is contained by nothing or no one. Infinite, eternal, omnipotent, omniscient, and omnipresent are words that describe, but still fall far short of describing the vastness of Spirit - yours and that of the Universe.

Whether you know *IT* or not, or experienced *IT* or not, matters not to the *Spirit*.

The Spirit *is,* regardless of your acknowledgment of it. Try to keep an open mind as you seek the Truth - when the time is right, the Truth will be revealed to you.

From the earliest days of the *Alcoholics Anonymous* program, the belief or disbelief in a *higher power* has plagued newcomers. Usually, non-believers, atheists, agnostics are mentored to start low - believe in something, anything higher than you, even a doorknob, until *the Absolute* is revealed.

You, of course, are encouraged to forge your own way forward - but here (at BBBC) we are going to start big - really big! And maybe save time on your path to freedom.

So, this week - you are going to focus on and study big philosophical topics.

Let's get started.

Focus Areas

The Absolute, Truth, Universe

Regularly reflect on the meanings and potential meanings of these words: *The Absolute, Truth, Universe*

- What do philosophers mean by the Absolute?
- The absolute what?
- Is it possible that there is an unambiguous absolute reality in or around the Universe?
- If there is a standard of non-ambiguity from which all things can be relative - then perhaps the world makes sense in the end.
- On the other hand, if there is only ambiguity - then maybe all meaning is relative.

I, for one, am a proponent of the former; there is a single Absolute, and we can gauge all things from it or God.

God

If there were no creation spawning from The Big Bang or from Genesis, there would be no *God*. God only has meaning in the context of manifested creation. The yogis found that before creation - God was the *unmanifested Spirit*. Once creation took place - the unmanifested Spirit manifested as *God*.

Do not get hung up *on the word* God or any of the connotations it has for you. It is just a word. Instead, when this word is used, consider that it, the word, represents everything that you do not know or understand yet. As you know more and more, perhaps you can begin whittling down the enormity of the word God and make it or Him more comprehensible; or, maybe it or Him will grow exponentially.

That which is beyond comprehension

Truth

There is a truth or the Truth - the Truth about the Universe, the Truth about you, and your place in the Universe, and the Truth for why you are here in the Universe. Truth may be synonymous with Absolute and Absolute with God, Truth, and Universe.

Universe

You often hear spiritual teachers and students alike refer to the Universe as the ultimate source of all things in the same way you may refer to God. There are many reasons for this. For now, allow *the words* God and the Universe be synonymous and if you have difficulty with the concept, then imagine that the Universe is made entirely of *God Stuff or within the mind of God*.

The Soul Identified as the Body Known as the Ego

Obviously, before your Soul entered your body, it was not identified as a body or an ego. However, once you were born, your Soul realized its embodiment, and it became fully identified as the body. This is due to many causes - but the prevalent ones are - social, cultural, ancestral, and survival-based reasons.

You were introduced to this concept in *The Power of Now*, reminded of it in *Polishing the Mirror*, and this week, you will gain more depth with *The Untethered Soul*.

Question yourself deeply; what is the ego really? A bundle of thoughts?

Is there more to it than that? If it is just thoughts, why am I so attached to it?

And, if it is just thoughts, then what or who am I really? Because I don't feel like just thoughts.

What is *my being*?

The Soul Identified as Spirit - the Reflected Image of God

Tugging against the *bundle of thoughts* called the ego in the material world, is the true reflection of God within, pulling you toward Him or It. The battle rages on day after day, week after week, year after year, incarnation after incarnation.

God's creation pulls your ego outward toward an idea of satisfaction via material achievement.

Meanwhile, God himself pulls at your Soul, inviting it to return home, to Him, its source for eternal joy and bliss.

Ego vs. Spirit. The battle will continue on until the day you finally merge back into Him. Of course, the path is tortuous and filled with obstacles such as *free will, karma, attachments, desires, Satan, accidents, and more.* Only after you overcome all of these obstacles, will you finally be freed from the bondage of perpetual embodiment.

Why Do I Exist?

This is a critical question for you to consider. It is safe to say that you probably did not create yourself; so, someone else or something else did. Who is it that would create a being like you without your consent, and then subject you to a mostly miserable existence? There's too much to this question to leave it alone:

Why - do - you - exist?

Once you find the answer, you can begin the march to freedom.

Study Areas

Remember - spend at least 30 minutes per day studying that day's topic. You are encouraged to spend more than 30 minutes and explore more than one topic provided that you complete all of your required activities, chores, steps and service work, etc.

The program requires commitment, integrity, and honesty. If you committed to this, then finish it with the highest personal integrity. You must be honest, always.

Day 1: Who or What is God?

Do some research here - and be diverse. Who do Buddhists, Taoists, Hindus, Jews, Muslims, Christians, say God is?

Start forming your own idea of God - and as you do consider the first verse of the *Tao te Ching*:

> "The Tao that can be told is not the eternal Tao;
> the name that can be named is not the eternal name.
> The Tao is both named and nameless;
> as nameless, it is the origin of all things; as named it is the mother of ten thousand things.
> Ever desireless one can see the mystery; ever desiring, one sees only the manifestations;
> and the mystery itself is the doorway to all understanding." (Dyer)

Day 2: What is the Soul?

You probably won't be surprised to know that no soul has ever been discovered in any autopsy - but then again neither has a mind - or for that matter any of the many emotions that we sometimes believe we possess. Yet we know, despite the lack of physical evidence, that these types of things exist - so much so that they dominate most of our daily lives.

So, what is the Soul? Again - look at the Tao teachings above.

You might find the yogi explanation of the Soul the most intriguing.

Day 3: Time and Space

In the physical dimension, where we believe we exist and that there is nothing beyond and everything is relative to something else. There can be no *space without an object, and there can be no time without at least two objects*. Discovering *where* you are is based on - or is relative to something else - such as the sun, or a mountain, or a street address. Determining *when* you are is relative to *when* something else is or was. For example, it is the year 2019 AD or 2,019 years after Christ. But in absolute terms - *when you are,* and *where you are,* are more difficult to ascertain.

Struggle with these questions this week. Not just in your study time, but all the time and in meditation:

- Who am I?
- What am I?
- Where am I?
- When am I?
- Why am I?

Day 4: What is or was the Big Bang?

The Big Bang was a scientific explanation of the time of creation, while the story of Genesis was considered not scientific. It is common these days for many churches to accept and teach *The Big Bang* as *how God did Genesis*. Find out answers to questions such as what is the Big Bang?

- When did it happen?
- How long did it take?
- What caused it?
- Where did its energy come from?
- Where did the masses of stars and planets come from?

Then consider this:

If there was nothing, and then the Big Bang brought forth everything that is, isn't it true that the atoms that make up your body were born at the time of the Big Bang?

Day 5: Why is it Here? Why Am I Here?

There is an absolute magnificence of this Universe and of you - far too much magnificence for your purpose to merely be *the best mom, or best spouse, or best employee*. If these were your purposes, the Universe, and you, could be far simpler, far less complicated, far less magnificent.

Couldn't you be the *best mom* on a simple Hollywood set for The Brady Bunch? We don't need all of this extraneous magnificence just to have you be the *best mom*.

So, there's something more, something much more meaningful as to *why you're here at this time in this place*.

Day 6: Religion vs. Spirituality

Today research and study the differences between religion and spirituality. As always, take the position of an academic, non-attached to wherever the research and your mind lead you. As a bonus, consider the question,

"Can religion be scientific?"

Day 7: Union, Oneness, Yoga

What is meant by the words Union or Unity, Oneness, and Yoga?

Required Activities

Again, the five required activities are always: *meditation, reading, aerobic exercise, flexibility exercise, and one recovery meeting*. These are things you would do every single day for 90 days and hopefully, the rest of your life.

Meditation

This week your meditation finally reaches 1 hour per day, and this amount of time is perfect. Ideally, two meditations of 30 minutes are suggested; however, few people with 5 weeks clean and sober can sit still for 30 solid minutes. So, this week we recommend three meditations of 20 minutes each, and if you want to try 30 minutes, you are encouraged to do so, but please be honest with yourself and get in one hour of meditation in no more than three meditations

Reading

It's already mentioned several times this week's reading is *The Untethered Soul* by Michael A. Singer. I've also suggested that you review *The Power of Now* from Week 3 and *Polishing the Mirror* from last week.

Try to concentrate on what you are reading; try to absorb the intent that the author has for you.

Aerobic Exercise

Also, this is the first week where you can increase the duration of your aerobic exercise above 30 minutes. Walk 35 minutes every day this week.

Flexibility and Mobility

This remains 10 minutes throughout the entire 90-day program. Remember never stretch a cold muscle. The best time to do these exercises is after aerobic activity.

Meeting

Every day for 90 days, one recovery meeting minimum. 60 Minutes of 100% recovery time just for you and those that you may help.

Needs, Habits, Healings, Affirmations, and Visualizations

Needs

This week's need is *personal growth and development*. With all living things, the old adage remains true; if you are not living, you are dying.

If you are not growing (living), you are dying.

Grow or die.

This program (BBBC) is technically a personal growth and development program. So is CrossFit, college, boot camp, and reading self-help books.

This week is a time for you to evaluate what skills, knowledge, education, and certifications you would like to gain in the future or might need in the future to help shape your chosen vocation.

Brainstorm this area. Don't box yourself into a corner. Be open; be creative; be imaginative. You can still be anything you want to be, it is never too late; in fact, you have an eternity.

Covey Habit 4: Think Win-Win

Focus this habit on all of your meaningful relationships - what does it mean to think win-win in a relationship?

Here's a hint:

1. If you argue with your significant other and force yourself into a win-lose outcome, where you win, and the other loses, then your relationship is **Win-Lose**; meaning 50% of your relationship now is a loser, and therefore *you are in a losing relationship*.

2. In the same argument, if you totally concede to the other, and let that person win, then you lose. Now you are in a **Lose-Win** relationship - again a 50% loser, and therefore *you are in a losing relationship*.

3. If the two of you give up in the argument without a negotiated outcome, and you sweep the dirt under the rug until another time, you both lose. **Lose-Lose** again *you are in a loser relationship*.

4. If on the other hand, you both exercise Habits 1, 2, 3, 4, and 5, in the process of respectful negotiated problem solving, you can create a **Win-Win**, a stronger relationship, a stronger character for yourself and a stronger character for the other and best of all *you are in a winning relationship*.

Healing Treatment Five

Do healing treatment 5, for 15 minutes, 3 times per day.

Affirmation and Visualization

The affirmation and visualization process should be well practiced by now. Continue to work with these at least three times per day. Use the process to build a *positive mental attitude* (PMA) toward your future and your goals.

Step and Service Work

This week you transition from the, *"Forgive Phase,"* toward the, *"Believe Phase."* Last week, you completed step 4, and this week *you must complete Step 5*. ***You Must complete Step 5.**_

As you will find, the completion of Step 5, results in the near-immediate completion of Step 6 and 7. It is in your best interest to complete these steps as outlined in the *Big Book*. Also, use the *12 and 12* for reference.

If you have written your Step 4 list properly, you should be able to trim the list of names of people that you've harmed or maybe who have harmed you from the content and the details of the harm done in either direction so that you can *burn the detail* and *keep the list of names*.

This is important! You want to keep the list because, in essence, the list is going to serve as your Step 8. However, you don't want to keep the details of your Step 4 laying around; you want to burn them (Step 4 details) or shred them.

As for service work, your habits and chores should be well-formed by now. Everything you started in week one should be continuing now. Your service work at meetings should be routine by now, and you should be offering to help those who have transportation difficulties make recovery meetings.

Prayer and Gratitude List

Continue to populate your *prayer and gratitude list* with people and things you are praying for or grateful for. Also, consider writing a short prayer of your own.

Once your complete step 7, which you should do this week, begin saying the *Step 7 Prayer* daily. You can still use the *Step 3 Prayer*, *The Lord's Prayer*, the *Serenity Prayer*, and any prayer where you simply have a conversation with God.

Wellness Checks

Continue your two times daily Wellness Checks and graph the results on the provided page in the back of the book.

Journaling

For your journaling activity this week, you are going to begin working on your long-range goals. These are *five-year goals, three-year goals, and one-year goals*. You will create your goals in each category of your being that we've covered so far: physical, mental/educational, relational/emotional, and spiritual.

The first run through the goal-setting process will be in reverse. The method is sometimes called *reverse engineering* here is what you should do:

For the first two days this week, days 29 and 30, create your 5-year goals in each of the four areas. Start with big-picture, broad terms through the first day, and then the second day get more specific and detailed.

Start asking yourself questions like:

1. Five years from now, what would I like my physical health to be? Education level to be? Knowledge of God to be? My significant relationships to be? And so on.
2. Just start writing and don't stop until you're out of ideas.

At the end of the second day, you are done - *for now* with your 5-year goals.

Then, for the next two days, days 31 and 32, you'll work on your three-year goals:

1. How do you want your life to be in the four areas three years from now?
2. Keep in mind that your 5-year goals depend on your 3-year progress - so what must be true in year three, for you to achieve your goals by year 5? For example, if you want a college degree by year five, you better be enrolled in college and halfway done by year three.

This is the reverse engineering part of the method.

If I am to achieve my 5-year goal of <u><Goal Name></u>, then I must have completed <u><Critical Step of Goal Name></u> by year 3

Be big picture and broad when you start on day 31 and get more detailed and specific on day 32. When you are finished on day 32, you are done with your three-year goals - for now.

On the next two days, days 33 and 34, you will work on your one-year goals - these are much *closer* than 3 and 5-year goals and much more critical tactically.

Start as you did with your five-year goals:

One year from now, I want <One Year Goal Name> in my, health, education, spirituality, relationships, etc., and you have to reverse-engineer from year 5 to year 3, and then from year 3 to year 1.

If year 3 goals are to be materialized, what must be true by the end of year 1?

On day 33, be big picture and broad, and on day 34, become more specific and detailed.

Once you finish your 1, 3, and 5-year goals, review them chronologically forward and determine how well they flow; then reverse chronologically, and determine how well they flow; work with them - forward and backward - like an accordion until they are well-written and understandable.

On day 35 - sit quietly with your draft 1, 3, and 5-year goals. Read them through once, then ask yourself,

What can I do right now in this instant to make progress toward at least one goal?

Whatever answer arises - do that activity or task **right now!**

Never leave the scene of a decision without taking definitive action. That's a Tony Robbins quote.

Always annotate daily what you're proud of, what you want to improve, what you learned, and what you'd like to teach.

The Lion Who Thought He Was a Sheep

Lesson: You are not what you think you are

There once was a very pregnant lion, and she was past due. She was to the point where she felt that if she didn't hunt before delivering her cub, she might not get another chance for some days after delivery. So, despite her condition, she decided to go hunting and because she didn't want to spend a lot of time away from the den once she came across a flock of sheep, she essentially just pounced right in the middle of the herd and landed on one of the sheep.

She came down so hard, and with all the chaos, she delivered the cub in the middle of that flock. She didn't realize it, and she dragged her prey back to the den, leaving her cub in the flock. The sheep being sheep elected to raise the lion cub as their own and they did that. The lion was male and grew into a fully-grown male lion; he spent his entire life, believing that he was a sheep. He grazed and frolicked just like all the other sheep; he even said baaaa just like a sheep would.

A year or so later, another adult male lion was hunting and came across the flock. He was astonished to see a fully-grown male lion frolicking in the herd and behaving like a sheep; he couldn't believe his eyes! He began his chase with his focus on the lion in the flock. All the sheep naturally scattered while he kept on the chase. He soon overcame the sheep lion and tackled him to the ground, and while he was on top of the sheep lion, the sheep lion squealed like a sheep and said, "Please don't kill me; I'm a nice sheep!"

The male lion said to his prey, "My friend, you are no sheep! You're not a sheep at all; you're a fully-grown male lion! Why do you live among the sheep?"

"I'm not a lion! Don't be ridiculous; I'm a sheep; I've been a sheep all my life!
With that, the male lion escorted the sheep-lion to the drinking pond and forced his head toward the water. Both lions stared at the reflection of the two fully grown lion heads reflected in the water. "Look! You see you're not a sheep! You're a lion!"

"I don't believe it," the sheep-lion said. The first lion then taught the sheep-lion how to roar, just like the king of the jungle should. After two or three tries the sheep-lion let out a huge, full-bodied lion roar. He really was a lion; he only thought he was a sheep. So, my friend, you're not a sheep; you're not just an addict; you are, in fact, a child of God who has forgotten his Divine heritage.

You are an incorruptible, invulnerable, immortal stainless soul. You only have to realize it. To realize it, you must not quit until you know the truth.

Awake lion, awake!

Day 29 Required Activities
Meditation: 20 Minutes 3 times
Reading: Untethered Soul 25 Pgs
Aerobic: 35 minutes once
Flexibility: 10 minutes once
Meeting: 60 minutes

Today's Study Areas
Who or what is God?

Week 5: This Week's Focus
Spiritual Wellbeing
The Absolute/God/Truth/Universe
Soul Identified as Body: Ego
Soul ID'd as Spirit: Image of God
Why Do I Exist?

Needs, Habits, Healings, Affirmations, & Visualizations

Needs: Personal Growth & Development (Expansion)

Covey Habit 4: Think Win-Win (in your relationships)

Healing Treatment Five

I positively expect goodness in my life because God is the True Life of my being and reality today and every day. I have a positive mental attitude in my conscious mind because the Mind of God within me is positive about everything in my life today and every day.

Step & Service Work

Phase 2 and 3: Forgive and Believe: Steps 5, 6, 7

Prayer & Gratitude List

"My Creator, I am now willing that you should have all of me, good and bad. I pray that you now remove from me every single defect of character which stands in the way of my usefulness to you and my fellows. Grant me strength, as I go out from here, to do your bidding. Amen." (AA Big Book).

Meetings and Appointments	
__00 / __30	
__00 / __30	
__00 / __30	
__00 / __30	
__00 / __30	
__00 / __30	
__00 / __30	
__00 / __30	
__00 / __30	
__00 / __30	
__00 / __30	
__00 / __30	
__00 / __30	
__00 / __30	
__00 / __30	
__00 / __30	
__00 / __30	

Notes, Numbers, & Future Appointments

Rev. Dr. Robert Hobbs
The Realization of Stainless Souls
www.StainlessSouls.com

Morning Wellness Check		
Physical		
Mental		
Emotional		
Relational		
Spiritual		
Lifestyle		
Immunity		

Evening Wellness Check		
Physical		
Mental		
Emotional		
Relational		
Spiritual		
Lifestyle		
Immunity		

Journaling		
Date:	Sobriety Date:	Number Days Clean & Sober:

My 5 Year Goals: Physical, Mental/Educational, Relational/Emotional, Spiritual

What I am Proud of/Happy About Today

What I Want to Improve/Remember

What Did I Learn

What Can I Teach Someone Like Me?

To Discuss with Sponsor, Doctor, Therapist, or Other Professional:

Day 30 Required Activities
Meditation: 20 Minutes 3 times
Reading: Untethered Soul 25 Pgs
Aerobic: 35 minutes once
Flexibility: 10 minutes once
Meeting: 60 minutes

Today's Study Areas
Who or what is God?
Who or what is a Soul?

Week 5: This Week's Focus
Spiritual Wellbeing
The Absolute/God/Truth/Universe
Soul Identified as Body: Ego
Soul ID'd as Spirit: Image of God
Why Do I Exist?

Needs, Habits, Healings, Affirmations, & Visualizations

Needs: Personal Growth & Development (Expansion)

Covey Habit 4: Think Win-Win (in your relationships)

Healing Treatment Five

Each and every day is lived in the Presence of my Higher God-Mind.

Step & Service Work

Phase 2 and 3: Forgive and Believe: Steps 5, 6, 7

Prayer & Gratitude List

"My Creator, I am now willing that you should have all of me, good and bad. I pray that you now remove from me every single defect of character which stands in the way of my usefulness to you and my fellows. Grant me strength, as I go out from here, to do your bidding. Amen." (AA Big Book).

Meetings and Appointments

__00 / __30	
__00 / __30	
__00 / __30	
__00 / __30	
__00 / __30	
__00 / __30	
__00 / __30	
__00 / __30	
__00 / __30	
__00 / __30	
__00 / __30	
__00 / __30	
__00 / __30	
__00 / __30	
__00 / __30	
__00 / __30	
__00 / __30	
__00 / __30	

Notes, Numbers, & Future Appointments

Rev. Dr. Robert Hobbs
The Realization of Stainless Souls
www.StainlessSouls.com

Morning Wellness Check		
Physical		
Mental		
Emotional		
Relational		
Spiritual		
Lifestyle		
Immunity		

Evening Wellness Check		
Physical		
Mental		
Emotional		
Relational		
Spiritual		
Lifestyle		
Immunity		

Journaling		
Date:	Sobriety Date:	Number Days Clean & Sober:

My 5 Year Goals: Physical, Mental/Educational, Relational/Emotional, Spiritual

What I am Proud of/Happy About Today

What I Want to Improve/Remember

What Did I Learn

What Can I Teach Someone Like Me?

To Discuss with Sponsor, Doctor, Therapist, or Other Professional:

Day 31 Required Activities	Today's Study Areas	Week 5: This Week's Focus
Meditation: 20 Minutes 3 times	Who or what is God?	Spiritual Wellbeing
Reading: Untethered Soul 25 Pgs	Who or what is a Soul?	The Absolute/God/Truth/Universe
Aerobic: 35 minutes once	Who, What, When, Why Am I?	Soul Identified as Body: Ego
Flexibility: 10 minutes once		Soul ID'd as Spirit: Image of God
Meeting: 60 minutes		Why Do I Exist?

Needs, Habits, Healings, Affirmations, & Visualizations	Meetings and Appointments	
Needs: Personal Growth & Development (Expansion)	__00 __30	
Covey Habit 4: Think Win-Win (in your relationships)	__00 __30	
Healing Treatment Five	__00 __30	
The Pure Spiritual Light of my True Self and my Soul is already dissolving unwanted thought patterns from my mind. For this, I give thanks, I let it be so, and so it is!	__00 __30	
	__00 __30	
Step & Service Work	__00 __30	
Phase 2 and 3: Forgive and Believe: Steps 5, 6, 7	__00 __30	
	__00 __30	
	__00 __30	
	__00 __30	
	__00 __30	
	__00 __30	
	__00 __30	
Prayer & Gratitude List	__00 __30	
	__00 __30	
	__00 __30	
"My Creator, I am now willing that you should have all of me, good and bad. I pray that you now remove from me every single defect of character which stands in the way of my usefulness to you and my fellows. Grant me strength, as I go out from here, to do your bidding. Amen." (AA Big Book).	__00 __30	
	__00 __30	
	__00 __30	

Notes, Numbers, & Future Appointments

Rev. Dr. Robert Hobbs
The Realization of Stainless Souls
www.StainlessSouls.com

Morning Wellness Check		
Physical		
Mental		
Emotional		
Relational		
Spiritual		
Lifestyle		
Immunity		

Evening Wellness Check		
Physical		
Mental		
Emotional		
Relational		
Spiritual		
Lifestyle		
Immunity		

Journaling		
Date:	Sobriety Date:	Number Days Clean & Sober:

To achieve my 5-year goals, I must within 3 years accomplish: My 3 Year Goals: Physical, Mental/Educational, Relational/Emotional, Spiritual

What I am Proud of/Happy About Today

What I Want to Improve/Remember

What Did I Learn

What Can I Teach Someone Like Me?

To Discuss with Sponsor, Doctor, Therapist, or Other Professional:

Day 32 Required Activities
Meditation: 20 Minutes 3 times
Reading: Untethered Soul 25 Pgs
Aerobic: 35 minutes once
Flexibility: 10 minutes once
Meeting: 60 minutes

Today's Study Areas
Who or what is God?
Who or what is a Soul?
Who, What, When, Why Am I?
What is/was the Big Bang?

Week 5: This Week's Focus
Spiritual Wellbeing
The Absolute/God/Truth/Universe
Soul Identified as Body: Ego
Soul ID'd as Spirit: Image of God
Why Do I Exist?

Needs, Habits, Healings, Affirmations, & Visualizations

Needs: Personal Growth & Development (Expansion)

Covey Habit 4: Think Win-Win (in your relationships)

Healing Treatment Five

Jesus said, "As a man thinketh in his heart, so is he." So, I am that which I thinketh in my heart and therefore I am a beacon of the pure Light, Life, and Love of God.

Step & Service Work

Phase 2 and 3: Forgive and Believe: Steps 5, 6, 7

Prayer & Gratitude List

"My Creator, I am now willing that you should have all of me, good and bad. I pray that you now remove from me every single defect of character which stands in the way of my usefulness to you and my fellows. Grant me strength, as I go out from here, to do your bidding. Amen." (AA Big Book).

Meetings and Appointments

__00 __30	
__00 __30	
__00 __30	
__00 __30	
__00 __30	
__00 __30	
__00 __30	
__00 __30	
__00 __30	
__00 __30	
__00 __30	
__00 __30	
__00 __30	
__00 __30	
__00 __30	
__00 __30	
__00 __30	
__00 __30	

Notes, Numbers, & Future Appointments

Rev. Dr. Robert Hobbs
The Realization of Stainless Souls
www.StainlessSouls.com

Morning Wellness Check		
Physical		
Mental		
Emotional		
Relational		
Spiritual		
Lifestyle		
Immunity		

Evening Wellness Check		
Physical		
Mental		
Emotional		
Relational		
Spiritual		
Lifestyle		
Immunity		

Journaling		
Date:	Sobriety Date:	Number Days Clean & Sober:

To achieve my 5-year goals, I must within 3 years accomplish: My 3 Year Goals: Physical, Mental/Educational, Relational/Emotional, Spiritual

What I am Proud of/Happy About Today

What I Want to Improve/Remember

What Did I Learn

What Can I Teach Someone Like Me?

To Discuss with Sponsor, Doctor, Therapist, or Other Professional:

Day 33 Required Activities
Meditation: 20 Minutes 3 times
Reading: Untethered Soul 25 Pgs
Aerobic: 35 minutes once
Flexibility: 10 minutes once
Meeting: 60 minutes

Today's Study Areas
Who or what is God?
Who or what is a Soul?
Who, What, When, Why Am I?
What is/was the Big Bang?
Why is it here/Why am I here?

Week 5: This Week's Focus
Spiritual Wellbeing
The Absolute/God/Truth/Universe
Soul Identified as Body: Ego
Soul ID'd as Spirit: Image of God
Why Do I Exist?

Needs, Habits, Healings, Affirmations, & Visualizations
Needs: Personal Growth & Development (Expansion)
Covey Habit 4: Think Win-Win (in your relationships)
Healing Treatment Five
The winning purpose of my soul inspires me and reverberates through my thoughts today and every day.

Meetings and Appointments	
__00 __30	
__00 __30	
__00 __30	
__00 __30	
__00 __30	
__00 __30	
__00 __30	
__00 __30	
__00 __30	
__00 __30	
__00 __30	
__00 __30	
__00 __30	
__00 __30	
__00 __30	
__00 __30	
__00 __30	
__00 __30	

Step & Service Work
Phase 2 and 3: Forgive and Believe: Steps 5, 6, 7

Prayer & Gratitude List
"My Creator, I am now willing that you should have all of me, good and bad. I pray that you now remove from me every single defect of character which stands in the way of my usefulness to you and my fellows. Grant me strength, as I go out from here, to do your bidding. Amen." (AA Big Book).

Notes, Numbers, & Future Appointments

Rev. Dr. Robert Hobbs
The Realization of Stainless Souls
www.StainlessSouls.com

Morning Wellness Check		
Physical		
Mental		
Emotional		
Relational		
Spiritual		
Lifestyle		
Immunity		

Evening Wellness Check		
Physical		
Mental		
Emotional		
Relational		
Spiritual		
Lifestyle		
Immunity		

Journaling		
Date:	Sobriety Date:	Number Days Clean & Sober:

To achieve my 3-year goals, I must within 1 year accomplish: My 1 Year Goals: Physical, Mental/Educational, Relational/Emotional, Spiritual

What I am Proud of/Happy About Today

What I Want to Improve/Remember

What Did I Learn

What Can I Teach Someone Like Me?

To Discuss with Sponsor, Doctor, Therapist, or Other Professional:

Day 34 Required Activities	Today's Study Areas	Week 5: This Week's Focus
Meditation: 20 Minutes 3 times	Who or what is a Soul?	Spiritual Wellbeing
Reading: Untethered Soul 25 Pgs	Who, What, When, Why Am I?	The Absolute/God/Truth/Universe
Aerobic: 35 minutes once	What is/was the Big Bang?	Soul Identified as Body: Ego
Flexibility: 10 minutes once	Why is it here/Why am I here?	Soul ID'd as Spirit: Image of God
Meeting: 60 minutes	Religion vs Spirituality	Why Do I Exist?

Needs, Habits, Healings, Affirmations, & Visualizations

Needs: Personal Growth & Development (Expansion)

Covey Habit 4: Think Win-Win (in your relationships)

Healing Treatment Five

Every meditation period opens my mind more and more to an awareness of my higher spiritual nature and soul.

Step & Service Work

Phase 2 and 3: Forgive and Believe: Steps 5, 6, 7

Prayer & Gratitude List

"My Creator, I am now willing that you should have all of me, good and bad. I pray that you now remove from me every single defect of character which stands in the way of my usefulness to you and my fellows. Grant me strength, as I go out from here, to do your bidding. Amen." (AA Big Book).

Meetings and Appointments

Time	
__00 __30	
__00 __30	
__00 __30	
__00 __30	
__00 __30	
__00 __30	
__00 __30	
__00 __30	
__00 __30	
__00 __30	
__00 __30	
__00 __30	
__00 __30	
__00 __30	
__00 __30	
__00 __30	
__00 __30	

Notes, Numbers, & Future Appointments

Rev. Dr. Robert Hobbs
The Realization of Stainless Souls
www.StainlessSouls.com

Morning Wellness Check		
Physical		
Mental		
Emotional		
Relational		
Spiritual		
Lifestyle		
Immunity		

Evening Wellness Check		
Physical		
Mental		
Emotional		
Relational		
Spiritual		
Lifestyle		
Immunity		

Journaling		
Date:	Sobriety Date:	Number Days Clean & Sober:

To achieve my 3-year goals, I must within 1 year accomplish: My 1 Year Goals: Physical, Mental/Educational, Relational/Emotional, Spiritual

What I am Proud of/Happy About Today

What I Want to Improve/Remember

What Did I Learn

What Can I Teach Someone Like Me?

To Discuss with Sponsor, Doctor, Therapist, or Other Professional:

Day 35 Required Activities	Today's Study Areas	Week 5: This Week's Focus
Meditation: 20 Minutes 3 times	Who, What, When, Why Am I?	Spiritual Wellbeing
Reading: Untethered Soul 25 Pgs	What is/was the Big Bang?	The Absolute/God/Truth/Universe
Aerobic: 35 minutes once	Why is it here/Why am I here?	Soul Identified as Body: Ego
Flexibility: 10 minutes once	Religion vs Spirituality	Soul ID'd as Spirit: Image of God
Meeting: 60 minutes	What is Union, Oneness, Yoga?	Why Do I Exist?

Needs, Habits, Healings, Affirmations, & Visualizations

Needs: Personal Growth & Development (Expansion)

Covey Habit 4: Think Win-Win (in your relationships)

Healing Treatment Five

In everything I am doing, I visualize it as being done by the Pure Inner Light, guided by the Pure Inner Love, through the Pure Eternal Life, that manifests as me throughout each moment of each day of my life.

Step & Service Work

Phase 2 and 3: Forgive and Believe: Steps 5, 6, 7

Prayer & Gratitude List

"My Creator, I am now willing that you should have all of me, good and bad. I pray that you now remove from me every single defect of character which stands in the way of my usefulness to you and my fellows. Grant me strength, as I go out from here, to do your bidding. Amen." (AA Big Book).

Meetings and Appointments

Time	
__00 __30	
__00 __30	
__00 __30	
__00 __30	
__00 __30	
__00 __30	
__00 __30	
__00 __30	
__00 __30	
__00 __30	
__00 __30	
__00 __30	
__00 __30	
__00 __30	
__00 __30	
__00 __30	
__00 __30	

Notes, Numbers, & Future Appointments

Rev. Dr. Robert Hobbs
The Realization of Stainless Souls
www.StainlessSouls.com

Morning Wellness Check		
Physical		
Mental		
Emotional		
Relational		
Spiritual		
Lifestyle		
Immunity		

Evening Wellness Check		
Physical		
Mental		
Emotional		
Relational		
Spiritual		
Lifestyle		
Immunity		

Journaling		
Date:	Sobriety Date:	Number Days Clean & Sober:

What can I do RIGHT NOW to start pursuing my goals?

What I am Proud of/Happy About Today

What I Want to Improve/Remember

What Did I Learn

What Can I Teach Someone Like Me?

To Discuss with Sponsor, Doctor, Therapist, or Other Professional:

Week 6 Lifestyle Wellness

High thinking; plain living

Perhaps no lesson in this 13-week program is more fundamental to your peace, serenity, tranquility, joy, happiness, and bliss, than this week's lesson on Lifestyle Wellness.

If you are an American, the odds are that you are working yourself to death. If you are not dying while working, you are probably worrying yourself to death. You are chasing after some form of material gain that you believe will give you happiness.

You've done this often. Once you acquired the desired item, you were happy for a while, but then due to boredom or worry (attachment) over the welfare of it, the happiness wore off. You then moved on to a new desire, and the cycle started again.

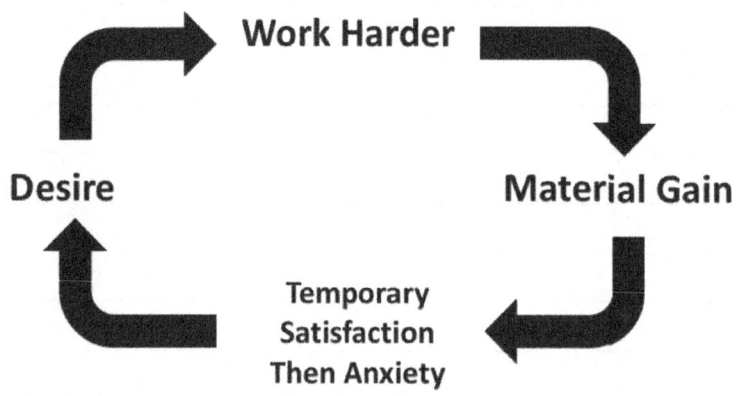

There is an alternative

Minimalism

Minimalism is often misunderstood. We are not advocating renunciation or austerity. We are suggesting that you learn quickly what your minimum needs are to live comfortably and simply. You will spend time learning about this practice in detail by reading the book *Minimalism: Living a Meaningful Life* by Joshua Fields Millburn and Ryan Nicodemus.

Essentialism

Minimalism and essentialism feed off each other. When you choose to *minimize*, you will find more freedom in your obligations at work. Ideally, you become willing and capable of doing only *what is essential* at work rather than signing up to do everything - even though you never could do everything. When you switch to an *essentialism mindset* - you are no longer compelled to do 100 projects, 1% well. Instead, you're able to take pride in the fact that you can do 1 project 100% well. If your material lifestyle is not minimalist, then you will be too afraid to *downsize* at work. However, once you know your *needs are addressed*, doing only essential work becomes less scary and much more fulfilling.

Rev. Dr. Robert Hobbs
The Realization of Stainless Souls
www.StainlessSouls.com

This week you will also begin reading the book *Essentialism: The Disciplined Pursuit of Less* by Greg McKeown.

Right away begin designing your life and lifestyle so that you can live simply, and think highly, and with total ability to be flexible.

Channel every energy toward happiness - not toward work - not toward stuff - not toward influence, fame, power.

One element of knowledge that you need to develop to begin creating a *high thinking, simple living mindset* is how to differentiate things that you want versus things that you need. Take your time with this topic - really evaluate what you need and what you want.

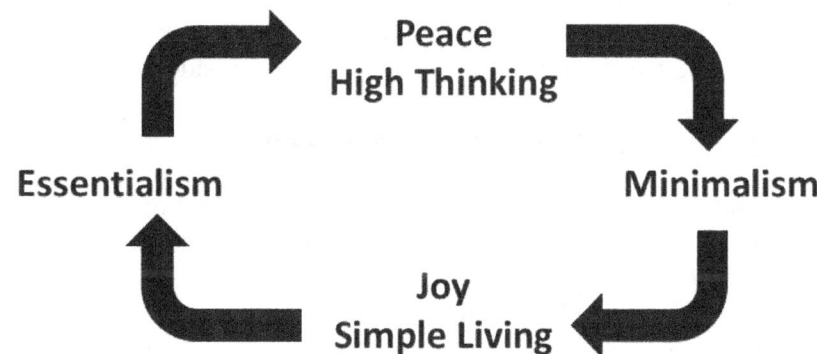

Typically, things you want will become cravings - you'll be so desirous of these things they will consume you until you have them. After you have them, you become overly worried about protecting them and taking care of them. All of this energy is wasted, and it contributes to a false sense of anxiety (anxiety is a form of fear, designed to keep you safe; it is misused when you worry about possessions).

Needs are something that you don't really have much of an attachment to such as toothpaste and toilet paper; you have them because you need them and you're not overly worried for their protection or how you're going to take care of them.

> *Abundance is not something we acquire;*
>
> *abundance is something we tune into!*
>
> ~Wayne Dyer

There are many examples we can review - you need a car - maybe to go back and forth to work. You want a BMW. From a happiness perspective, you will be far happier with the basic car that you need, rather than the BMW (and all it entails) that you want.

Finally, the last topic in this week's focus list is PMA (positive mental attitude). Napoleon Hill introduced us to PMA in nearly all of his writings since *Think and Grow Rich*. There could be an entire 90-day program worth of work we could do on PMA alone. I'd like you to become an expert on how to leverage PMA to create a better life for yourself and those in it. I'll leave it to you to find out how, but we have been weaving PMA into your life daily since day one.

Study Areas

The study areas this week are really a study of you, of what you are and of what you want to become. You really must evaluate whether or not you need a 5,000 square foot-house, or if you could settle for an 800 square-foot house. Whether you need an $80,000 car, or will an $8,000 car do. Everything you add to your life will distract you and redirect (misdirect) your energy. If you keep your stuff simple, your relationships simple, and your vocation simple, you can have more focus and energy to enjoy high thinking, and in high thinking, you can find the joy, bliss, and happiness of plain living. This is the only place, the only way, true happiness can be found in the physical realm.

Day 1: Covey Habit 3: Put First Things First.

As I mentioned before, Habit 3 is my favorite of the seven, and there are several excellent YouTube videos available where Dr. Covey demonstrates the thesis of *putting first things first*. He also teaches, as a part of Habit 3 that weekly planning or planning by the week, is the optimum for productivity. Enjoy learning about Habit 3, but more importantly, enjoy the freedom that Habit 3 provides when adequately utilized.

What Are the First Things?

As an aside, but as a part of *putting first things first*, Covey also talks about the quadrants of productivity where the axes of the four quadrants are *urgency and importance*. He has the participants in his demonstration categorize all the different things that they do at work across the scale of *not important to very important and not urgent to very urgent*. What Covey found was that most people spend time working on things that are urgent and *not important*. He teaches that it is because they do, that crises generally occur where tasks become *very important and very critical*. There is a little opportunity, when people work this way, to be proactive and to manage the work, instead of having the work manage them.

So, another demonstration that you can look at as you study Habit 3 is the demonstration on Quadrant 2.

Day 2: What do I Really Need to Survive?

After reading *Minimalism*, this will make more sense to you, but to start down this road, you need to know what the bare minimum resources are that you need to survive. Food, water, shelter, and.....what else? This will serve as your baseline. You will always have security knowing that if you have these things, you can survive, and if you can survive, you can pursue your life's purpose. Everything above the baseline level of need can be considered convenience items or luxury items or *wants*.

Few people will choose to live long with the bare minimums, and that is understandable. Take comfort in knowing that everything above the baseline level is not necessary; and if you lose it, there will be no threat to your survival. Therefore, there is no valid fear or anxiety.

Day 3: How Hard Do I Really Have to Work?

As you scale down to *what you need,* obviously you scaled-down costs. As you scale down expenses, you can scale down how much you need to earn to afford those costs. This is the *link between minimalism and essentialism*.

The necessity of special stress-inducing projects and hours at work is alleviated as the cost of living is smartly reduced.

So, embrace some *level of minimalism*, and then some *degree of essentialism*, so that any work you do is absolutely essential to meet your minimum needs. Everything else is the icing on the cake.

Day 4: What is Real Happiness

This is something only you can answer, but I encourage you never to accept today's answer because as you grow in wisdom, your definition of real happiness will evolve. While you begin contemplating, allow me to give you a few pointers:

1. Happiness is not found in places or things
2. Other people cannot provide you with joy
3. Happiness might be something you can actually take with you after you die - you cannot take people, places, or things
4. Happiness may happen many lifetimes later

Day 5: How to Plan Weekly

Watch Covey videos on this and on Quadrant 2. In the meantime, here is a brief primer:

1. Set up time weekly to plan the coming week - usually Sunday.
2. Write in the things most important to you. First, the big stuff like school meetings, child activities, vacation, community service, etc.
3. Write in important meetings and appointments
4. Write in your 7 AA meetings, one each day
5. Write in study time, meditation time, etc. After filling in your agenda with these priority items, fill in if necessary, brain-dead items such as *watch TV, send an email, etc. Or, Preferably, fill in all wasted time with meditation!*

Day 6: How to be Productive

Watch videos on *Getting Things Done*, by James Allen, *First Things First* and *Essentialism*.

Day 7: Learn About the Subconscious Mind

· Where is it?
· What does it do?
· How powerful is it compared with the conscious mind?

Required Activities

Meditation

If you can sit for 30 minutes, do your meditations two times a day for 30 minutes each; if you find this routine comfortable for you, you don't need to change it again.

Reading

Minimalism for the first six days, *essentialism* on the seventh day.

Aerobic Exercise/Flexibility

40 minutes of walking once each day followed by 10 minutes of flexibility and mobility

Recovery Meeting

As it is for daily in this 90-day program, attend one recovery meeting every single day.

Needs, Habits, Healings, Affirmations, and Visualizations

Needs

This week you continue looking at your personal growth and development needs.

Where do you want to improve your life?

- Physical: Lose weight, run a marathon, do CrossFit, do keto?
- Mental: Get a degree, read a book, learn a language, study a topic.
- Emotional: Fix relationship, control anger, spend more time with children, get a less stressful job.
- Spiritual. Learn how to meditate, do yoga, pray better, find God.
- Grow or die - ABG: Always Be Growing

Habit 3: Put First Things First

We've already discussed Habit 3.

Healing Treatment Six

As you have for five weeks, do your healing treatment for 15 minutes 3 times a day. Begin to look for opportunities to blend or integrate your affirmations and visualizations with your healing treatments and meditations.

Affirmations and Visualizations

Remember how Genesis describes God's process of creation:

In the beginning, God created the heavens and the earth, and the earth was without form and void,

Think about this statement, what does it mean when an object is void of form? It indicates *it was just thought*, doesn't it? If it exists without form? It only exists as a thought.

Contemplate This!

So, first is a thought. When you do your affirmations, first form them as thoughts.

And then,

<u>*God said…*</u>

God spoke; He created a sound and vibrational energy that represented His **<u>thought</u>** and,

As He spoke - **His breath, His life force**, was embedded in the sound vibrations; the sound vibrations were imbued with the ***<u>Life Energy of God</u>***…

"Let there be light!"

With this statement, God created a *visualization of his thought*. So, the creation hierarchy, if you will, is:

Thought energy | Sound energy | Vibrational energy | Life energy | Light energy

In the same way, you are asked to bring your dreams and goals into reality, and to *real physical form*. This is one purpose of your affirmation and visualization practice. Developing PMA is another.

Advanced Prayer

You may be used to considering *prayer* things you say from memory before meals or bedtime. For most people the petitions are not imbued with energy or emotion; they're usually not even personal, they're just words you've heard and now recite from memory.

If a friend were talking to you in such a detached and indifferent way, would you be motivated by their words?

Do you think God would be motivated by your indifferent and uninspired words?

God will not answer your prayer until he recognizes your prayer as authentic, sincere, and meaningful.

Pray as Jesus did; so earnestly that sweat falls from your head like drops of blood. Then you will know what it means to put your whole self, mind, body, heart, and soul into the prayer.

No matter what your prayer request, pray with your whole self. Fully merge into your true spirit, and thus into the Spirit of God.

Know that when,

You and the Father are One,

He already knows what you seek before you ask because *He is present within you. He is One with your thoughts and feelings.*

Also, consider this when praying for the resources that you will need to carry out your Divine Purpose: Your authentic Divine Purpose was placed within your intuitive awareness by the Divine - hence - Divine Purpose.

Because He sanctioned you for your purpose, it is up to Him to provision you with the resources you need to be successful. He would not sanction you without provisioning you. Because of this, you can pray with confidence, in fact, with *the expectation* that your prayers will be answered. In this case as God's child on a Divine Mission, you do not need to approach like a beggar, you approach as a child, as an heir, and you demand that which you are entitled.

Finally, consider this too. All prayer comes from God. He already knows what we need He writes our prayers on our hearts through intuition while in deep meditation. We, in turn, take his intuitive guidance and turn it into words. Then, through affirmation and visualization, we reaffirm and program both our rational and subconscious minds with His Divine Will for our lives.

In other words, we don't pray our prayers because God needs to hear them; we pray our prayers because we need to hear them.

Step and Service Work

This week you enter the *Believe Phase*. Often reflect on *what you believe* and what your beliefs are.

Thought - Sound - Vibration - Life - Light

Step 7

Last week, just after Step 5, you completed Steps 6 and 7. This week spend some time with the information available to you in Step 7. Say *Step 7 Prayer* often. Make yourself available to serve others; be totally grateful at all times for your spirituality and sobriety.

Use the blank spaces here to add new service ideas or suggestions that you can implement in addition to everything else you've been doing since week 1.

Prayer and Gratitude List

Never end a day without a prayer of gratitude for the people, places, and things that have made your life better. The *Step 7 Prayer* is provided for you for your benefit this week.

Wellness Checks

Continue your twice-daily wellness checks in each of the seven areas. Have you noticed any trends? Any correlations? If you have, write about your experiences in your notebook.

Journaling

As a reminder, write down your sobriety date and number of days clean and sober every day in the journaling section of the planner. Also, do so with an attitude of gratitude.

What's Next?

Day 36

One day, these 90 days are going to conclude. On the 91st day, you will feel a void and an emptiness once all these daily activities and exercises are no longer prevalent. The point of this program is to teach you that you can fill a day with recovery - and that often a day seems too short to do all you want to do. Decide now how you are going to spend day 91; and then, how you're going to spend day 92 and 93 through day 182.

Make a commitment to yourself now that you will live your life in a specified manner *as dictated by you* beginning on day 91, and then every day for the rest of your life.

Day 37

Put some descriptions around your commitment from yesterday. How, in detail, will you live your life in weeks 14 through 26?

Days 39 through 42

You have drafted your 1, 3, and 5-year plans, have completed most of the topics in this program, and have begun thinking about life after the *Brown Bag, Blue Collar Recovery Planner*. Now and for the rest of this week plan out in detail your *90-day plan for the 90 days following this program*. The areas to plan in particular are the same as those covered here. Have a plan for your *physical, mental, emotional, relational, spiritual, and lifestyle wellness, as well as a blueprint for relapse prevention.*

Don't skimp here. Get into the details.

- Where are you weak?
- Where are you strong?
- What are your goals?

Rev. Dr. Robert Hobbs
The Realization of Stainless Souls
www.StainlessSouls.com

You already have your 1-year goals, so these 90-day objectives should be aligned and consistent with those goals, and then with your three and five-year goals.

Finally, everyday fill in your:

- Happy and proud moments and the
- Issues you want to improve
- Something you learned
- Something you can teach later

Day 36 Required Activities
Meditation: 30 Minutes 2 times
Reading: Minimalism 25 Pages
Aerobic: 40 minutes once
Flexibility: 10 minutes once
Meeting: 60 minutes

Today's Study Areas
Covey Habit 3: Put 1st things 1st

Week 6: This Week's Focus
Lifestyle: Minimal & Essential
Minimalism
Essentialism
Wants vs Needs
PMA: Positive Mental Attitude

Needs, Habits, Healings, Affirmations, & Visualizations
Needs: Personal Growth & Development (Expansion)
Covey Habit 3: Put First Things First
Healing Treatment Six
Because the power of God and the Universe prosper me, I am confidently living a life of peace and tranquility.

Step & Service Work
Phase 3: Believe: Step 7

Prayer & Gratitude List
"My Creator, I am now willing that you should have all of me, good and bad. I pray that you now remove from me every single defect of character which stands in the way of my usefulness to you and my fellows. Grant me strength, as I go out from here, to do your bidding. Amen." (AA Big Book).

Meetings and Appointments	
__00 __30	
__00 __30	
__00 __30	
__00 __30	
__00 __30	
__00 __30	
__00 __30	
__00 __30	
__00 __30	
__00 __30	
__00 __30	
__00 __30	
__00 __30	
__00 __30	
__00 __30	
__00 __30	
__00 __30	
__00 __30	

Notes, Numbers, & Future Appointments

Rev. Dr. Robert Hobbs
The Realization of Stainless Souls
www.StainlessSouls.com

Morning Wellness Check		
Physical		
Mental		
Emotional		
Relational		
Spiritual		
Lifestyle		
Immunity		

Evening Wellness Check		
Physical		
Mental		
Emotional		
Relational		
Spiritual		
Lifestyle		
Immunity		

Journaling		
Date:	Sobriety Date:	Number Days Clean & Sober:

What am I going to do at the end of these 90 days? A commitment to me!

What I am Proud of/Happy About Today

What I Want to Improve/Remember

What Did I Learn

What Can I Teach Someone Like Me?

To Discuss with Sponsor, Doctor, Therapist, or Other Professional:

Day 37 Required Activities	Today's Study Areas	Week 6: This Week's Focus
Meditation: 30 Minutes 2 times	Covey Habit 3: Put 1st things 1st	Lifestyle: Minimal & Essential
Reading: Minimalism 25 Pages	What do I REALLY need to survive	Minimalism
Aerobic: 40 minutes once		Essentialism
Flexibility: 10 minutes once		Wants vs Needs
Meeting: 60 minutes		PMA: Positive Mental Attitude

Needs, Habits, Healings, Affirmations, & Visualizations

Needs: Personal Growth & Development (Expansion)

Covey Habit 3: Put First Things First

Healing Treatment Six

The Higher-Power within me is greater than any feeling of unworthiness within me; I surrender my mind & body to the Higher God-Power within. The Higher-Power within gives me the poise and confidence to get up and go live up to the potential instilled in me by my Creator.

Step & Service Work

Phase 3: Believe: Step 7

Prayer & Gratitude List

"My Creator, I am now willing that you should have all of me, good and bad. I pray that you now remove from me every single defect of character which stands in the way of my usefulness to you and my fellows. Grant me strength, as I go out from here, to do your bidding. Amen." (AA Big Book).

Meetings and Appointments

__00 __30	
__00 __30	
__00 __30	
__00 __30	
__00 __30	
__00 __30	
__00 __30	
__00 __30	
__00 __30	
__00 __30	
__00 __30	
__00 __30	
__00 __30	
__00 __30	
__00 __30	
__00 __30	
__00 __30	
__00 __30	

Notes, Numbers, & Future Appointments

Rev. Dr. Robert Hobbs
The Realization of Stainless Souls
www.StainlessSouls.com

Morning Wellness Check		
Physical		
Mental		
Emotional		
Relational		
Spiritual		
Lifestyle		
Immunity		

Evening Wellness Check		
Physical		
Mental		
Emotional		
Relational		
Spiritual		
Lifestyle		
Immunity		

Journaling		
Date:	Sobriety Date:	Number Days Clean & Sober:

How I intend to live my life in weeks 14-26

What I am Proud of/Happy About Today

What I Want to Improve/Remember

What Did I Learn

What Can I Teach Someone Like Me?

To Discuss with Sponsor, Doctor, Therapist, or Other Professional:

Day 38 Required Activities
Meditation: 30 Minutes 2 times
Reading: Minimalism 25 Pages
Aerobic: 40 minutes once
Flexibility: 10 minutes once
Meeting: 60 minutes

Today's Study Areas
Covey Habit 3: Put 1st things 1st
What do I REALLY need to survive
What must I REALLY do at work

Week 6: This Week's Focus
Lifestyle: Minimal & Essential
Minimalism
Essentialism
Wants vs Needs
PMA: Positive Mental Attitude

Needs, Habits, Healings, Affirmations, & Visualizations

Needs: Personal Growth & Development (Expansion)

Covey Habit 3: Put First Things First

Healing Treatment Six

I rely on The Presence of God's Power and Will for my life, and I am thereby relaxed and poised in all that my life may bring.

Step & Service Work

Phase 3: Believe: Step 7

Prayer & Gratitude List

"My Creator, I am now willing that you should have all of me, good and bad. I pray that you now remove from me every single defect of character which stands in the way of my usefulness to you and my fellows. Grant me strength, as I go out from here, to do your bidding. Amen." (AA Big Book).

Meetings and Appointments

Time	
__00 __30	
__00 __30	
__00 __30	
__00 __30	
__00 __30	
__00 __30	
__00 __30	
__00 __30	
__00 __30	
__00 __30	
__00 __30	
__00 __30	
__00 __30	
__00 __30	
__00 __30	
__00 __30	
__00 __30	

Notes, Numbers, & Future Appointments

Rev. Dr. Robert Hobbs
The Realization of Stainless Souls
www.StainlessSouls.com

Morning Wellness Check		
Physical		
Mental		
Emotional		
Relational		
Spiritual		
Lifestyle		
Immunity		

Evening Wellness Check		
Physical		
Mental		
Emotional		
Relational		
Spiritual		
Lifestyle		
Immunity		

Journaling		
Date:	Sobriety Date:	Number Days Clean & Sober:

Draft 90-day plan for weeks 14-26 (days 91 – 182) Physical, Mental, Emotional/Relational, Spiritual, Lifestyle, Relapse Prevention

What I am Proud of/Happy About Today

What I Want to Improve/Remember

What Did I Learn

What Can I Teach Someone Like Me?

To Discuss with Sponsor, Doctor, Therapist, or Other Professional:

Day 39 Required Activities	Today's Study Areas	Week 6: This Week's Focus
Meditation: 30 Minutes 2 times	Covey Habit 3: Put 1st things 1st	Lifestyle: Minimal & Essential
Reading: Minimalism 25 Pages	What do I REALLY need to survive	Minimalism
Aerobic: 40 minutes once	What must I REALLY do at work	Essentialism
Flexibility: 10 minutes once	What is REAL HAPPINESS?	Wants vs Needs
Meeting: 60 minutes		PMA: Positive Mental Attitude

Needs, Habits, Healings, Affirmations, & Visualizations

Needs: Personal Growth & Development (Expansion)

Covey Habit 3: Put First Things First

Healing Treatment Six

The Mind and Wisdom of my Higher Mind direct me, in every way, to success and happiness through intuition and creative ideas today and every day.

Step & Service Work

Phase 3: Believe: Step 7

Prayer & Gratitude List

"My Creator, I am now willing that you should have all of me, good and bad. I pray that you now remove from me every single defect of character which stands in the way of my usefulness to you and my fellows. Grant me strength, as I go out from here, to do your bidding. Amen." (AA Big Book).

Meetings and Appointments

__00 __30	
__00 __30	
__00 __30	
__00 __30	
__00 __30	
__00 __30	
__00 __30	
__00 __30	
__00 __30	
__00 __30	
__00 __30	
__00 __30	
__00 __30	
__00 __30	
__00 __30	
__00 __30	
__00 __30	
__00 __30	

Notes, Numbers, & Future Appointments

Rev. Dr. Robert Hobbs
The Realization of Stainless Souls
www.StainlessSouls.com

Morning Wellness Check		
Physical		
Mental		
Emotional		
Relational		
Spiritual		
Lifestyle		
Immunity		

Evening Wellness Check		
Physical		
Mental		
Emotional		
Relational		
Spiritual		
Lifestyle		
Immunity		

Journaling		
Date:	Sobriety Date:	Number Days Clean & Sober:

Draft 90-day plan for weeks 14-26 (days 91 – 182) Physical, Mental, Emotional/Relational, Spiritual, Lifestyle, Relapse Prevention

What I am Proud of/Happy About Today

What I Want to Improve/Remember

What Did I Learn

What Can I Teach Someone Like Me?

To Discuss with Sponsor, Doctor, Therapist, or Other Professional:

Day 40 Required Activities
Meditation: 30 Minutes 2 times
Reading: Minimalism 25 Pages
Aerobic: 40 minutes once
Flexibility: 10 minutes once
Meeting: 60 minutes

Today's Study Areas
Covey Habit 3: Put 1st things 1st
What do I REALLY need to survive
What must I REALLY do at work
What is REAL HAPPINESS?
How to plan weekly

Week 6: This Week's Focus
Lifestyle: Minimal & Essential
Minimalism
Essentialism
Wants vs Needs
PMA: Positive Mental Attitude

Needs, Habits, Healings, Affirmations, & Visualizations

Needs: Personal Growth & Development (Expansion)

Covey Habit 3: Put First Things First

Healing Treatment Six

I am one, now and always, with financial abundance through the Infinite Source of Supply within me.

Meetings and Appointments

__00 __30	
__00 __30	
__00 __30	
__00 __30	
__00 __30	
__00 __30	
__00 __30	
__00 __30	
__00 __30	
__00 __30	
__00 __30	
__00 __30	
__00 __30	
__00 __30	
__00 __30	
__00 __30	
__00 __30	
__00 __30	
__00 __30	

Step & Service Work

Phase 3: Believe: Step 7

Prayer & Gratitude List

"My Creator, I am now willing that you should have all of me, good and bad. I pray that you now remove from me every single defect of character which stands in the way of my usefulness to you and my fellows. Grant me strength, as I go out from here, to do your bidding. Amen." (AA Big Book).

Notes, Numbers, & Future Appointments

Rev. Dr. Robert Hobbs
The Realization of Stainless Souls
www.StainlessSouls.com

Morning Wellness Check		
Physical		
Mental		
Emotional		
Relational		
Spiritual		
Lifestyle		
Immunity		

Evening Wellness Check		
Physical		
Mental		
Emotional		
Relational		
Spiritual		
Lifestyle		
Immunity		

Journaling		
Date:	Sobriety Date:	Number Days Clean & Sober:

Draft 90-day plan for weeks 14-26 (days 91 – 182) Physical, Mental, Emotional/Relational, Spiritual, Lifestyle, Relapse Prevention

What I am Proud of/Happy About Today

What I Want to Improve/Remember

What Did I Learn

What Can I Teach Someone Like Me?

To Discuss with Sponsor, Doctor, Therapist, or Other Professional:

Day 41 Required Activities	Today's Study Areas	Week 6: This Week's Focus
Meditation: 30 Minutes 2 times	What do I REALLY need to survive	Lifestyle: Minimal & Essential
Reading: Minimalism 25 Pages	What must I REALLY do at work	Minimalism
Aerobic: 40 minutes once	What is REAL HAPPINESS?	Essentialism
Flexibility: 10 minutes once	How to plan weekly	Wants vs Needs
Meeting: 60 minutes	How to be productive	PMA: Positive Mental Attitude

Needs, Habits, Healings, Affirmations, & Visualizations

Needs: Personal Growth & Development (Expansion)

Covey Habit 3: Put First Things First

Healing Treatment Six

I am One with perfect fulfillment of my potential and purposefully chosen life immediately, today, and every day!

Step & Service Work

Phase 3: Believe: Step 7

Prayer & Gratitude List

"My Creator, I am now willing that you should have all of me, good and bad. I pray that you now remove from me every single defect of character which stands in the way of my usefulness to you and my fellows. Grant me strength, as I go out from here, to do your bidding. Amen." (AA Big Book).

Meetings and Appointments

__00 __30	
__00 __30	
__00 __30	
__00 __30	
__00 __30	
__00 __30	
__00 __30	
__00 __30	
__00 __30	
__00 __30	
__00 __30	
__00 __30	
__00 __30	
__00 __30	
__00 __30	
__00 __30	
__00 __30	

Notes, Numbers, & Future Appointments

Rev. Dr. Robert Hobbs
The Realization of Stainless Souls
www.StainlessSouls.com

Morning Wellness Check		
Physical		
Mental		
Emotional		
Relational		
Spiritual		
Lifestyle		
Immunity		

Evening Wellness Check		
Physical		
Mental		
Emotional		
Relational		
Spiritual		
Lifestyle		
Immunity		

Journaling		
Date:	Sobriety Date:	Number Days Clean & Sober:

Draft 90-day plan for weeks 14-26 (days 91 – 182) Physical, Mental, Emotional/Relational, Spiritual, Lifestyle, Relapse Prevention

What I am Proud of/Happy About Today

What I Want to Improve/Remember

What Did I Learn

What Can I Teach Someone Like Me?

To Discuss with Sponsor, Doctor, Therapist, or Other Professional:

Day 42 Required Activities	Today's Study Areas	Week 6: This Week's Focus
Meditation: 30 Minutes 2 times	What must I REALLY do at work	Lifestyle: Minimal & Essential
Reading: Essentialism 25 Pages	What is REAL HAPPINESS?	Minimalism
Aerobic: 40 minutes once	How to plan weekly	Essentialism
Flexibility: 10 minutes once	How to be productive	Wants vs Needs
Meeting: 60 minutes	What is the subconscious mind?	PMA: Positive Mental Attitude

Needs, Habits, Healings, Affirmations, & Visualizations

Needs: Personal Growth & Development (Expansion)

Covey Habit 3: Put First Things First

Healing Treatment Six

Today and every day, I will be presently conscious of doing everything I do - differently, better, and with more awareness, than I ever have before. I am Universally directed to live up to the Divine potential within me. For this, I give thanks, I let it be so, and so it is!

Step & Service Work

Phase 3: Believe: Step 7

Prayer & Gratitude List

"My Creator, I am now willing that you should have all of me, good and bad. I pray that you now remove from me every single defect of character which stands in the way of my usefulness to you and my fellows. Grant me strength, as I go out from here, to do your bidding. Amen." (AA Big Book).

Meetings and Appointments

__ 00 __ 30	
__ 00 __ 30	
__ 00 __ 30	
__ 00 __ 30	
__ 00 __ 30	
__ 00 __ 30	
__ 00 __ 30	
__ 00 __ 30	
__ 00 __ 30	
__ 00 __ 30	
__ 00 __ 30	
__ 00 __ 30	
__ 00 __ 30	
__ 00 __ 30	
__ 00 __ 30	
__ 00 __ 30	
__ 00 __ 30	
__ 00 __ 30	

Notes, Numbers, & Future Appointments

Rev. Dr. Robert Hobbs
The Realization of Stainless Souls
www.StainlessSouls.com

Morning Wellness Check		
Physical		
Mental		
Emotional		
Relational		
Spiritual		
Lifestyle		
Immunity		

Evening Wellness Check		
Physical		
Mental		
Emotional		
Relational		
Spiritual		
Lifestyle		
Immunity		

Journaling		
Date:	Sobriety Date:	Number Days Clean & Sober:

Draft 90-day plan for weeks 14-26 (days 91 – 182) Physical, Mental, Emotional/Relational, Spiritual, Lifestyle, & Relapse Prevention

What I am Proud of/Happy About Today

What I Want to Improve/Remember

What Did I Learn

What Can I Teach Someone Like Me?

To Discuss with Sponsor, Doctor, Therapist, or Other Professional:

Week 7 Immunity & Defense

Defending Your Sobriety; Relapse Prevention; Building a Moat

Welcome to the last week of the first six-week semester. So far, you have accomplished quite a bit. You have completed detox and orientation as well as studied topics on well-being, including:

· Physical
· Mental
· Emotional
· Spiritual
· Lifestyle

You have been:

· Meditating,
· Reading,
· Walking,
· Stretching,
· Studying,
· Serving others, and even
· Making your bed

You have much to be proud of. However, your work is not done. In fact, it is never done.

Recovery will take the rest of your life

You have come so far and accomplished so much; it is now time to build a moat around your new way of life. The moat acts as a barrier. It keeps unhealthy things (or threats to your sobriety) outside while fostering and nurturing those things that are good for you inside. Visualize yourself as a castle surrounded by a moat with everything dangerous for you on the *outside* and everything right for you on the *inside*.

Occasionally, there may be some good things that should be allowed into your kingdom. If you are sure it's okay, you can lower your drawbridge temporarily to permit the right stuff to cross. Once they are inside, you raise the bridge and maintain your immunity.

Occasionally, there may be a few things on the inside that need let out; these items can be let go by lowering the drawbridge; once they're gone raise the bridge that protects your immunity.

This Week's Focus

*Sobriety Immunity **equals** Relapse Prevention*

The things that can harm us can be called poison or toxic. This week you'll spend time self-analyzing the toxins that will poison your sobriety and result in relapse. You may consider toxins and triggers to be synonymous, but generally speaking, toxins are toxic to everyone, and triggers are specific to you and your addiction.

By now, you should expect that your analysis will be done across 4 areas - physical toxins, mental toxins, emotional toxins, and spiritual toxins.

Rev. Dr. Robert Hobbs
The Realization of Stainless Souls
www.StainlessSouls.com

Study Areas

Day 1: Define Immunity, Relapse Prevention, Defense, and Moat

How do these terms apply to your sobriety?

Day 2: Find Your mTriggers (Mental Triggers)

These are triggers or stimuli that cause your *mind* or consciousness to go on a run - uncontrolled and undefined toward some unhealthy outcome.

To recognize these or any triggers, you must be fully present (mindful) when they arise.

To defend against these triggers, which are driving you to an unwanted outcome, you must exercise *integrity in the moment (gap) of choice.* The *integrity* is your personal honesty; the *gap* is the time between stimulus and response, the *desired response* is the one that is in accordance with your *values and beliefs.*

To avoid these uncontrolled runs, you sometimes have to be observing your mind in the same way an air traffic controller manages the airways. You have to be present and have an awareness and sensitivity of what might go wrong based on the patterns of planes in the sky (or emotions in your mind) and then be proactive in making some adjustments that will place you in a place of safety with integrity toward your values and beliefs.

Take some time while you're in a positive state to identify the cause of your mTriggers. Often these are from stimuli such as movies, music, media, social media, and people.

When you identify a likely trigger, your defense is to eliminate it and its source from your life. In early recovery, *Surrender and Retreat,* also known as *avoidance*, are perfectly acceptable guards while you build up your more elegant and longer-term immunities.

Day 3: eTriggers (Emotional Triggers)

Today evaluate carefully what your eTriggers are. What stimuli in your life, such as propaganda, advertising, perfumes, etc., stir your emotions in such a way that could result in a spontaneous relapse? Emotional triggers are tricky because they can quickly arrive in stealth mode; the first feeling might be innocent, but the chain reaction that follows can be deadly. As discussed with mTriggers, *you have to be mindful*, and *you have to exercise integrity in the moment of choice.* You cannot be caught unprepared for this type of attack, or you might relapse. So, spend today, provided you're in a positive state, analyzing your eTriggers, and then determine the sources and then work to eliminate them from your life.

Day 4: sTriggers (Spiritual Triggers)

Spiritual triggers are stimuli that draw you deeper into the material world and further away from the spiritual. Material is synonymous with physical, so you can assume that *desires and attachments* to people, places, and things would be prevalent here. Note the way we worded the previous sentence; it is the *desire or attachment*, not the people place or thing that is the trigger.

The most apparent stimuli here are sexual in nature: porn, racy shows, risqué company, could all be categorized as sTriggers. Anything that weakens you spiritually can be considered a spiritual trigger. Find out what yours are, and design defenses against them. Remember *avoidance (Surrender and Retreat)* is best in early recovery. Later, when you have more skill and experience - you can design more elegant defenses against sTriggers.

Day 5: pTriggers (Physical Triggers)

pTriggers are physical triggers, and in this case, quite literally they are physical objects that might trigger a string or chain of events that lead to relapse. You must know what these objects are and have a commitment to *breaking the chain* before the last link - the relapse link.

Alcoholics Anonymous teaches physical triggers are people, places, and things, and that until one is firm in their recovery triggering people, places, and things, should be avoided.

Day 6: Mentorship and Leadership

Part of *Alcoholics Anonymous'* success is due to its focus on serving others. If you are going to be successful in recovery, at some point, you are going to have to lead (sponsor, coach, mentor) someone through the recovery process.

If you are going to complete this recovery program, you're going to actually teach someone (like you) at least one of the significant areas of study that you have worked with. In fact, by the end of next week, you will be teaching someone something you learned about physical well-being.

Teaching is fundamental to leadership. It is a critical element. Your service work during the last seven weeks, and this teaching will prepare you to begin leading and mentoring. Spend the day learning about the terms leadership and mentorship.

Day 7: What is Concentration

On the surface, this topic might seem a little out of place. After all, we are working with relapse prevention and triggers. What role could concentration possibly play?

Well, if you could concentrate your mind, at will, on any object you choose, then you have conquered the topic of relapse prevention. It would work like this:

- · Because you are mindful,
- · You *instantly notice a relapse trigger* arising in your mind or senses,
- · You *immediately exercise integrity in the moment of choice*, and then
- · *Concentrate your mind on an object* totally unrelated to the relapse trigger

If your concentration is 100%, you would not be able to relapse; it is foolproof.

So, study concentration

Required Activities

Meditation

Twice each day for 30 minutes

Reading

The Universe has Your Back by Gabby Bernstein. This is a book that brought me out of a very dark time in 2016; read it with an open mind and adopt any meditative practices that speak to you.

Aerobic Exercise

45 minutes one time. Some people will be able to walk 3 miles in 45 minutes!

Flexibility

10 minutes.

Recovery Meeting

60 Minutes

Needs, Habits, Healings, Affirmation, and Visualization

Needs

This is your last week focusing on *growth and development*. Be sure to review the previous three weeks and write down clear, concise statements of what or how you want to develop.

Grow or die
ABG: Always Be Growing

Covey Habit 6: Synergize or Napoleon Hill Mastermind

There are two offerings this week. Because Dr. Covey did such a great job getting out the *synergize* message, it became one of those words no one wanted to use anymore - it had become too cliché. The concept was initially introduced by Napoleon Hill, author of *Think and Grow Rich* under the moniker *Mastermind*.

In both cases, the idea is that two heads are better than one, or that one plus one is three. When you apply more minds to a problem, you can improve the potential solution set, and thus the eventual solution. Review these two terms this week and brainstorm on how they can help you; there are plenty of videos available on YouTube.

Healing Treatment Seven

Practice this week's healing for 15 minutes 3 times per day.

Affirmation and Visualization

Practice each day's affirmation 3 times.

Remember there are 90+ short-form affirmations available for use in the back of this planner. You can use these when you're driving or running or walking or doing anything that you can do while putting your mind toward an affirmation.

Step and Service Work

Three weeks ago, you completed Step 4. If you were thorough, you created a list of offenses that you may have committed, and part of that list was the names of who you offended. If you were smart, you kept the names and destroyed the offenses. If you did, you did Step 8 with Step 4; so, Step 8 is done.

Step 9 is the amends step; though you may be eager, you should take your time. Be studious. Re-read steps 8, 9, and 10, in both the *Big Book* and the *12 and 12*. There are some amends you should begin making right away, with those who are closest usually, and probably those are the people you've hurt the most.

However, it is my experience that you should slow roll those that are not as close or as harmed. This is not permission to miss an opportunity to apologize, but rather advice that Step 9 may take years to complete. For that reason, steps 9, 10, 11, and 12, are worked simultaneously by all addicts and alcoholics in recovery.

This week, re-read Step 9, review your list from Step 4, which is now your Step 8, and talk to your sponsor and a few others about how they did Step 9. Ask how you should start. Another tip is don't start with your hardest most challenging relationship. Practice your approach a few times on those who you may owe slightly more than an apology. Learn what you can and then plan your attack for those essential relationships that might be more complicated.

Remember no amends you ever make should ever cause harm to yourself or others; sometimes it's better to let a dog sleep.

Prayer and Gratitude

This section is on you again this week.

- What are you grateful for?
- Who are you praying for?
- What prayers are you saying?

You might want to consider learning the *Prayer of Saint Francis of Assisi* as it is popular in recovery.

Twice-daily Wellness Checks

Do your checks and plot results.

Journaling

Use the journaling section to record any triggers you run across in the course of your daily life.

Note that the *Step 9 Promises*, from Pages 84 to 85 of the *AA Big Book*, are provided for you to ponder this week. If you're going to meetings, you are likely reading these at least once each day anyway.

Continue to record your:

- Happy items,
- Things to improve
- Things learned
- Something you can teach

Tony Robbins teaches,

A life worth living is a life worth recording.

Record your beautiful life.

And now friends, congratulations! You've made it to the end of the first semester of the Brown Bag Blue Collar Recovery System, now we move on to week 8, and the second 6-week semester.

Notes and Sketches

Day 43 Required Activities
Meditation: 30 Minutes 2 times
Read: Universe has ur Back 25 Pg
Aerobic: 45 minutes once
Flexibility: 10 minutes once
Meeting: 60 minutes

Today's Study Areas
Defending Sobriety (with a moat)

Week 7: This Week's Focus
Immunity: Relapse Prevention
Mental Toxins
Emotional Toxins
Spiritual Toxins
Physical Toxins

Needs, Habits, Healings, Affirmations, & Visualizations

Needs: Personal Growth & Development (Expansion)

Covey Habit 6: Synergize or Napoleon Hill: Mastermind

Healing Treatment Seven

Carl Jung said, "One doesn't solve problems; one outgrows them," and therefore, rather than continuing to struggle always for solutions to my difficulties, I intend from now on to use the Infinite Power of my Higher Mind to rise above and outgrow them.

Step & Service Work

Phase 3: Believe; Steps 8, 9

Prayer & Gratitude List

Meetings and Appointments	
__00 __30	
__00 __30	
__00 __30	
__00 __30	
__00 __30	
__00 __30	
__00 __30	
__00 __30	
__00 __30	
__00 __30	
__00 __30	
__00 __30	
__00 __30	
__00 __30	
__00 __30	
__00 __30	
__00 __30	
__00 __30	
__00 __30	

Notes, Numbers, & Future Appointments

Rev. Dr. Robert Hobbs
The Realization of Stainless Souls
www.StainlessSouls.com

Morning Wellness Check		
Physical		
Mental		
Emotional		
Relational		
Spiritual		
Lifestyle		
Immunity		

Evening Wellness Check		
Physical		
Mental		
Emotional		
Relational		
Spiritual		
Lifestyle		
Immunity		

Journaling		
Date:	Sobriety Date:	Number Days Clean & Sober:

If we are painstaking about this phase of our development, we will be amazed before we are halfway through. We are going to know a new freedom and a new happiness. We will not regret the past nor wish to shut the door on it. We will comprehend the word serenity and we will know peace. No matter how far down the scale we have gone, we will see how our experience can benefit others. That feeling of uselessness and self-pity will disappear. We will lose interest in selfish things and gain interest in our fellows. Self-seeking will slip away. Our whole attitude and outlook upon life will change. Fear of people and of economic insecurity will leave us. We will intuitively know how to handle situations which used to baffle us. We will suddenly realize that God is doing for us what we could not do for ourselves. Are these extravagant promises? We think not. They are being fulfilled among us—sometimes quickly, sometimes slowly. They will always materialize if we work for them (AA Big Book).

What I am Proud of/Happy About Today

What I Want to Improve/Remember

What Did I Learn

What Can I Teach Someone Like Me?

To Discuss with Sponsor, Doctor, Therapist, or Other Professional:

Day 44 Required Activities
Meditation: 30 Minutes 2 times
Read: Universe has ur Back 25 Pg
Aerobic: 45 minutes once
Flexibility: 10 minutes once
Meeting: 60 minutes

Today's Study Areas
Defending Sobriety (with a moat)
mTriggers: Movies, People, Media

Week 7: This Week's Focus
Immunity: Relapse Prevention
Mental Toxins
Emotional Toxins
Spiritual Toxins
Physical Toxins

Needs, Habits, Healings, Affirmations, & Visualizations

Needs: Personal Growth & Development (Expansion)

Covey Habit 6: Synergize or Napoleon Hill: Mastermind

Healing Treatment Seven

The Power of God within me will overcome any habit or thought pattern I desire to be liberated of, and through that Power within me, my mind is continuously revitalized, rejuvenated, and made anew. For this, I give thanks, I let it be so, and so it is!

Step & Service Work

Phase 3: Believe; Steps 8, 9

Prayer & Gratitude List

Meetings and Appointments

__00 __30	
__00 __30	
__00 __30	
__00 __30	
__00 __30	
__00 __30	
__00 __30	
__00 __30	
__00 __30	
__00 __30	
__00 __30	
__00 __30	
__00 __30	
__00 __30	
__00 __30	
__00 __30	
__00 __30	
__00 __30	
__00 __30	

Notes, Numbers, & Future Appointments

Rev. Dr. Robert Hobbs
The Realization of Stainless Souls
www.StainlessSouls.com

Morning Wellness Check		
Physical		
Mental		
Emotional		
Relational		
Spiritual		
Lifestyle		
Immunity		

Evening Wellness Check		
Physical		
Mental		
Emotional		
Relational		
Spiritual		
Lifestyle		
Immunity		

Journaling		
Date:	Sobriety Date:	Number Days Clean & Sober:

What I am Proud of/Happy About Today

What I Want to Improve/Remember

What Did I Learn

What Can I Teach Someone Like Me?

To Discuss with Sponsor, Doctor, Therapist, or Other Professional:

Day 45 Required Activities	Today's Study Areas	Week 7: This Week's Focus
Meditation: 30 Minutes 2 times	Defending Sobriety (with a moat)	Immunity: Relapse Prevention
Read: Universe has ur Back 25 Pg	mTriggers: Movies, People, Media	Mental Toxins
Aerobic: 45 minutes once	eTriggers: Media Propaganda, Ads	Emotional Toxins
Flexibility: 10 minutes once		Spiritual Toxins
Meeting: 60 minutes		Physical Toxins

Needs, Habits, Healings, Affirmations, & Visualizations

Needs: Personal Growth & Development (Expansion)

Covey Habit 6: Synergize or Napoleon Hill: Mastermind

Healing Treatment Seven

My subconscious mind creates and identifies with a visual image of me as a healthy, clean and sober, prosperous, and content person with every breath I draw from the Universe every moment of my life.

Step & Service Work

Phase 3: Believe; Steps 8, 9

Prayer & Gratitude List

Meetings and Appointments

Time	
__00 / __30	
__00 / __30	
__00 / __30	
__00 / __30	
__00 / __30	
__00 / __30	
__00 / __30	
__00 / __30	
__00 / __30	
__00 / __30	
__00 / __30	
__00 / __30	
__00 / __30	
__00 / __30	
__00 / __30	
__00 / __30	
__00 / __30	

Notes, Numbers, & Future Appointments

Rev. Dr. Robert Hobbs
The Realization of Stainless Souls
www.StainlessSouls.com

Morning Wellness Check		
Physical		
Mental		
Emotional		
Relational		
Spiritual		
Lifestyle		
Immunity		

Evening Wellness Check		
Physical		
Mental		
Emotional		
Relational		
Spiritual		
Lifestyle		
Immunity		

Journaling		
Date:	Sobriety Date:	Number Days Clean & Sober:

If we are painstaking about this phase of our development, we will be amazed before we are halfway through. We are going to know a new freedom and a new happiness. We will not regret the past nor wish to shut the door on it. We will comprehend the word serenity and we will know peace. No matter how far down the scale we have gone, we will see how our experience can benefit others. That feeling of uselessness and self-pity will disappear. We will lose interest in selfish things and gain interest in our fellows. Self-seeking will slip away. Our whole attitude and outlook upon life will change. Fear of people and of economic insecurity will leave us. We will intuitively know how to handle situations which used to baffle us. We will suddenly realize that God is doing for us what we could not do for ourselves. Are these extravagant promises? We think not. They are being fulfilled among us—sometimes quickly, sometimes slowly. They will always materialize if we work for them (AA Big Book).

What I am Proud of/Happy About Today

What I Want to Improve/Remember

What Did I Learn

What Can I Teach Someone Like Me?

To Discuss with Sponsor, Doctor, Therapist, or Other Professional:

Day 46 Required Activities
Meditation: 30 Minutes 2 times
Read: Universe has ur Back 25 Pg
Aerobic: 45 minutes once
Flexibility: 10 minutes once
Meeting: 60 minutes

Today's Study Areas
Defending Sobriety (with a moat)
mTriggers: Movies, People, Media
eTriggers: Media Propaganda, Ads
sTriggers: Desires, Attachments

Week 7: This Week's Focus
Immunity: Relapse Prevention
Mental Toxins
Emotional Toxins
Spiritual Toxins
Physical Toxins

Needs, Habits, Healings, Affirmations, & Visualizations
Needs: Personal Growth & Development (Expansion)
Covey Habit 6: Synergize or Napoleon Hill: Mastermind
Healing Treatment Seven
I am grateful to the Higher-Power of my mind for providing me with Self-Mastery

Meetings and Appointments	
__00 __30	
__00 __30	
__00 __30	
__00 __30	
__00 __30	
__00 __30	
__00 __30	
__00 __30	
__00 __30	
__00 __30	
__00 __30	
__00 __30	
__00 __30	
__00 __30	
__00 __30	
__00 __30	
__00 __30	

Step & Service Work
Phase 3: Believe; Steps 8, 9

Prayer & Gratitude List

Notes, Numbers, & Future Appointments

Rev. Dr. Robert Hobbs
The Realization of Stainless Souls
www.StainlessSouls.com

Morning Wellness Check		
Physical		
Mental		
Emotional		
Relational		
Spiritual		
Lifestyle		
Immunity		

Evening Wellness Check		
Physical		
Mental		
Emotional		
Relational		
Spiritual		
Lifestyle		
Immunity		

Journaling		
Date:	Sobriety Date:	Number Days Clean & Sober:

What I am Proud of/Happy About Today

What I Want to Improve/Remember

What Did I Learn

What Can I Teach Someone Like Me?

To Discuss with Sponsor, Doctor, Therapist, or Other Professional:

Day 47 Required Activities	Today's Study Areas	Week 7: This Week's Focus
Meditation: 30 Minutes 2 times	Defending Sobriety (with a moat)	Immunity: Relapse Prevention
Read: Universe has ur Back 25 Pg	mTriggers: Movies, People, Media	Mental Toxins
Aerobic: 45 minutes once	eTriggers: Media Propaganda, Ads	Emotional Toxins
Flexibility: 10 minutes once	sTriggers: Desires, Attachments	Spiritual Toxins
Meeting: 60 minutes	pTriggers: People, Places, Things	Physical Toxins

Needs, Habits, Healings, Affirmations, & Visualizations

Needs: Personal Growth & Development (Expansion)

Covey Habit 6: Synergize or Napoleon Hill: Mastermind

Healing Treatment Seven

I constantly, consciously and subconsciously visualize myself as a person who creates, behaves, and carries on as a person with a wonderfully contented life today and every day.

Step & Service Work

Phase 3: Believe; Steps 8, 9

Prayer & Gratitude List

Meetings and Appointments

__00 __30	
__00 __30	
__00 __30	
__00 __30	
__00 __30	
__00 __30	
__00 __30	
__00 __30	
__00 __30	
__00 __30	
__00 __30	
__00 __30	
__00 __30	
__00 __30	
__00 __30	
__00 __30	
__00 __30	

Notes, Numbers, & Future Appointments

Rev. Dr. Robert Hobbs
The Realization of Stainless Souls
www.StainlessSouls.com

Morning Wellness Check		
Physical		
Mental		
Emotional		
Relational		
Spiritual		
Lifestyle		
Immunity		

Evening Wellness Check		
Physical		
Mental		
Emotional		
Relational		
Spiritual		
Lifestyle		
Immunity		

Journaling		
Date:	Sobriety Date:	Number Days Clean & Sober:

If we are painstaking about this phase of our development, we will be amazed before we are halfway through. We are going to know a new freedom and a new happiness. We will not regret the past nor wish to shut the door on it. We will comprehend the word serenity and we will know peace. No matter how far down the scale we have gone, we will see how our experience can benefit others. That feeling of uselessness and self-pity will disappear. We will lose interest in selfish things and gain interest in our fellows. Self-seeking will slip away. Our whole attitude and outlook upon life will change. Fear of people and of economic insecurity will leave us. We will intuitively know how to handle situations which used to baffle us. We will suddenly realize that God is doing for us what we could not do for ourselves. Are these extravagant promises? We think not. They are being fulfilled among us—sometimes quickly, sometimes slowly. They will always materialize if we work for them (AA Big Book).

What I am Proud of/Happy About Today

What I Want to Improve/Remember

What Did I Learn

What Can I Teach Someone Like Me?

To Discuss with Sponsor, Doctor, Therapist, or Other Professional:

Day 48 Required Activities	Today's Study Areas	Week 7: This Week's Focus
Meditation: 30 Minutes 2 times	mTriggers: Movies, People, Media	Immunity: Relapse Prevention
Read: Universe has ur Back 25 Pg	eTriggers: Media Propaganda, Ads	Mental Toxins
Aerobic: 45 minutes once	sTriggers: Desires, Attachments	Emotional Toxins
Flexibility: 10 minutes once	pTriggers: People, Places, Things	Spiritual Toxins
Meeting: 60 minutes	Mentorship & Leadership	Physical Toxins

Needs, Habits, Healings, Affirmations, & Visualizations

Needs: Personal Growth & Development (Expansion)

Covey Habit 6: Synergize or Napoleon Hill: Mastermind

Healing Treatment Seven

By releasing all past negativity, I release my God-Directed mind – into a positive future.

Step & Service Work

Phase 3: Believe; Steps 8, 9

Prayer & Gratitude List

Meetings and Appointments

__00 __30	
__00 __30	
__00 __30	
__00 __30	
__00 __30	
__00 __30	
__00 __30	
__00 __30	
__00 __30	
__00 __30	
__00 __30	
__00 __30	
__00 __30	
__00 __30	
__00 __30	
__00 __30	
__00 __30	
__00 __30	
__00 __30	

Notes, Numbers, & Future Appointments

Rev. Dr. Robert Hobbs
The Realization of Stainless Souls
www.StainlessSouls.com

Morning Wellness Check		
Physical		
Mental		
Emotional		
Relational		
Spiritual		
Lifestyle		
Immunity		

Evening Wellness Check		
Physical		
Mental		
Emotional		
Relational		
Spiritual		
Lifestyle		
Immunity		

Journaling		
Date:	Sobriety Date:	Number Days Clean & Sober:

What I am Proud of/Happy About Today

What I Want to Improve/Remember

What Did I Learn

What Can I Teach Someone Like Me?

To Discuss with Sponsor, Doctor, Therapist, or Other Professional:

Day 49 Required Activities
Meditation: 30 Minutes 2 times
Read: Universe has ur Back 25 Pg
Aerobic: 45 minutes once
Flexibility: 10 minutes once
Meeting: 60 minutes

Today's Study Areas
eTriggers: Media Propaganda, Ads
sTriggers: Desires, Attachments
pTriggers: People, Places, Things
Mentorship & Leadership
What is concentration?

Week 7: This Week's Focus
Immunity: Relapse Prevention
Mental Toxins
Emotional Toxins
Spiritual Toxins
Physical Toxins

Needs, Habits, Healings, Affirmations, & Visualizations

Needs: Personal Growth & Development (Expansion)

Covey Habit 6: Synergize or Napoleon Hill: Mastermind

Healing Treatment Seven

The God-Power within me is greater than any obstacle before me.

Step & Service Work

Phase 3: Believe; Steps 8, 9

Prayer & Gratitude List

Meetings and Appointments

Time	
__00 __30	
__00 __30	
__00 __30	
__00 __30	
__00 __30	
__00 __30	
__00 __30	
__00 __30	
__00 __30	
__00 __30	
__00 __30	
__00 __30	
__00 __30	
__00 __30	
__00 __30	
__00 __30	
__00 __30	
__00 __30	

Notes, Numbers, & Future Appointments

Rev. Dr. Robert Hobbs
The Realization of Stainless Souls
www.StainlessSouls.com

Morning Wellness Check		
Physical		
Mental		
Emotional		
Relational		
Spiritual		
Lifestyle		
Immunity		

Evening Wellness Check		
Physical		
Mental		
Emotional		
Relational		
Spiritual		
Lifestyle		
Immunity		

Journaling		
Date:	Sobriety Date:	Number Days Clean & Sober:

If we are painstaking about this phase of our development, we will be amazed before we are halfway through. We are going to know a new freedom and a new happiness. We will not regret the past nor wish to shut the door on it. We will comprehend the word serenity and we will know peace. No matter how far down the scale we have gone, we will see how our experience can benefit others. That feeling of uselessness and self-pity will disappear. We will lose interest in selfish things and gain interest in our fellows. Self-seeking will slip away. Our whole attitude and outlook upon life will change. Fear of people and of economic insecurity will leave us. We will intuitively know how to handle situations which used to baffle us. We will suddenly realize that God is doing for us what we could not do for ourselves. Are these extravagant promises? We think not. They are being fulfilled among us—sometimes quickly, sometimes slowly. They will always materialize if we work for them (AA Big Book).

What I am Proud of/Happy About Today

What I Want to Improve/Remember

What Did I Learn

What Can I Teach Someone Like Me?

To Discuss with Sponsor, Doctor, Therapist, or Other Professional:

Week 8: Teach Detox and Physical Wellness

It's hard to believe, isn't it? You've already completed seven weeks. If you were disciplined, they were pretty intense. The thing about a program like this is its completion requires 100% honesty and integrity on your part, you must - MUST hold yourself accountable. I compare it to people who want to run a marathon; you can't do it just because you decide to. You must choose to, then set some goals, make a plan, execute the plan, continue running no matter how bad you feel, show up on race day, and then run the full 26.2 miles. If you fall short, by just one foot, no medal, and you are not considered a marathoner; you have to complete the whole thing.

There is no one *making* the marathon runner run. There is no one *watching over* the runner's shoulder, making sure they put in all the required miles on the required days.

There is only the runner and his or her vision to complete a milestone. S/he is self-motivated and self-inspired.

A program like this one can absolutely work for you if you're willing to be honest and accountable to the most important person in the Universe,

You

This week's primary task is to pick a topic from weeks 1 or 2, then review the curriculum in your notes from those weeks, then spend 30 minutes teaching the selected subject to another human - preferably one who suffers as you do. It would be even more ideal if you could find another person using the Brown Bag Blue Collar System and teach them your topic.

If you do find another BBBC student willing to work with you, you can work together creating lessons and teaching each other the material.

Your lesson plan can be simple. It should have

- A title
- 3 - 5 learning objectives
- A short discussion on each of the objectives
- A list of references or source material
- A summary
- A time for questions and answers
- Contact information so that your student can contact you later if questions persist

Each week for the rest of this program, you will teach one 30-minute lesson for a total of six lessons. Remember, if you want to master something, teach it!

Additionally - each day of this week corresponds to a day in weeks 1 or 2. Review and study those areas again for 30 minutes, try to remember important points while advancing your knowledge by doing research. At the end of 7 days, you should be quite comfortable with the topics studied.

Finally - the deliverable for this week is to create your Physical Wellness Plan. Don't confuse goals with plans.

Goals are visions.

Plans are action items with dates that help you arrive at your target.

Rev. Dr. Robert Hobbs
The Realization of Stainless Souls
www.StainlessSouls.com

To create your personal Physical Wellness Plan, begin by reviewing your 90-day, 1-year, 3-year, 5-year, physical wellness goals established throughout the first semester and then transpose those goals to a new section of your notebook.

Planning takes a certain amount of ingenuity and creativity. Here is how to proceed.

1. Write down your 90-day goals (or whatever period you are working on)
2. Ask yourself, "*What is the last step, that if completed successfully, will assure me with complete confidence that I will achieve this goal?*"
3. Write down that last step
4. Assign a date to when that last step should be completed for you to achieve your 90-day goal on time (or whatever period you are working on)
5. Now step back one week *before* the completion of your last step. Write down everything that must be completed in that week to complete that last step. Put dates next to each of these tasks. Obviously, the dates should fall within the week in question
6. Now step back one more week, evaluate everything that must be done *in this week* for you to complete *next week's* tasks as written in Step 5; put dates next to these tasks. All the dates should fall within the calendar dates of this week
7. Continue to step back one week at a time, adding the tasks that are necessary as prerequisites to be completed for the following week's tasks to be started and completed
8. The stepping back process will bring you back from *your completion date* to *today* in 1-week increments. There are 13 weeks in a 90-day period.
9. Your plan should look something like this:

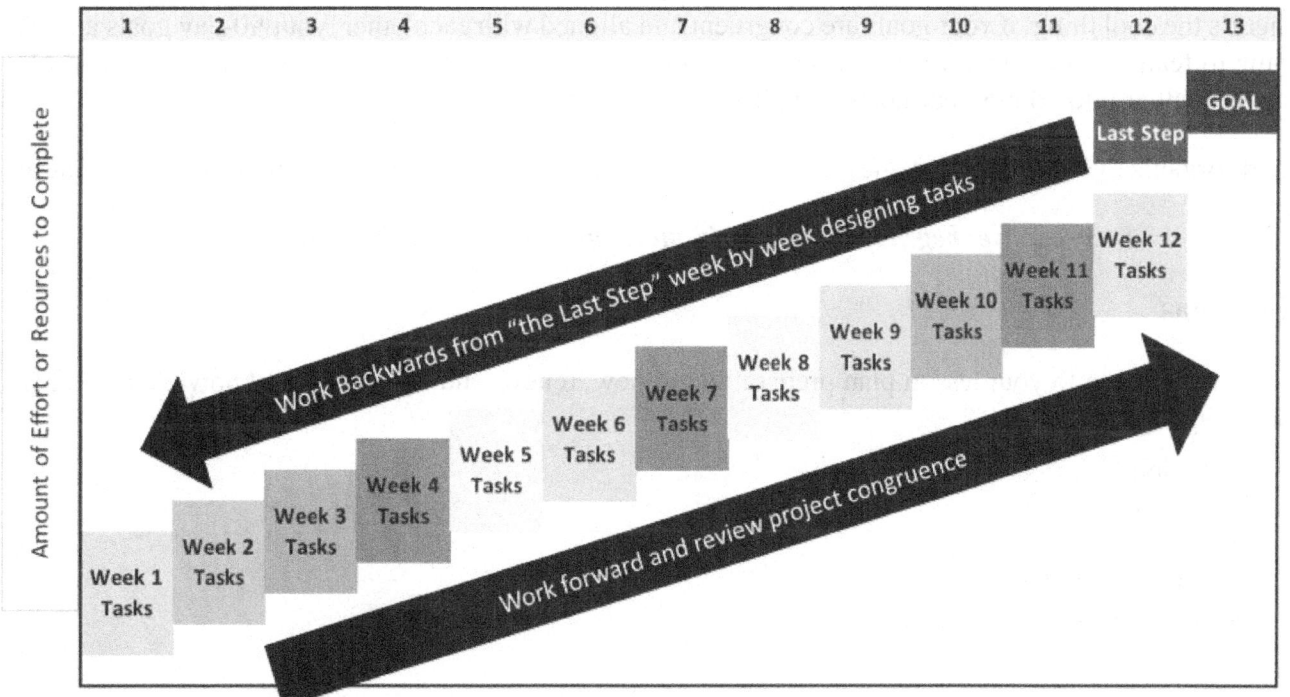

10. Once you have your tasks and dates completed, working from the goal backward through today, read the plan from today *forward*, making sure it is practical, sensible, and comprehensible. Make any adjustments in the forward direction that seem to improve the plan. Then perform all the tasks in reverse again, and then forward again making any improvements as you go forward and back and forward again.

11. Add milestones. Most plans, such as running or weight-loss, have naturally occurring *milestones* along the path. For example, if you want to lose 60 pounds in 13 weeks, you will have to lose about 5 pounds each week. You can measure your weekly progress to the goal by measuring your weekly milestones in this case, - 5 lb., - 10 lb., - 15 lb., - 20 lb., and so on. If you are not on track, you will make suitable adjustments to your plan, or to your expected outcome, (goal) or to the completion date. By continuously modifying your plan (with honesty and integrity), you will never fail at anything ever again, you will always be improving one day at a time.

12. Now, walk through your plan one more time from today through completion, making sure it is S - M - A - R - T or smart. Are your goals in the associated plan:
    · Specific
    · Measurable
    · Attainable
    · Relevant, and
    · Time-based

If your plan makes sense, recopy it into a neat, legible format and keep it with your planner or notebook.

Begin executing your plan immediately

The steps to planning the achievement of your goals used for your 90-day goals are easily modified for your 1-year, 3-year, and 5-year goals. When you *chunk down* projects, you can *chunk in* quarters (13 weeks, 3 months, or 90 days), months, or weeks. For your 5-year goals, you might want to chunk in years.

Now here's the cool thing, if your goals are congruent and aligned with each other, your 90-day goals and plans are going to feather into your 1-year goals and strategies, which will feather into your 3-year goals and plans, which will feather into your 5-year goals and plans.

Be smart; organize your goals, strategies, and plans to support each other and your ultimate objectives in life.

Be proactive; begin with the end in mind, and always put first things first.

Study Areas

Each day, in addition to your lesson plan preparation, review, renew, and advance your knowledge on each of the following topics:

1. Hydration
2. Breathing
3. Eating
4. Exercise and endorphins
5. Heroin - - MAT - - abstinence

Required Activities

Meditation

You can relax now and settle in on your meditation schedule of 30 minutes two times per day.

Rev. Dr. Robert Hobbs
The Realization of Stainless Souls
www.StainlessSouls.com

Exercise

Soon *aerobic exercise* will level out at 60 minutes per day, but this week you are to walk 50 minutes each day. *Flexibility and mobility exercises* remain 10 minutes - best done while warmed-up after your aerobic activity.

Meeting

Your recovery meeting requirement remains one per day for 60 Minutes.

Reading

This week begin reading the spiritual classic, *Autobiography of a Yogi,* by Paramahansa Yogananda. This is a longer book, so read 30 pages per day this week, and then you will revisit this volume again in week 11.

Needs, Habits, Healings, Affirmations, and Visualizations

Needs

There are six human needs, per Anthony Robbins and Chloe Madanes. They are:

1. Certainty
2. Connection
3. Growth
4. Variety
5. Contribution
6. Significance

Some of these are polar; for example,

· *Certainty* opposes *variety* (uncertainty),
· *Connection* opposes *significance*,
· *Growth* opposes *contribution*

I say polar because a person focused on certainty and security cannot simultaneously focus on uncertainty and variety. Likewise, one focused on love and connection cannot concentrate on personal significance. Finally, one focused on personal growth and development, cannot focus on contribution. In practice, we focus on all six to varying degrees during a typical day and average lifetime.

This week's need is the need to contribute to society or our community. *Karma yogis* focus almost exclusively on service - offering *everything they do* to God without concern for the outcome of the activity. Through service work, one can find freedom on a small mortal scale; this is proven in AA. On the big scale, service work has proven beneficial by saints and avatars (like Jesus, for example).

For 7 weeks now, if you are working per this plan, you have done quite a bit of service work, especially relative to service work you did before your recovery.

Recognize too, that *to give something away* you must have it in the first place. We discussed earlier in the program that you cannot love someone unless you have love to give; you wouldn't be willing to part with it unless you have it in abundance. The same holds true for any services you provide. You wouldn't provide services of the type you provide unless you had them or their benefits in abundance. So, the Paradox holds; it always does if you want something, give it away, and it will be given back abundantly.

This week study precisely that - *the philosophy of giving*, and how giving results in receiving.

It is said a man with a closed or clenched fist can never receive anything but a man with an open hand cannot contain all he will be given.

Covey Habit 7: Sharpen the Saw

We started the program and detox with Habit 7: Sharpen the Saw. It wasn't fair to Habit 7 that you were so distracted with your withdrawal. So, this week, revisit Habit 7: *Sharpen the Saw*. Integrate the maintenance of your production capability with your building of a moat.

Healing Treatment Eight

Do the Healing Practice three times for 15 minutes each day.

Affirmations and Visualizations

Do your daily affirmation and visualization practices as you've been taught and have been practicing. Remember to consider your affirmations and healings as *advanced forms of prayer*.

Remember, Jesus said, when teaching His Apostles how to pray,

When you pray, go into the closet, close the door, pray in secret and the heavenly Father who hears in secret will reward you abundantly.

Step and Service Work

Last week we discussed the practical reality that most people in recovery are almost always on Steps 9, 10, 11, and 12. Sometimes, Step 9 could take a decade or more to complete. Steps 10, 11, and 12, are *every day for the rest of your life steps*. Re-read *Into Action* and *Working with Others* as well as Steps 10, 11, and 12, in the *12 and 12*.

In addition to all the service work you are doing daily - teach someone how to do a simple 5-minute meditation. Don't overcomplicate it; but, realize that when it comes to meditation, you now know far more than any ordinary person.

Prayer and Gratitude List

Again, this week, it is up to you to create your *prayer and gratitude list*.

- · Who and what are you praying for?
- · What prayer do you want to pray?
- · And what or who are you grateful for?

This section should never ever be blank for someone in early recovery.

Wellness Checks

Continue to score your well-being in the seven areas listed twice per day and graph your results on the 90-day graph in the back of this book.

Finally, always record something you were:

- · Happy or proud of
- · Something you want to improve

- Something you learned
- Something you might want to teach

Day 50 Required Activities
Meditation: 30 Minutes 2 times
Read: Autobiography of Yogi 30pg
Aerobic: 50 minutes once
Flexibility: 10 minutes once
Meeting: 60 minutes

Today's Study Areas
Hydration: Why it matters
Breathing: How to Breathe Proper
Eating: The Spiritual Side
Exercise & Endorphins
Heroin - MAT - Abstinence

Week 8: This Week's Focus
Teach: Detox & Physical Wellness

Deliverable
Creating a Life: Develop your
Personal Physical Wellness Plan

Needs, Habits, Healings, Affirmations, & Visualizations

Needs: Community Service/Contribution (and Abundance)

Covey Habit 7: Sharpen the Saw

Healing Treatment Eight

My subconscious mind creates and identifies with a visual image of myself as a radiant, healthy, wealthy, fulfilled, and joyful child of the Universe with every beat of my heart, today and every day of my life.

Step & Service Work

Phase 4: Serve; Steps 9, 10, 11, 12

Show someone how to meditate

Prayer & Gratitude List

Meetings and Appointments

__00 / __30	
__00 / __30	
__00 / __30	
__00 / __30	
__00 / __30	
__00 / __30	
__00 / __30	
__00 / __30	
__00 / __30	
__00 / __30	
__00 / __30	
__00 / __30	
__00 / __30	
__00 / __30	
__00 / __30	
__00 / __30	
__00 / __30	
__00 / __30	

Notes, Numbers, & Future Appointments

Rev. Dr. Robert Hobbs
The Realization of Stainless Souls
www.StainlessSouls.com

Morning Wellness Check		
Physical		
Mental		
Emotional		
Relational		
Spiritual		
Lifestyle		
Immunity		

Evening Wellness Check		
Physical		
Mental		
Emotional		
Relational		
Spiritual		
Lifestyle		
Immunity		

Journaling		
Date:	Sobriety Date:	Number Days Clean & Sober:

What I am Proud of/Happy About Today

What I Want to Improve/Remember

What Did I Learn

What Can I Teach Someone Like Me?

To Discuss with Sponsor, Doctor, Therapist, or Other Professional:

Day 51 Required Activities
Meditation: 30 Minutes 2 times
Read: Autobiography of Yogi 30pg
Aerobic: 50 minutes once
Flexibility: 10 minutes once
Meeting: 60 minutes

Today's Study Areas
Hydration: Why it matters
Breathing: How to Breathe Proper
Eating: The Spiritual Side
Exercise & Endorphins
Heroin - MAT - Abstinence

Week 8: This Week's Focus
Teach: Detox & Physical Wellness
Deliverable
Creating a Life: Develop your
Personal Physical Wellness Plan

Needs, Habits, Healings, Affirmations, & Visualizations
Needs: Community Service/Contribution (and Abundance)
Covey Habit 7: Sharpen the Saw
Healing Treatment Eight
As it automatically operates all the systems of my body, my subconscious mind creates and identifies with a visual image of myself as a person possessing vitality, prosperity, love, and awareness.

Step & Service Work
Phase 4: Serve; Steps 9, 10, 11, 12
Show someone how to meditate

Prayer & Gratitude List

Meetings and Appointments	
__00 __30	
__00 __30	
__00 __30	
__00 __30	
__00 __30	
__00 __30	
__00 __30	
__00 __30	
__00 __30	
__00 __30	
__00 __30	
__00 __30	
__00 __30	
__00 __30	
__00 __30	
__00 __30	
__00 __30	

Notes, Numbers, & Future Appointments

Rev. Dr. Robert Hobbs
The Realization of Stainless Souls
www.StainlessSouls.com

Morning Wellness Check		
Physical		
Mental		
Emotional		
Relational		
Spiritual		
Lifestyle		
Immunity		

Evening Wellness Check		
Physical		
Mental		
Emotional		
Relational		
Spiritual		
Lifestyle		
Immunity		

Journaling		
Date:	Sobriety Date:	Number Days Clean & Sober:

What I am Proud of/Happy About Today

What I Want to Improve/Remember

What Did I Learn

What Can I Teach Someone Like Me?

To Discuss with Sponsor, Doctor, Therapist, or Other Professional:

Day 52 Required Activities	Today's Study Areas	Week 8: This Week's Focus
Meditation: 30 Minutes 2 times	Hydration: Why it matters	Teach: Detox & Physical Wellness
Read: Autobiography of Yogi 30pg	Breathing: How to Breathe Proper	
Aerobic: 50 minutes once	Eating: The Spiritual Side	**Deliverable**
Flexibility: 10 minutes once	Exercise & Endorphins	Creating a Life: Develop your
Meeting: 60 minutes	Heroin - MAT - Abstinence	Personal Physical Wellness Plan

Needs, Habits, Healings, Affirmations, & Visualizations

Needs: Community Service/Contribution (and Abundance)

Covey Habit 7: Sharpen the Saw

Healing Treatment Eight

I am grateful for the Unity of my mind and body with all through the Power of my Higher-Mind and the Healing Intelligence in my body.

Meetings and Appointments

__00 __30	
__00 __30	
__00 __30	
__00 __30	
__00 __30	
__00 __30	
__00 __30	
__00 __30	
__00 __30	
__00 __30	
__00 __30	
__00 __30	
__00 __30	
__00 __30	
__00 __30	
__00 __30	
__00 __30	
__00 __30	

Step & Service Work

Phase 4: Serve; Steps 9, 10, 11, 12

Show someone how to meditate

Prayer & Gratitude List

Notes, Numbers, & Future Appointments

Rev. Dr. Robert Hobbs
The Realization of Stainless Souls
www.StainlessSouls.com

Morning Wellness Check		
Physical		
Mental		
Emotional		
Relational		
Spiritual		
Lifestyle		
Immunity		

Evening Wellness Check		
Physical		
Mental		
Emotional		
Relational		
Spiritual		
Lifestyle		
Immunity		

Journaling		
Date:	Sobriety Date:	Number Days Clean & Sober:

What I am Proud of/Happy About Today

What I Want to Improve/Remember

What Did I Learn

What Can I Teach Someone Like Me?

To Discuss with Sponsor, Doctor, Therapist, or Other Professional:

Day 53 Required Activities
Meditation: 30 Minutes 2 times
Read: Autobiography of Yogi 30pg
Aerobic: 50 minutes once
Flexibility: 10 minutes once
Meeting: 60 minutes

Today's Study Areas
Hydration: Why it matters
Breathing: How to Breathe Proper
Eating: The Spiritual Side
Exercise & Endorphins
Heroin - MAT - Abstinence

Week 8: This Week's Focus
Teach: Detox & Physical Wellness

Deliverable
Creating a Life: Develop your
Personal Physical Wellness Plan

Needs, Habits, Healings, Affirmations, & Visualizations
Needs: Community Service/Contribution (and Abundance)
Covey Habit 7: Sharpen the Saw
Healing Treatment Eight
I am One with perfect health of every living cell of my body immediately, today, and every day.

Meetings and Appointments
__00 __30
__00 __30
__00 __30
__00 __30
__00 __30
__00 __30
__00 __30
__00 __30
__00 __30
__00 __30
__00 __30
__00 __30
__00 __30
__00 __30
__00 __30
__00 __30
__00 __30
__00 __30
__00 __30
__00 __30

Step & Service Work
Phase 4: Serve; Steps 9, 10, 11, 12
Teach someone how to meditate

Prayer & Gratitude List

Notes, Numbers, & Future Appointments

Rev. Dr. Robert Hobbs
The Realization of Stainless Souls
www.StainlessSouls.com

Morning Wellness Check		
Physical		
Mental		
Emotional		
Relational		
Spiritual		
Lifestyle		
Immunity		

Evening Wellness Check		
Physical		
Mental		
Emotional		
Relational		
Spiritual		
Lifestyle		
Immunity		

Journaling		
Date:	Sobriety Date:	Number Days Clean & Sober:

What I am Proud of/Happy About Today

What I Want to Improve/Remember

What Did I Learn

What Can I Teach Someone Like Me?

To Discuss with Sponsor, Doctor, Therapist, or Other Professional:

Day 54 Required Activities	Today's Study Areas	Week 8: This Week's Focus
Meditation: 30 Minutes 2 times	Hydration: Why it matters	Teach: Detox & Physical Wellness
Read: Autobiography of Yogi 30pg	Breathing: How to Breathe Proper	
Aerobic: 50 minutes once	Eating: The Spiritual Side	**Deliverable**
Flexibility: 10 minutes once	Exercise & Endorphins	Creating a Life: Develop your
Meeting: 60 minutes	Heroin - MAT - Abstinence	Personal Physical Wellness Plan

Needs, Habits, Healings, Affirmations, & Visualizations

Needs: Community Service/Contribution (and Abundance)

Covey Habit 7: Sharpen the Saw

Healing Treatment Eight

I am One with harmony, tranquility, and serenity in my body, life, and consciousness, immediately, today, and every day!

Meetings and Appointments

__00 __30	
__00 __30	
__00 __30	
__00 __30	
__00 __30	
__00 __30	
__00 __30	
__00 __30	
__00 __30	
__00 __30	
__00 __30	
__00 __30	
__00 __30	
__00 __30	
__00 __30	
__00 __30	
__00 __30	

Step & Service Work

Phase 4: Serve; Steps 9, 10, 11, 12

Teach someone how to meditate

Prayer & Gratitude List

Notes, Numbers, & Future Appointments

Rev. Dr. Robert Hobbs
The Realization of Stainless Souls
www.StainlessSouls.com

Morning Wellness Check		
Physical		
Mental		
Emotional		
Relational		
Spiritual		
Lifestyle		
Immunity		

Evening Wellness Check		
Physical		
Mental		
Emotional		
Relational		
Spiritual		
Lifestyle		
Immunity		

Journaling		
Date:	Sobriety Date:	Number Days Clean & Sober:

What I am Proud of/Happy About Today

What I Want to Improve/Remember

What Did I Learn

What Can I Teach Someone Like Me?

To Discuss with Sponsor, Doctor, Therapist, or Other Professional:

Day 55 Required Activities	Today's Study Areas	Week 8: This Week's Focus
Meditation: 30 Minutes 2 times	Hydration: Why it matters	Teach: Detox & Physical Wellness
Read: Autobiography of Yogi 30pg	Breathing: How to Breathe Proper	
Aerobic: 50 minutes once	Eating: The Spiritual Side	**Deliverable**
Flexibility: 10 minutes once	Exercise & Endorphins	Creating a Life: Develop your
Meeting: 60 minutes	Heroin - MAT - Abstinence	Personal Physical Wellness Plan

Needs, Habits, Healings, Affirmations, & Visualizations

Needs: Community Service/Contribution (and Abundance)

Covey Habit 7: Sharpen the Saw

Healing Treatment Eight

I am a living manifestation in the physical world of the omniscient Mind of God.

Step & Service Work

Phase 4: Serve; Steps 9, 10, 11, 12

Show someone how to meditate

Prayer & Gratitude List

Meetings and Appointments

__00 __30	
__00 __30	
__00 __30	
__00 __30	
__00 __30	
__00 __30	
__00 __30	
__00 __30	
__00 __30	
__00 __30	
__00 __30	
__00 __30	
__00 __30	
__00 __30	
__00 __30	
__00 __30	
__00 __30	

Notes, Numbers, & Future Appointments

Rev. Dr. Robert Hobbs
The Realization of Stainless Souls
www.StainlessSouls.com

Date:_____ Day: M T W Th F S Su

Morning Wellness Check		
Physical		
Mental		
Emotional		
Relational		
Spiritual		
Lifestyle		
Immunity		

Evening Wellness Check		
Physical		
Mental		
Emotional		
Relational		
Spiritual		
Lifestyle		
Immunity		

Journaling		
Date:	Sobriety Date:	Number Days Clean & Sober:

What I am Proud of/Happy About Today

What I Want to Improve/Remember

What Did I Learn

What Can I Teach Someone Like Me?

To Discuss with Sponsor, Doctor, Therapist, or Other Professional:

Day 56 Required Activities
Meditation: 30 Minutes 2 times
Read: Autobiography of Yogi 30pg
Aerobic: 50 minutes once
Flexibility: 10 minutes once
Meeting: 60 minutes

Today's Study Areas
Hydration: Why it matters
Breathing: How to Breathe Proper
Eating: The Spiritual Side
Exercise & Endorphins
Heroin - MAT - Abstinence

Week 8: This Week's Focus
Teach: Detox & Physical Wellness
Deliverable
Creating a Life: Develop your
Personal Physical Wellness Plan

Needs, Habits, Healings, Affirmations, & Visualizations

Needs: Community Service/Contribution (and Abundance)

Covey Habit 7: Sharpen the Saw

Healing Treatment Eight

My mind and body are the canvas for the creative expression of my Higher Mind in everything I do, today and every day.

Step & Service Work

Phase 4: Serve; Steps 9, 10, 11, 12

Show someone how to meditate

Prayer & Gratitude List

Meetings and Appointments

__00 __30	
__00 __30	
__00 __30	
__00 __30	
__00 __30	
__00 __30	
__00 __30	
__00 __30	
__00 __30	
__00 __30	
__00 __30	
__00 __30	
__00 __30	
__00 __30	
__00 __30	
__00 __30	
__00 __30	
__00 __30	

Notes, Numbers, & Future Appointments

Rev. Dr. Robert Hobbs
The Realization of Stainless Souls
www.StainlessSouls.com

Morning Wellness Check		
Physical		
Mental		
Emotional		
Relational		
Spiritual		
Lifestyle		
Immunity		

Evening Wellness Check		
Physical		
Mental		
Emotional		
Relational		
Spiritual		
Lifestyle		
Immunity		

Journaling		
Date:	Sobriety Date:	Number Days Clean & Sober:

What I am Proud of/Happy About Today

What I Want to Improve/Remember

What Did I Learn

What Can I Teach Someone Like Me?

To Discuss with Sponsor, Doctor, Therapist, or Other Professional:

Week 9: Teach Mental/Intellectual Health

Who Am I? Who are You, Really?

By the end of this week, you will teach a lesson on one of the topics you studied in week 3. Pick a topic that you are curious about. Remember to look through the *"What Can I Teach"* boxes at the end of each day in week 3. Review the work you did and your notes from your independent research and study.

Remember the lessons on *your ego* and the many reading assignments that have touched on your ego. Try to conceptualize what *your identity really is*, what the *identity you hold for a loved one really is*, and what the *relationship between your identity and their identity really is*.

Generally, we identify ourselves with a story or a *bundle of organized thoughts*. Rarely do we share 100% of our story with others; therefore, it is impossible for someone to get to know us. Likewise, as little as we know about ourselves, we know even less about others.

> *Every time I look in the mirror,*
>
> *God looks back!*
>
> *~Liam Gallagher*

Our view of other people or another person is really just another story or *bundle of organized thoughts*. Our perspective is almost always based on a *bundle of thoughts <u>that the other person chooses to reveal to us</u>*, which may or may not be an accurate representation of who they are or think they are.

The relationship, of course, is just <u>*another*</u> *bundle of thoughts* - our thoughts on what our relationship is and then the other person's ideas about the relationship. So again, you can see that there are many opportunities for error that corrupt our most meaningful relationships. The ego is *in the way* on multiple levels and is preventing us from developing the oft sought, but ever elusive *soul-mate relationship*.

For instructions on drafting lesson plans and how to plan, see the introduction to week 8. One of your assignments this week is preparing to teach a lesson plan on mental wellness.

Creating a life

Remember you already have created 90-day, 1, 3, and 5-year goals for your mental/intellectual well-being. *This week review your goals and then transpose them to your notebook*. Then transform your goals to plans by following the suggested process in the week 8 introduction.

Required Study Areas

Revisit your study of the relevant topics from week 3. Specifically, after reviewing your work, strengthen and deepen your knowledge by doing additional research on the items listed in the *study areas box*.

Required Activities

Meditation.

Rev. Dr. Robert Hobbs
The Realization of Stainless Souls
www.StainlessSouls.com

You are stable at 2, 30-minute meditations per day.

Reading

Your reading this week is a really quick read by Tony Robbins called *Notes From a Friend*. You only have to read 15 pages per day.

Aerobic Exercise

You are up to 55 minutes of walking per day! Imagine that!

Flexibility

10 minutes focused on forward and backward spinal column bends and only after warming up.

Meetings

Still one recovery meeting per week; usually one hour in duration.

Needs, Habits, Healings, Affirmations, and Visualizations

Needs

Spend another week looking at the relationship between giving (first) and receiving (second) abundance. Understand the theory behind the concept.

Assessment

Take the *StrengthsFinder 2.0* test and review the results. This one costs a little money, but it is worth the $20 or $50 to have the results from an assessment of your strengths.

The best way to get the test is to buy the *Strengths Finder 2.0* Kindle book, by Tom Rath. The publisher will send you a code to take the test for free. Otherwise, you will pay $50 for just the test. If you are in a relationship, you may want to have your significant other take the test as well - it is fun to compare the results.

Healing Treatment Nine

Are you noticing any results from the healing treatments? Have you realized yet that healing treatments are a form of affirmation and therefore serve as an *advanced prayer*? Continue to practice healing treatments three times per day for 15 minutes and *always maintain that PMA*!!

Affirmation and Visualization

Every day you get a brand-new, unique affirmation to use to help you manifest the abundant good the Universe has to offer. Don't be afraid to modify these if you'd like to - just keep the basic format. Always remember there are short-form affirmations in the back of the book and dozens more recorded at www.TheStainlessSoulsPodcast.com

Thought - Sound - Vibration - Life - Light

Step and Service Work

For your service activity this week, ask your homegroup or sponsor, if it would be okay for you to lead or chair a meeting this week or soon. If you are allowed, prepare a topic following the group's tradition, show up early, greet the attendees, and then do your best, and forget the rest.

For step work, Steps 9-12 are usually simultaneous and perpetual, focus on implementing Step 10 into your daily life. I would assume you'd rather not go through the Steps 4 and 5 processes again. The way to avoid it is to practice the concepts of Steps 4 and 5 in your everyday life (Step 10).

When you are *mindful* and *exercising integrity in the moment of choice*, you will find Step 10 to be a great benefit to you. The greatest gift perhaps is that you'll rarely go to bed with regrets or while second-guessing yourself.

When you are *mindful* you notice when you are wrong; when you *exercise integrity in the moment of choice*, you promptly admit that you've erred and seek to make any necessary amends (provided you do not do additional harm with the amends). Never again will you have to do a deep moral inventory or a deep dive into your dark past, because you're keeping your side of the street clean.

Prayer and Gratitude List

This section is up to you to write in:

- Those for whom you are praying
- That for which you are grateful
- Your own short heartfelt prayers

Twice-daily Wellness Checks

Keep entering your quick wellness scores and plot them on the bubble chart.

Journaling

Continue to record your sobriety date and the number of days clean and sober. Keep track of meaningful, creative, intuitive thoughts and ideas you have.

Record your:

- Proud/happy moments each day, perhaps you're grateful for these?
- What you've learned each day, maybe you're thankful for this too?
- What you want to improve, and build that into your goals and planning exercises
- What you think you might like to teach in the future

Rev. Dr. Robert Hobbs
The Realization of Stainless Souls
www.StainlessSouls.com

Notes and Sketches

Day 57 Required Activities
Meditation: 30 Minutes 2 times
Read: Notes from a Friend 15 pgs
Aerobic: 55 minutes once
Flexibility: 10 minutes once
Meeting: 60 minutes

Today's Study Areas
The Ego: The Thought of Me
The Future: Real or just a thought
My Story = My Identity?
My Story of You = Your Identity?
If stories & thoughts don't exist?

Week 9: This Week's Focus
Teach: Mental/Intellectual Health
Who Am I, Who Are You, Really?
Deliverable
Creating a Life: Develop Personal
Mental-Educational Wellness Plan

Needs, Habits, Healings, Affirmations, & Visualizations

Needs: Community Service/Contribution (and Abundance)

Take Strengths Finder Test

Healing Treatment Nine

My Higher Mind performs all things and is unlimited in what it can do.

Step & Service Work

Phase 4: Serve; Steps 9, 10, 11, 12

Chair/Lead a Meeting

Prayer & Gratitude List

Meetings and Appointments

__00 __30	
__00 __30	
__00 __30	
__00 __30	
__00 __30	
__00 __30	
__00 __30	
__00 __30	
__00 __30	
__00 __30	
__00 __30	
__00 __30	
__00 __30	
__00 __30	
__00 __30	
__00 __30	
__00 __30	

Notes, Numbers, & Future Appointments

Morning Wellness Check		
Physical		
Mental		
Emotional		
Relational		
Spiritual		
Lifestyle		
Immunity		

Evening Wellness Check		
Physical		
Mental		
Emotional		
Relational		
Spiritual		
Lifestyle		
Immunity		

Journaling		
Date:	Sobriety Date:	Number Days Clean & Sober:

What I am Proud of/Happy About Today

What I Want to Improve/Remember

What Did I Learn

What Can I Teach Someone Like Me?

To Discuss with Sponsor, Doctor, Therapist, or Other Professional:

Day 58 Required Activities	Today's Study Areas	Week 9: This Week's Focus
Meditation: 30 Minutes 2 times	The Ego: The Thought of Me	Teach: Mental/Intellectual Health
Read: Notes from a Friend 15 pgs	The Future: Real or just a thought	Who Am I, Who Are You, Really?
Aerobic: 55 minutes once	My Story = My Identity?	**Deliverable**
Flexibility: 10 minutes once	My Story of You = Your Identity?	Creating a Life: Develop Personal
Meeting: 60 minutes	If stories & thoughts don't exist?	Mental-Educational Wellness Plan

Needs, Habits, Healings, Affirmations, & Visualizations

Needs: Community Service/Contribution (and Abundance)

Review/Reflect on Strengths Finder Test

Healing Treatment Nine

I am One Mind with the Mind of God within me.

Step & Service Work

Phase 4: Serve; Steps 9, 10, 11, 12

Chair/Lead a Meeting

Prayer & Gratitude List

Meetings and Appointments

Time	
__00 __30	
__00 __30	
__00 __30	
__00 __30	
__00 __30	
__00 __30	
__00 __30	
__00 __30	
__00 __30	
__00 __30	
__00 __30	
__00 __30	
__00 __30	
__00 __30	
__00 __30	
__00 __30	
__00 __30	
__00 __30	

Notes, Numbers, & Future Appointments

Rev. Dr. Robert Hobbs
The Realization of Stainless Souls
www.StainlessSouls.com

Morning Wellness Check		
Physical		
Mental		
Emotional		
Relational		
Spiritual		
Lifestyle		
Immunity		

Evening Wellness Check		
Physical		
Mental		
Emotional		
Relational		
Spiritual		
Lifestyle		
Immunity		

Journaling		
Date:	Sobriety Date:	Number Days Clean & Sober:

What I am Proud of/Happy About Today

What I Want to Improve/Remember

What Did I Learn

What Can I Teach Someone Like Me?

To Discuss with Sponsor, Doctor, Therapist, or Other Professional:

Day 59 Required Activities	Today's Study Areas	Week 9: This Week's Focus
Meditation: 30 Minutes 2 times	The Ego: The Thought of Me	Teach: Mental/Intellectual Health
Read: Notes from a Friend 15 pgs	The Future: Real or just a thought	Who Am I, Who Are You, Really?
Aerobic: 55 minutes once	My Story = My Identity?	**Deliverable**
Flexibility: 10 minutes once	My Story of You = Your Identity?	Creating a Life: Develop Personal
Meeting: 60 minutes	If stories & thoughts don't exist?	Mental-Educational Wellness Plan

Needs, Habits, Healings, Affirmations, & Visualizations

Needs: Community Service/Contribution (and Abundance)

Review/Reflect on Strengths Finder Test

Healing Treatment Nine

St. Paul said, "Let the Mind be in you that was in Christ." I now invite the Mind that was in Christ into my mind.

Meetings and Appointments

__00 __30	
__00 __30	
__00 __30	
__00 __30	
__00 __30	
__00 __30	
__00 __30	
__00 __30	
__00 __30	
__00 __30	
__00 __30	
__00 __30	
__00 __30	
__00 __30	
__00 __30	
__00 __30	
__00 __30	
__00 __30	

Step & Service Work

Phase 4: Serve; Steps 9, 10, 11, 12

Chair/Lead a Meeting

Prayer & Gratitude List

Notes, Numbers, & Future Appointments

Rev. Dr. Robert Hobbs
The Realization of Stainless Souls
www.StainlessSouls.com

Morning Wellness Check		
Physical		
Mental		
Emotional		
Relational		
Spiritual		
Lifestyle		
Immunity		

Evening Wellness Check		
Physical		
Mental		
Emotional		
Relational		
Spiritual		
Lifestyle		
Immunity		

Journaling		
Date:	Sobriety Date:	Number Days Clean & Sober:

What I am Proud of/Happy About Today

What I Want to Improve/Remember

What Did I Learn

What Can I Teach Someone Like Me?

To Discuss with Sponsor, Doctor, Therapist, or Other Professional:

Day 60 Required Activities	Today's Study Areas	Week 9: This Week's Focus
Meditation: 30 Minutes 2 times	The Ego: The Thought of Me	Teach: Mental/Intellectual Health
Read: Notes from a Friend 15 pgs	The Future: Real or just a thought	Who Am I, Who Are You, Really?
Aerobic: 55 minutes once	My Story = My Identity?	**Deliverable**
Flexibility: 10 minutes once	My Story of You = Your Identity?	Creating a Life: Develop Personal
Meeting: 60 minutes	If stories & thoughts don't exist?	Mental-Educational Wellness Plan

Needs, Habits, Healings, Affirmations, & Visualizations

Needs: Community Service/Contribution (and Abundance)

Review/Reflect on Strengths Finder Test

Healing Treatment Nine

I now summon from the nucleus of my mind and from the Power of the Universe that resides there, that His Healing Energy radiates new, positive, and Divine thought patterns into all layers of my mind. I give thanks that I am heard, I let it be so, and so it is!

Step & Service Work

Phase 4: Serve; Steps 9, 10, 11, 12

Chair/Lead a Meeting

Prayer & Gratitude List

Meetings and Appointments	
__00 __30	
__00 __30	
__00 __30	
__00 __30	
__00 __30	
__00 __30	
__00 __30	
__00 __30	
__00 __30	
__00 __30	
__00 __30	
__00 __30	
__00 __30	
__00 __30	
__00 __30	
__00 __30	
__00 __30	
__00 __30	

Notes, Numbers, & Future Appointments

Rev. Dr. Robert Hobbs
The Realization of Stainless Souls
www.StainlessSouls.com

Morning Wellness Check		
Physical		
Mental		
Emotional		
Relational		
Spiritual		
Lifestyle		
Immunity		

Evening Wellness Check		
Physical		
Mental		
Emotional		
Relational		
Spiritual		
Lifestyle		
Immunity		

Journaling		
Date:	Sobriety Date:	Number Days Clean & Sober:

What I am Proud of/Happy About Today

What Did I Learn

What I Want to Improve/Remember

What Can I Teach Someone Like Me?

To Discuss with Sponsor, Doctor, Therapist, or Other Professional:

Day 61 Required Activities	Today's Study Areas	Week 9: This Week's Focus
Meditation: 30 Minutes 2 times	The Ego: The Thought of Me	Teach: Mental/Intellectual Health
Read: Notes from a Friend 15 pgs	The Future: Real or just a thought	Who Am I, Who Are You, Really?
Aerobic: 55 minutes once	My Story = My Identity?	**Deliverable**
Flexibility: 10 minutes once	My Story of You = Your Identity?	Creating a Life: Develop Personal
Meeting: 60 minutes	If stories & thoughts don't exist?	Mental-Educational Wellness Plan

Needs, Habits, Healings, Affirmations, & Visualizations	Meetings and Appointments
Needs: Community Service/Contribution (and Abundance)	__00 __30
Review/Reflect on Strengths Finder Test	__00 __30
Healing Treatment Nine	__00 __30
My positive mental attitude is a result of the positivity of the Presence of God's Spirit within me, and it sublimates all negative thoughts into positive ones today and every day.	__00 __30
	__00 __30
	__00 __30
Step & Service Work	__00 __30
Phase 4: Serve; Steps 9, 10, 11, 12	__00 __30
	__00 __30
	__00 __30
	__00 __30
Chair/Lead a Meeting	__00 __30
	__00 __30
	__00 __30
Prayer & Gratitude List	__00 __30
	__00 __30
	__00 __30
	__00 __30
	__00 __30
	__00 __30

Notes, Numbers, & Future Appointments

Rev. Dr. Robert Hobbs
The Realization of Stainless Souls
www.StainlessSouls.com

Morning Wellness Check		
Physical		
Mental		
Emotional		
Relational		
Spiritual		
Lifestyle		
Immunity		

Evening Wellness Check		
Physical		
Mental		
Emotional		
Relational		
Spiritual		
Lifestyle		
Immunity		

Journaling		
Date:	Sobriety Date:	Number Days Clean & Sober:

What I am Proud of/Happy About Today

What I Want to Improve/Remember

What Did I Learn

What Can I Teach Someone Like Me?

To Discuss with Sponsor, Doctor, Therapist, or Other Professional:

Day 62 Required Activities	Today's Study Areas	Week 9: This Week's Focus
Meditation: 30 Minutes 2 times	The Ego: The Thought of Me	Teach: Mental/Intellectual Health
Read: Notes from a Friend 15 pgs	The Future: Real or just a thought	Who Am I, Who Are You, Really?
Aerobic: 55 minutes once	My Story = My Identity?	**Deliverable**
Flexibility: 10 minutes once	My Story of You = Your Identity?	Creating a Life: Develop Personal
Meeting: 60 minutes	If stories & thoughts don't exist?	Mental-Educational Wellness Plan

Needs, Habits, Healings, Affirmations, & Visualizations

Needs: Community Service/Contribution (and Abundance)

Review/Reflect on Strengths Finder Test

Healing Treatment Nine

I am at peace with myself now and eternally through the peace in the God-Mind within me.

Step & Service Work

Phase 4: Serve; Steps 9, 10, 11, 12

Chair/Lead a Meeting

Prayer & Gratitude List

Meetings and Appointments

__00 __30	
__00 __30	
__00 __30	
__00 __30	
__00 __30	
__00 __30	
__00 __30	
__00 __30	
__00 __30	
__00 __30	
__00 __30	
__00 __30	
__00 __30	
__00 __30	
__00 __30	
__00 __30	
__00 __30	
__00 __30	

Notes, Numbers, & Future Appointments

Rev. Dr. Robert Hobbs
The Realization of Stainless Souls
www.StainlessSouls.com

Morning Wellness Check		
Physical		
Mental		
Emotional		
Relational		
Spiritual		
Lifestyle		
Immunity		

Evening Wellness Check		
Physical		
Mental		
Emotional		
Relational		
Spiritual		
Lifestyle		
Immunity		

Journaling		
Date:	Sobriety Date:	Number Days Clean & Sober:

What I am Proud of/Happy About Today

What I Want to Improve/Remember

What Did I Learn

What Can I Teach Someone Like Me?

To Discuss with Sponsor, Doctor, Therapist, or Other Professional:

Day 63 Required Activities	Today's Study Areas	Week 9: This Week's Focus
Meditation: 30 Minutes 2 times	The Ego: The Thought of Me	Teach: Mental/Intellectual Health
Read: Notes from a Friend 15 pgs	The Future: Real or just a thought	Who Am I, Who Are You, Really?
Aerobic: 55 minutes once	My Story = My Identity?	**Deliverable**
Flexibility: 10 minutes once	My Story of You = Your Identity?	Creating a Life: Develop Personal
Meeting: 60 minutes	If stories & thoughts don't exist?	Mental-Educational Wellness Plan

Needs, Habits, Healings, Affirmations, & Visualizations

Needs: Community Service/Contribution (and Abundance)

Review/Reflect on Strengths Finder Test

Healing Treatment Nine

My Divine Self is building new healthier thought patterns consistent with a positive mental attitude in my mind, right now, and I open myself that these new patterns are already mine. For this, I give thanks, I let it be so, and so it is!

Step & Service Work

Phase 4: Serve; Steps 9, 10, 11, 12

Chair/Lead a Meeting

Prayer & Gratitude List

Meetings and Appointments	
__00 __30	
__00 __30	
__00 __30	
__00 __30	
__00 __30	
__00 __30	
__00 __30	
__00 __30	
__00 __30	
__00 __30	
__00 __30	
__00 __30	
__00 __30	
__00 __30	
__00 __30	
__00 __30	
__00 __30	
__00 __30	

Notes, Numbers, & Future Appointments

Rev. Dr. Robert Hobbs
The Realization of Stainless Souls
www.StainlessSouls.com

Morning Wellness Check		
Physical		
Mental		
Emotional		
Relational		
Spiritual		
Lifestyle		
Immunity		

Evening Wellness Check		
Physical		
Mental		
Emotional		
Relational		
Spiritual		
Lifestyle		
Immunity		

Journaling		
Date:	Sobriety Date:	Number Days Clean & Sober:

What I am Proud of/Happy About Today

What Did I Learn

What I Want to Improve/Remember

What Can I Teach Someone Like Me?

To Discuss with Sponsor, Doctor, Therapist, or Other Professional:

Week 10: Teach Relational and Emotional Well-being

Objectives:

- Understand feelings and love
- Create emotional plans: 90-days, 1-year, 3-year, 5-year
- Create a draft budget for days 91 to 180
- Teach a class on one topic

Revisit your work, notes, and assignments from week 4, and this week dig deeper into the following items:

1. Covey Habit 5: Seek first to understand, before seeking to be understood
2. Empathetic listening
3. Emotions - your *inner guide* (see *The Universe Has Your Back*)
4. My emotional triggers
5. My significant other's emotional triggers

Choose a topic that you were curious and confident about and prepare and teach a lesson plan on that topic. Review week 4 for potential teaching topics and notes. For instructions on how to create a lesson plan review the intro to week 8.

Also, this week in *creating a life* build your 90-day, 1-year, 3-year, and 5-year emotional/relational *goals into* 90-day, 1-year, 3-year, and 5-year *plans*. For instructions on how to create plans, review the introduction to week 8.

This week you also create a financial budget for the 13 weeks - 3 months immediately following this 90-day program. (Weeks 14-26).

For simplicity, follow a format similar to this one from MS Excel to begin budgeting:

Rev. Dr. Robert Hobbs
The Realization of Stainless Souls
www.StainlessSouls.com

Personal Monthly Budget

Projected Monthly Income	
Income 1	$4,300.00
Extra income	$300.00
Total monthly income	$4,600.00

Actual Monthly Income	
Income 1	$4,000.00
Extra income	$300.00
Total monthly income	$4,300.00

Projected Balance (Projected income minus expenses)	$3,405.00
Actual Balance (Actual income minus expenses)	$3,064.00
Difference (Actual minus projected)	($341.00)

HOUSING	Projected Cost	Actual Cost	Difference
Mortgage or rent	$1,000.00	$1,000.00	$0.00
Phone	$54.00	$100.00	-$46.00
Electricity	$44.00	$56.00	-$12.00
Gas	$22.00	$28.00	-$6.00
Water and sewer	$8.00	$8.00	$0.00
Cable	$34.00	$34.00	$0.00
Waste removal	$10.00	$10.00	$0.00
Maintenance or repairs	$23.00	$0.00	$23.00
Supplies	$0.00	$0.00	$0.00
Other	$0.00	$0.00	$0.00
Subtotal			-$41.00

TRANSPORTATION	Projected Cost	Actual Cost	Difference
Vehicle payment			$0.00
Bus/taxi fare			$0.00
Insurance			$0.00
Licensing			$0.00
Fuel			$0.00
Maintenance			$0.00
Other			$0.00
Subtotal			$0.00

INSURANCE	Projected Cost	Actual Cost	Difference
Home			$0.00
Health			$0.00
Life			$0.00
Other			$0.00
Subtotal			$0.00

FOOD	Projected Cost	Actual Cost	Difference
Groceries			$0.00
Dining out			$0.00
Other			$0.00
Subtotal			$0.00

PETS	Projected Cost	Actual Cost	Difference
Food			$0.00
Medical			$0.00
Grooming			$0.00
Toys			$0.00
Other			$0.00
Subtotal			$0.00

PERSONAL CARE	Projected Cost	Actual Cost	Difference
Medical			$0.00
Hair/nails			$0.00
Clothing			$0.00
Dry cleaning			$0.00
Health club			$0.00
Organization dues or fees			$0.00
Other			$0.00
Subtotal			$0.00

ENTERTAINMENT	Projected Cost	Actual Cost	Difference
Video/DVD			$0.00
CDs			$0.00
Movies			$0.00
Concerts			$0.00
Sporting events			$0.00
Live theater			$0.00
Other			$0.00
Other			$0.00
Other			$0.00
Subtotal			$0.00

LOANS	Projected Cost	Actual Cost	Difference
Personal			$0.00
Student			$0.00
Credit card			$0.00
Credit card			$0.00
Credit card			$0.00
Other			$0.00
Subtotal			$0.00

TAXES	Projected Cost	Actual Cost	Difference
Federal			$0.00
State			$0.00
Local			$0.00
Other			$0.00
Subtotal			$0.00

SAVINGS OR INVESTMENTS	Projected Cost	Actual Cost	Difference
Retirement account			$0.00
Investment account			$0.00
Other			$0.00
Subtotal			$0.00

GIFTS AND DONATIONS	Projected Cost	Actual Cost	Difference
Charity 1			$0.00
Charity 2			$0.00
Charity 3			$0.00
Subtotal			$0.00

LEGAL	Projected Cost	Actual Cost	Difference
Attorney			$0.00
Alimony			$0.00
Payments on lien or judgment			$0.00
Other			$0.00
Subtotal			$0.00

Total Projected Cost	$1,195.00
Total Actual Cost	$1,236.00
Total Difference	($41.00)

If positive save or work less

If negative economize or increase income.

Required Activities

Meditate

Two times per day for 30 minutes

Read

Heroin - Living and Dying with an Addict You Love, How to Survive When Everyone Dies. Evaluate your impact on your loved ones. Practice empathy when dealing with them and their issues regarding your life and your addiction.

Aerobic Exercise

It took 10 weeks, but here you are at the summit. You have allocated one hour of every day to *moving your body*, and now you're ready to begin an advanced physical activity such as cycling, running, swimming, or all of these. Be a triathlete, join CrossFit, run a marathon, but until you choose, keep walking. You can walk two times per day for 30 minutes each or once per day for 60 minutes.

Flexibility

10 minutes is the standard; keep bending.

Meetings.

In less than 30 days, you will have completed 90 in 90! Keep it up! Do your service work!

Needs, Habits, Healing, Affirmation, and Visualization

Need

This week your focus shifts to your need for variety, your need for taking risks, imaginative and creative. This need is the polar opposite of your need for certainty and security.

The idea is: if everything in life is guaranteed, you would be bored. There would be no spice. As much as we all pray and wish for a "Peace of Mind," we really don't want it for very long. We crave variety too. This week evaluate yourself on how vital *variety* may be to you. What are *"uncertain"* activities that you desire? Want to jump out of an airplane? Sail around the world? What is it that you want to do?

You don't have to act on any of the ideas that you write down just yet, and you probably shouldn't. Instead, try to reconcile your need for security with your need for variety. Come up with some ideas on how you can balance these competing parts of you.

Love Languages Test

A fella by the name of Gary Chapman wrote a book called *The Five Love Languages*. It describes how every human expresses and prefers to receive love in five distinct ways. Although all five love languages are a part of all humans, we each have a propensity or a preference for one or two above all others.

The theory is also that a given human prefers to express and receive love in the same language, so if my love language is *words of affirmation,* then the only way you can show me love, and I can receive it is if you provide *words of affirmation.* If you try to express with *physical touch,* or *quality time,* or *gifts,* or *acts of service,* I will not feel that you love me.

Further, if your love language is not *words of affirmation,* no matter how many great things I say about you, you will not feel that I love you. The problem is - I do love you, and you do love me - but our signals are crossed, and we are both frustrated and confused.

Dr. Chapman is so awesome that he has developed a free online quiz that you can take to determine your love language. You can have your significant other, and children, and other loved ones take the test and find out how their love language compares to yours. Often the results are stunning. Two people who have been married for 30 or more years suddenly find out they haven't had a harmonious relationship because their love languages are mismatched. This does not mean their marriage was a mistake, but their approach to each other was in error.

The fix to this disharmony is simple. You have to love your significant other *in their love language,* and they have to love you *in your love language.* If you do this - then you will find great harmony for the rest of your lives together. Take the test, share the results, and improve your relationships.

Healing Treatment Ten

Complete healing treatment ten

Affirmation and Visualization

Complete the affirmations and visualizations following the instructions; do the work; don't cheat.

> *The minute I heard my first love story, I started looking for you,*
>
> *not knowing how blind that was.*
>
> *Lovers don't finally meet somewhere;*
>
> *they are in each other all along.*
>
> *~Rumi*

Step and Service Work

This is the final transition week where you transition from *Phase 4 Serve* - to *Phase 5 Integrate.* You are also working, as we all do, Steps 9, 10, 11, and 12, simultaneously. This week focus on Step 11. It should not be difficult for you, as you have been practicing prayers and meditation every day since day one.

Read Step 11 in the *Big Book* and in the *12 and 12.* Contemplate on *conscious contact with God.* What does that mean? What does it mean to you? Recognize that if it is possible to make *conscious contact with God,* don't you think it might be a good idea to figure out how?

What if God has a will for you and for your life and you don't know what it is? Wouldn't you be wasting your time and your life? And indeed, you must trust that if He does have a will for your life, He will give you what you need to carry it out? Wouldn't this make your prayers easier? Knowing He must help you with His will for you? And if it makes you or prayers easier, wouldn't it make your life easier?

Don't just go through the motions with step work, prayer, or meditation. It is not sufficient to sit quietly for 2 minutes and toss up your petitions. Make contact, get intimate, and in that contact, He will *see what you pray for in secret, and He will answer your prayers with His abundance*.

Service

You are in week 10. You have gotten to make coffee, help set up and tear down, and maybe even chaired a meeting. This week add another service activity to your resume by *greeting all newcomers.* Welcome them warmly and make sure they have a *newcomer's packet* from your group or at least several phone numbers from some of the members of the same gender. If you can afford to, buy them a *Big Book,* and put your phone number inside the front cover. If you see them again, welcome them back, and invite them to meet you for coffee before the next meeting you will both attend.

Fellowship

Start building a fellowship for yourself and others by welcoming people to the meetings you attend.

Prayer and Gratitude List

Again, Who are you praying for? What are you grateful for? Learn the *Prayer of Saint Francis*.

Wellness Checks

Keep scoring yourself and keep plotting the results

Journaling

Keep writing down your thoughts, inspirations, hopes, and ideas. Expand on them in your notebook.

At the end of each day record

- What you are happy or proud of
- What you want to improve
- What you learned
- What you might want to teach

Rev. Dr. Robert Hobbs
The Realization of Stainless Souls
www.StainlessSouls.com

Notes and Sketches

Day 64 Required Activities	Today's Study Areas	Week 10: This Week's Focus
Meditation: 30 Minutes 2 times	Covey Habit 5	Teach: Relation/Emotional Health
Read: Heroin Living&Dying 25 pgs	Empathetic Listening	Feelings & Love
Aerobic: 60 min 1x or 30 min 2x	Emotions: Your Inner Guide	**Deliverables**
Flexibility: 10 minutes once	Emotional Triggers: Mine	1-Creating a Life: Emotional Plan
Meeting: 60 minutes	Emotional Triggers: Signif other	2-Create Budget for days 90-180

Needs, Habits, Healings, Affirmations, & Visualizations

Needs: Creativity/Freedom/Variety

Take Love Language Test

Healing Treatment Ten

The Love and Life of the Universe which permeates all things and is channeled as Light through God's Mind within me transmits the magnetic power of Love through me today and every day.

Step & Service Work

Phase 4 and 5: Serve and Integrate; Steps 9, 10, 11, 12

Meet and Greet Newcomers, Make sure they have phone numbers

Prayer & Gratitude List

Meetings and Appointments

__00 __30	
__00 __30	
__00 __30	
__00 __30	
__00 __30	
__00 __30	
__00 __30	
__00 __30	
__00 __30	
__00 __30	
__00 __30	
__00 __30	
__00 __30	
__00 __30	
__00 __30	
__00 __30	
__00 __30	

Notes, Numbers, & Future Appointments

Rev. Dr. Robert Hobbs
The Realization of Stainless Souls
www.StainlessSouls.com

Date:_____ Day: M T W Th F S Su

Morning Wellness Check		
Physical		
Mental		
Emotional		
Relational		
Spiritual		
Lifestyle		
Immunity		

Evening Wellness Check		
Physical		
Mental		
Emotional		
Relational		
Spiritual		
Lifestyle		
Immunity		

Journaling		
Date:	Sobriety Date:	Number Days Clean & Sober:

What I am Proud of/Happy About Today

What I Want to Improve/Remember

What Did I Learn

What Can I Teach Someone Like Me?

To Discuss with Sponsor, Doctor, Therapist, or Other Professional:

Day 65 Required Activities
Meditation: 30 Minutes 2 times
Read: Heroin Living&Dying 25 pgs
Aerobic: 60 min 1x or 30 min 2x
Flexibility: 10 minutes once
Meeting: 60 minutes

Today's Study Areas
Covey Habit 5
Empathetic Listening
Emotions: Your Inner Guide
Emotional Triggers: Mine
Emotional Triggers: Signif other

Week 10: This Week's Focus
Teach: Relation/Emotional Health
Feelings & Love

Deliverables
1-Creating a Life: Emotional Plan
2-Create Budget for days 90-180

Needs, Habits, Healings, Affirmations, & Visualizations

Needs: Creativity/Freedom/Variety

Review/Reflect on Love Language Test

Healing Treatment Ten

I am One with the Love of God within me. One Love.

Meetings and Appointments

__00 __30	
__00 __30	
__00 __30	
__00 __30	
__00 __30	
__00 __30	
__00 __30	
__00 __30	
__00 __30	
__00 __30	
__00 __30	
__00 __30	
__00 __30	
__00 __30	
__00 __30	
__00 __30	
__00 __30	
__00 __30	

Step & Service Work

Phase 4 and 5: Serve and Integrate; Steps 9, 10, 11, 12

Meet and Greet Newcomers, Make sure they have phone numbers

Prayer & Gratitude List

Notes, Numbers, & Future Appointments

Rev. Dr. Robert Hobbs
The Realization of Stainless Souls
www.StainlessSouls.com

Morning Wellness Check		
Physical		
Mental		
Emotional		
Relational		
Spiritual		
Lifestyle		
Immunity		

Evening Wellness Check		
Physical		
Mental		
Emotional		
Relational		
Spiritual		
Lifestyle		
Immunity		

Journaling		
Date:	Sobriety Date:	Number Days Clean & Sober:

What I am Proud of/Happy About Today

What I Want to Improve/Remember

What Did I Learn

What Can I Teach Someone Like Me?

To Discuss with Sponsor, Doctor, Therapist, or Other Professional:

Day 66 Required Activities	Today's Study Areas	Week 10: This Week's Focus
Meditation: 30 Minutes 2 times	Covey Habit 5	Teach: Relation/Emotional Health
Read: Heroin Living&Dying 25 pgs	Empathetic Listening	Feelings & Love
Aerobic: 60 min 1x or 30 min 2x	Emotions: Your Inner Guide	**Deliverables**
Flexibility: 10 minutes once	Emotional Triggers: Mine	1-Creating a Life: Emotional Plan
Meeting: 60 minutes	Emotional Triggers: Signif other	2-Create Budget for days 90-180

Needs, Habits, Healings, Affirmations, & Visualizations

Needs: Creativity/Freedom/Variety

Share Love Language Test Results with Important/Significant People

Healing Treatment Ten

Every time I see a person in love, I will see myself in my own mind as having the same kind of loving relationship today and each moment of each day of my life.

Step & Service Work

Phase 4 and 5: Serve and Integrate; Steps 9, 10, 11, 12

Meet and Greet Newcomers, Make sure they have phone numbers

Prayer & Gratitude List

Meetings and Appointments

__00 __30	
__00 __30	
__00 __30	
__00 __30	
__00 __30	
__00 __30	
__00 __30	
__00 __30	
__00 __30	
__00 __30	
__00 __30	
__00 __30	
__00 __30	
__00 __30	
__00 __30	
__00 __30	
__00 __30	
__00 __30	

Notes, Numbers, & Future Appointments

Rev. Dr. Robert Hobbs
The Realization of Stainless Souls
www.StainlessSouls.com

Morning Wellness Check		
Physical		
Mental		
Emotional		
Relational		
Spiritual		
Lifestyle		
Immunity		

Evening Wellness Check		
Physical		
Mental		
Emotional		
Relational		
Spiritual		
Lifestyle		
Immunity		

Journaling		
Date:	Sobriety Date:	Number Days Clean & Sober:

What I am Proud of/Happy About Today

What I Want to Improve/Remember

What Did I Learn

What Can I Teach Someone Like Me?

To Discuss with Sponsor, Doctor, Therapist, or Other Professional:

Day 67 Required Activities	Today's Study Areas	Week 10: This Week's Focus
Meditation: 30 Minutes 2 times	Covey Habit 5	Teach: Relation/Emotional Health
Read: Heroin Living&Dying 25 pgs	Empathetic Listening	Feelings & Love
Aerobic: 60 min 1x or 30 min 2x	Emotions: Your Inner Guide	**Deliverables**
Flexibility: 10 minutes once	Emotional Triggers: Mine	1-Creating a Life: Emotional Plan
Meeting: 60 minutes	Emotional Triggers: Signif other	2-Create Budget for days 90-180

Needs, Habits, Healings, Affirmations, & Visualizations

Needs: Creativity/Freedom/Variety

Share Love Language Test Results with Important/Significant People

Healing Treatment Ten

I am One with the perfect love of all beings in my life – immediately, today, and every day!

Step & Service Work

Phase 4 and 5: Serve and Integrate; Steps 9, 10, 11, 12

Meet and Greet Newcomers, Make sure they have phone numbers

Prayer & Gratitude List

Meetings and Appointments

__00 __30	
__00 __30	
__00 __30	
__00 __30	
__00 __30	
__00 __30	
__00 __30	
__00 __30	
__00 __30	
__00 __30	
__00 __30	
__00 __30	
__00 __30	
__00 __30	
__00 __30	
__00 __30	

Notes, Numbers, & Future Appointments

Rev. Dr. Robert Hobbs
The Realization of Stainless Souls
www.StainlessSouls.com

Morning Wellness Check		
Physical		
Mental		
Emotional		
Relational		
Spiritual		
Lifestyle		
Immunity		

Evening Wellness Check		
Physical		
Mental		
Emotional		
Relational		
Spiritual		
Lifestyle		
Immunity		

Journaling		
Date:	Sobriety Date:	Number Days Clean & Sober:

What I am Proud of/Happy About Today

What I Want to Improve/Remember

What Did I Learn

What Can I Teach Someone Like Me?

To Discuss with Sponsor, Doctor, Therapist, or Other Professional:

Day 68 Required Activities	Today's Study Areas	Week 10: This Week's Focus
Meditation: 30 Minutes 2 times	Covey Habit 5	Teach: Relation/Emotional Health
Read: Heroin Living&Dying 25 pgs	Empathetic Listening	Feelings & Love
Aerobic: 60 min 1x or 30 min 2x	Emotions: Your Inner Guide	**Deliverables**
Flexibility: 10 minutes once	Emotional Triggers: Mine	1-Creating a Life: Emotional Plan
Meeting: 60 minutes	Emotional Triggers: Signif other	2-Create Budget for days 90-180

Needs, Habits, Healings, Affirmations, & Visualizations

Needs: Creativity/Freedom/Variety

Ask Important/Significant People to Take Love Language Test

Healing Treatment Ten

As God-Mind within me continues to grow in consciousness, I release the past and enjoin myself to partaking in a perfect future.

Meetings and Appointments	
__00 __30	
__00 __30	
__00 __30	
__00 __30	
__00 __30	
__00 __30	
__00 __30	
__00 __30	
__00 __30	
__00 __30	
__00 __30	
__00 __30	
__00 __30	
__00 __30	
__00 __30	
__00 __30	
__00 __30	
__00 __30	

Step & Service Work

Phase 4 and 5: Serve and Integrate; Steps 9, 10, 11, 12

Meet and Greet Newcomers, Make sure they have phone numbers

Prayer & Gratitude List

Notes, Numbers, & Future Appointments

Rev. Dr. Robert Hobbs
The Realization of Stainless Souls
www.StainlessSouls.com

Morning Wellness Check		
Physical		
Mental		
Emotional		
Relational		
Spiritual		
Lifestyle		
Immunity		

Evening Wellness Check		
Physical		
Mental		
Emotional		
Relational		
Spiritual		
Lifestyle		
Immunity		

Journaling		
Date:	Sobriety Date:	Number Days Clean & Sober:

What I am Proud of/Happy About Today

What I Want to Improve/Remember

What Did I Learn

What Can I Teach Someone Like Me?

To Discuss with Sponsor, Doctor, Therapist, or Other Professional:

Day 69 Required Activities	Today's Study Areas	Week 10: This Week's Focus
Meditation: 30 Minutes 2 times	Covey Habit 5	Teach: Relation/Emotional Health
Read: Heroin Living&Dying 25 pgs	Empathetic Listening	Feelings & Love
Aerobic: 60 min 1x or 30 min 2x	Emotions: Your Inner Guide	**Deliverables**
Flexibility: 10 minutes once	Emotional Triggers: Mine	1-Creating a Life: Emotional Plan
Meeting: 60 minutes	Emotional Triggers: Signif other	2-Create Budget for days 90-180

Needs, Habits, Healings, Affirmations, & Visualizations

Needs: Creativity/Freedom/Variety

Ask Important/Significant People to Take Love Language Test

Healing Treatment Ten

My reality is success and happiness in life and is made possible by my Higher Mind.

Meetings and Appointments

___00 / ___30	
___00 / ___30	
___00 / ___30	
___00 / ___30	
___00 / ___30	
___00 / ___30	
___00 / ___30	
___00 / ___30	
___00 / ___30	
___00 / ___30	
___00 / ___30	
___00 / ___30	
___00 / ___30	
___00 / ___30	
___00 / ___30	
___00 / ___30	
___00 / ___30	
___00 / ___30	

Step & Service Work

Phase 4 and 5: Serve and Integrate; Steps 9, 10, 11, 12

Meet and Greet Newcomers, Make sure they have phone numbers

Prayer & Gratitude List

Notes, Numbers, & Future Appointments

Rev. Dr. Robert Hobbs
The Realization of Stainless Souls
www.StainlessSouls.com

Morning Wellness Check		
Physical		
Mental		
Emotional		
Relational		
Spiritual		
Lifestyle		
Immunity		

Evening Wellness Check		
Physical		
Mental		
Emotional		
Relational		
Spiritual		
Lifestyle		
Immunity		

Journaling		
Date:	Sobriety Date:	Number Days Clean & Sober:

What I am Proud of/Happy About Today

What I Want to Improve/Remember

What Did I Learn

What Can I Teach Someone Like Me?

To Discuss with Sponsor, Doctor, Therapist, or Other Professional:

Day 70 Required Activities	Today's Study Areas	Week 10: This Week's Focus
Meditation: 30 Minutes 2 times	Covey Habit 5	Teach: Relation/Emotional Health
Read: Heroin Living&Dying 25 pgs	Empathetic Listening	Feelings & Love
Aerobic: 60 min 1x or 30 min 2x	Emotions: Your Inner Guide	**Deliverables**
Flexibility: 10 minutes once	Emotional Triggers: Mine	1-Creating a Life: Emotional Plan
Meeting: 60 minutes	Emotional Triggers: Signif other	2-Create Budget for days 90-180

Needs, Habits, Healings, Affirmations, & Visualizations

Needs: Creativity/Freedom/Variety

Compare LL Results – Together How Can You Improve Relationships

Healing Treatment Ten

Because I am cognizant and connected to the very nucleus and center of my mind, where the Intelligence of the Universe pours into me and from which I continuously emerge, I am confident about my future, regardless of what is occurring at this moment.

Step & Service Work

Phase 4 and 5: Serve and Integrate; Steps 9, 10, 11, 12

Meet and Greet Newcomers, Make sure they have phone numbers

Prayer & Gratitude List

Meetings and Appointments

Time	
__00 __30	
__00 __30	
__00 __30	
__00 __30	
__00 __30	
__00 __30	
__00 __30	
__00 __30	
__00 __30	
__00 __30	
__00 __30	
__00 __30	
__00 __30	
__00 __30	
__00 __30	
__00 __30	
__00 __30	
__00 __30	

Notes, Numbers, & Future Appointments

Rev. Dr. Robert Hobbs
The Realization of Stainless Souls
www.StainlessSouls.com

Morning Wellness Check		
Physical		
Mental		
Emotional		
Relational		
Spiritual		
Lifestyle		
Immunity		

Evening Wellness Check		
Physical		
Mental		
Emotional		
Relational		
Spiritual		
Lifestyle		
Immunity		

Journaling		
Date:	Sobriety Date:	Number Days Clean & Sober:

What I am Proud of/Happy About Today

What I Want to Improve/Remember

What Did I Learn

What Can I Teach Someone Like Me?

To Discuss with Sponsor, Doctor, Therapist, or Other Professional:

Week 11: Teach Spiritual Well-being

This week, contemplate and maybe decide, to the best of your ability, what is *the Absolute, God, Truth, or Universe?* It doesn't matter what I think, or your preacher thinks, or what you think scripture says. It matters *what you know*, what you intuitively know to be true.

Surely your perspective will change with practice and with wisdom.

But at any point, before you are fully realized, you should have a firm and articulate idea of what *The Absolute* is. You need to recognize that there is no right or wrong perspective; there is only the perspective you have now. Write it out - record it - have it available to you so you can develop it and build on it.

Also, this week, you will write out the 90-day, 1-year, 3-year, and 5-year plans based on your spiritual goals following the instructions provided in week 8.

You will also formally write out the following.

- A draft version of your definite Divine Purpose
- Your values and beliefs
- Your eulogy: what will be said about you once you were gone based on the life you are designing for yourself now

You will also review your notes and work from week 5, and deepen your understanding through additional research and study on the following topics

- Who or *what is God?*
- *Who or what is a Soul?*
- *Who or what, when, and why, am I?*
- *Soul identified as body/spirit*
- *Religion versus* spirituality

Additionally, you will prepare and teach a lesson plan (see week 8) on a topic that you are curious about regarding spiritual well-being.

Is a diamond any less valuable because it is covered in mud?

God sees the endless, changeless, stainless beauty of our Souls.

He knows we are not our mistakes.

~Paramahansa Yogananda-ji, Jai Guru!

Required Activities

Your meditation practice, aerobic activity, flexibility exercise, and recovery meeting requirements, are the same as last week and will remain so during the balance of this 90-day program.

Your reading assignment this week is the second half of the spiritual classic *An Autobiography of Yogi* by Paramahansa Yogananda. Read 30 pages per day. Remember you read the first half of the volume in week 8.

Needs, Healing, Habits, Affirmations, and Visualizations

Needs

This week you will continue to evaluate your need for risk, adventure, variety, creativity, and uncertainty. Remember, it is a group of needs which is tugging you away from fulfilling your opposing need for certainty and security. How can you balance these two different needs while maintaining a contented life?

Healing Treatment Eleven

Follow the instructions and practice the healing treatment three times per day for 15 minutes.

Affirmation and Visualization

Practice affirmations and visualizations following the instructions provided throughout this course

Step and Service Work

This week you enter the final phase of the *Brown Bag Blue Collar Recovery System*. This is the *integration phase* where you begin the practice of integrating everything you have learned in this 90-day course.

Though you should review these phases carefully, they are listed here for your convenience

1. Surrender
2. Forgive
3. Believe
4. Serve
5. Integrate

Phase 5 is nothing more than incorporating the first four phases into your everyday life:

1. Daily surrender
2. Daily forgiveness
3. Daily affirmation of beliefs
4. Daily service
5. All integrated in a balanced way

Although anytime an opportunity arises to make amends per step 9 with someone from your past, for all intents and purposes, we will focus on steps 10, 11, and 12, these last few weeks.

This week's primary step is Step 12. Re-read the *Big Book* chapter *Working with Others* and Step 12 in the *12 and 12*. If you want to keep what you have, you have to give it away to someone else. You don't need to force your service work on anyone; when the time is right, opportunities will present themselves to you. It should be your practice (with virtually everything in your recovery) to run any occasion and decision by your sponsor. As s/he is in the best position to guide you properly.

Step 12 says a lot, it assumes:

·   *A Spiritual Awakening*
·   That you *try* to carry the message to those who need to hear it, and
·   That you *practice* the recovery principles in all of your affairs

If you do these things without concern for perfection, you will have what you need to serve others in the highest way. Until then, focus on the service work you have done until this point. It is your intent that matters.

Be honest.
Do your best; forget the rest

Prayer and Gratitude List

Begin to write your own prayers for yourself, for others, and for devotion to the Absolute. Always have gratitude every day and express it sincerely.

Twice-daily Wellness Checks

Continue scoring and plotting your Wellness two times per day. Now, in the end, hopefully, the trend from day 1 to day 75 is upward. You should now be feeling better in all areas of your life.

Assess how the trends track against each other:

- Which ones move in the same direction?
- Which ones move in the opposite direction?
- How about at opposite ends of the day?
- Do your days begin and end in the same way?
- Do you wake up feeling better than you went to bed?
- Do you wake up feeling worse?

Take a close look at yourself; get to know yourself. As you more deeply evaluate yourself, more will be revealed, and the more control you can gain of reactions to the challenging stimuli of this existence.

Notes and Sketches

Day 71 Required Activities
Meditation: 30 Minutes 2 times
Read: Autobiography of Yogi 30pg
Aerobic: 60 min 1x or 30 min 2x
Flexibility: 10 minutes once
Meeting: 60 minutes

Today's Study Areas
Who or what is God?
Who or what is a Soul?
Who, What, When, Why Am I?
Soul Identified as Body/as Spirit
Religion vs. Spirituality

Week 11: This Week's Focus
Teach: Spiritual Wellbeing
The Absolute/God/Truth/Universe
Deliverables
Creating a Life: Personal Spiritual
Wellness Plan **AND** see Journal

Needs, Habits, Healings, Affirmations, & Visualizations

Needs: Creativity/Freedom/Variety

Healing Treatment Eleven

God is welling up from within me; my inner body is filled with the Infinite Mind of God as an Infinite Light – within and all around my body.

Step & Service Work

Phase 5: Integrate; Steps 10, 11, 12 every day for the rest of your life.

Prayer & Gratitude List

Meetings and Appointments

Time	
__00 __30	
__00 __30	
__00 __30	
__00 __30	
__00 __30	
__00 __30	
__00 __30	
__00 __30	
__00 __30	
__00 __30	
__00 __30	
__00 __30	
__00 __30	
__00 __30	
__00 __30	
__00 __30	
__00 __30	

Notes, Numbers, & Future Appointments

Rev. Dr. Robert Hobbs
The Realization of Stainless Souls
www.StainlessSouls.com

Morning Wellness Check		
Physical		
Mental		
Emotional		
Relational		
Spiritual		
Lifestyle		
Immunity		

Evening Wellness Check		
Physical		
Mental		
Emotional		
Relational		
Spiritual		
Lifestyle		
Immunity		

Journaling		
Date:	Sobriety Date:	Number Days Clean & Sober:

Deliverables: DRAFT Version (On separate parchment):

My Definite (Divine, Life's) Purpose (Why I am):

My Values and Beliefs (How I am What I am):

My Eulogy:

What I am Proud of/Happy About Today

What I Want to Improve/Remember

What Did I Learn

What Can I Teach Someone Like Me?

To Discuss with Sponsor, Doctor, Therapist, or Other Professional:

Day 72 Required Activities	Today's Study Areas	Week 11: This Week's Focus
Meditation: 30 Minutes 2 times	Who or what is God?	Teach: Spiritual Wellbeing
Read: Autobiography of Yogi 30pg	Who or what is a Soul?	The Absolute/God/Truth/Universe
Aerobic: 60 min 1x or 30 min 2x	Who, What, When, Why Am I?	**Deliverables**
Flexibility: 10 minutes once	Soul Identified as Body/as Spirit	Creating a Life: Personal Spiritual
Meeting: 60 minutes	Religion vs. Spirituality	Wellness Plan **AND** see Journal

Needs, Habits, Healings, Affirmations, & Visualizations

Needs: Creativity/Freedom/Variety

Healing Treatment Eleven

I am One with the Presence of God within me.

Step & Service Work

Phase 5: Integrate; Steps 10, 11, 12 every day for the rest of your life.

Prayer & Gratitude List

Meetings and Appointments

__00 __30	
__00 __30	
__00 __30	
__00 __30	
__00 __30	
__00 __30	
__00 __30	
__00 __30	
__00 __30	
__00 __30	
__00 __30	
__00 __30	
__00 __30	
__00 __30	
__00 __30	
__00 __30	
__00 __30	
__00 __30	

Notes, Numbers, & Future Appointments

Rev. Dr. Robert Hobbs
The Realization of Stainless Souls
www.StainlessSouls.com

Morning Wellness Check		
Physical		
Mental		
Emotional		
Relational		
Spiritual		
Lifestyle		
Immunity		

Evening Wellness Check		
Physical		
Mental		
Emotional		
Relational		
Spiritual		
Lifestyle		
Immunity		

Journaling		
Date:	Sobriety Date:	Number Days Clean & Sober:

Deliverables: DRAFT Version (On separate parchment):

My Definite (Divine, Life's) Purpose (Why I am):

My Values and Beliefs (How I am What I am):

My Eulogy:

What I am Proud of/Happy About Today

What I Want to Improve/Remember

What Did I Learn

What Can I Teach Someone Like Me?

To Discuss with Sponsor, Doctor, Therapist, or Other Professional:

Day 73 Required Activities	Today's Study Areas	Week 11: This Week's Focus
Meditation: 30 Minutes 2 times	Who or what is God?	Teach: Spiritual Wellbeing
Read: Autobiography of Yogi 30pg	Who or what is a Soul?	The Absolute/God/Truth/Universe
Aerobic: 60 min 1x or 30 min 2x	Who, What, When, Why Am I?	**Deliverables**
Flexibility: 10 minutes once	Soul Identified as Body/as Spirit	Creating a Life: Personal Spiritual
Meeting: 60 minutes	Religion vs. Spirituality	Wellness Plan **AND** see Journal

Needs, Habits, Healings, Affirmations, & Visualizations

Needs: Creativity/Freedom/Variety

Healing Treatment Eleven

I am One in Spirit with the Spirit of God within me.

Step & Service Work

Phase 5: Integrate; Steps 10, 11, 12 every day for the rest of your life.

Prayer & Gratitude List

Meetings and Appointments

__00 __30	
__00 __30	
__00 __30	
__00 __30	
__00 __30	
__00 __30	
__00 __30	
__00 __30	
__00 __30	
__00 __30	
__00 __30	
__00 __30	
__00 __30	
__00 __30	
__00 __30	
__00 __30	
__00 __30	
__00 __30	

Notes, Numbers, & Future Appointments

Rev. Dr. Robert Hobbs
The Realization of Stainless Souls
www.StainlessSouls.com

Morning Wellness Check		
Physical		
Mental		
Emotional		
Relational		
Spiritual		
Lifestyle		
Immunity		

Evening Wellness Check		
Physical		
Mental		
Emotional		
Relational		
Spiritual		
Lifestyle		
Immunity		

Journaling		
Date:	Sobriety Date:	Number Days Clean & Sober:

Deliverables: DRAFT Version (On separate parchment):

My Definite (Divine, Life's) Purpose (Why I am):

My Values and Beliefs (How I am What I am):

My Eulogy:

What I am Proud of/Happy About Today

What I Want to Improve/Remember

What Did I Learn

What Can I Teach Someone Like Me?

To Discuss with Sponsor, Doctor, Therapist, or Other Professional:

Day 74 Required Activities
Meditation: 30 Minutes 2 times
Read: Autobiography of Yogi 30pg
Aerobic: 60 min 1x or 30 min 2x
Flexibility: 10 minutes once
Meeting: 60 minutes

Today's Study Areas
Who or what is God?
Who or what is a Soul?
Who, What, When, Why Am I?
Soul Identified as Body/as Spirit
Religion vs. Spirituality

Week 11: This Week's Focus
Teach: Spiritual Wellbeing
The Absolute/God/Truth/Universe
Deliverables
Creating a Life: Personal Spiritual
Wellness Plan **AND** see Journal

Needs, Habits, Healings, Affirmations, & Visualizations

Needs: Creativity/Freedom/Variety

Healing Treatment Eleven

Every thought, today and every day, is guided by the Mind of God.

Step & Service Work

Phase 5: Integrate; Steps 10, 11, 12 every day for the rest of your life.

Prayer & Gratitude List

Meetings and Appointments

__00 __30	
__00 __30	
__00 __30	
__00 __30	
__00 __30	
__00 __30	
__00 __30	
__00 __30	
__00 __30	
__00 __30	
__00 __30	
__00 __30	
__00 __30	
__00 __30	
__00 __30	
__00 __30	
__00 __30	
__00 __30	
__00 __30	

Notes, Numbers, & Future Appointments

Rev. Dr. Robert Hobbs
The Realization of Stainless Souls
www.StainlessSouls.com

Morning Wellness Check		
Physical		
Mental		
Emotional		
Relational		
Spiritual		
Lifestyle		
Immunity		

Evening Wellness Check		
Physical		
Mental		
Emotional		
Relational		
Spiritual		
Lifestyle		
Immunity		

Journaling		
Date:	Sobriety Date:	Number Days Clean & Sober:

Deliverables: DRAFT Version (On separate parchment):

My Definite (Divine, Life's) Purpose (Why I am):

My Values and Beliefs (How I am What I am):

My Eulogy:

What I am Proud of/Happy About Today

What I Want to Improve/Remember

What Did I Learn

What Can I Teach Someone Like Me?

To Discuss with Sponsor, Doctor, Therapist, or Other Professional:

Day 75 Required Activities	Today's Study Areas	Week 11: This Week's Focus
Meditation: 30 Minutes 2 times	Who or what is God?	Teach: Spiritual Wellbeing
Read: Autobiography of Yogi 30pg	Who or what is a Soul?	The Absolute/God/Truth/Universe
Aerobic: 60 min 1x or 30 min 2x	Who, What, When, Why Am I?	**Deliverables**
Flexibility: 10 minutes once	Soul Identified as Body/as Spirit	Creating a Life: Personal Spiritual
Meeting: 60 minutes	Religion vs. Spirituality	Wellness Plan **AND** see Journal

Needs, Habits, Healings, Affirmations, & Visualizations

Needs: Creativity/Freedom/Variety

Healing Treatment Eleven

The God-Power within me has raised my consciousness above the consciousness of my problem. <<<Repeat 3x. For the elevation of my consciousness, I give thanks to the God-Power within me, I let it be so, and so it is!

Step & Service Work

Phase 5: Integrate; Steps 10, 11, 12 every day for the rest of your life.

Prayer & Gratitude List

Meetings and Appointments

__00 __30	
__00 __30	
__00 __30	
__00 __30	
__00 __30	
__00 __30	
__00 __30	
__00 __30	
__00 __30	
__00 __30	
__00 __30	
__00 __30	
__00 __30	
__00 __30	
__00 __30	
__00 __30	
__00 __30	

Notes, Numbers, & Future Appointments

Rev. Dr. Robert Hobbs
The Realization of Stainless Souls
www.StainlessSouls.com

Morning Wellness Check		
Physical		
Mental		
Emotional		
Relational		
Spiritual		
Lifestyle		
Immunity		

Evening Wellness Check		
Physical		
Mental		
Emotional		
Relational		
Spiritual		
Lifestyle		
Immunity		

Journaling		
Date:	Sobriety Date:	Number Days Clean & Sober:

Deliverables: DRAFT Version (On separate parchment):

My Definite (Divine, Life's) Purpose (Why I am):

My Values and Beliefs (How I am What I am):

My Eulogy:

What I am Proud of/Happy About Today

What I Want to Improve/Remember

What Did I Learn

What Can I Teach Someone Like Me?

To Discuss with Sponsor, Doctor, Therapist, or Other Professional:

Day 76 Required Activities	Today's Study Areas	Week 11: This Week's Focus
Meditation: 30 Minutes 2 times	Who or what is God?	Teach: Spiritual Wellbeing
Read: Autobiography of Yogi 30pg	Who or what is a Soul?	The Absolute/God/Truth/Universe
Aerobic: 60 min 1x or 30 min 2x	Who, What, When, Why Am I?	**Deliverables**
Flexibility: 10 minutes once	Soul Identified as Body/as Spirit	Creating a Life: Personal Spiritual
Meeting: 60 minutes	Religion vs. Spirituality	Wellness Plan **AND** see Journal

Needs, Habits, Healings, Affirmations, & Visualizations

Needs: Creativity/Freedom/Variety

Healing Treatment Eleven

Universal flexibility exists in my mind and thereby opens numerous channels through which good (and God) can reach me.

Step & Service Work

Phase 5: Integrate; Steps 10, 11, 12 every day for the rest of your life.

Prayer & Gratitude List

Meetings and Appointments

Time	
__00 / __30	
__00 / __30	
__00 / __30	
__00 / __30	
__00 / __30	
__00 / __30	
__00 / __30	
__00 / __30	
__00 / __30	
__00 / __30	
__00 / __30	
__00 / __30	
__00 / __30	
__00 / __30	
__00 / __30	
__00 / __30	
__00 / __30	
__00 / __30	

Notes, Numbers, & Future Appointments

Rev. Dr. Robert Hobbs
The Realization of Stainless Souls
www.StainlessSouls.com

Morning Wellness Check		
Physical		
Mental		
Emotional		
Relational		
Spiritual		
Lifestyle		
Immunity		

Evening Wellness Check		
Physical		
Mental		
Emotional		
Relational		
Spiritual		
Lifestyle		
Immunity		

Journaling		
Date:	Sobriety Date:	Number Days Clean & Sober:

Deliverables: DRAFT Version (On separate parchment):

My Definite (Divine, Life's) Purpose (Why I am):

My Values and Beliefs (How I am What I am):

My Eulogy:

What I am Proud of/Happy About Today

What I Want to Improve/Remember

What Did I Learn

What Can I Teach Someone Like Me?

To Discuss with Sponsor, Doctor, Therapist, or Other Professional:

Day 77 Required Activities	Today's Study Areas	Week 11: This Week's Focus
Meditation: 30 Minutes 2 times	Who or what is God?	Teach: Spiritual Wellbeing
Read: Autobiography of Yogi 30pg	Who or what is a Soul?	The Absolute/God/Truth/Universe
Aerobic: 60 min 1x or 30 min 2x	Who, What, When, Why Am I?	**Deliverables**
Flexibility: 10 minutes once	Soul Identified as Body/as Spirit	Creating a Life: Personal Spiritual
Meeting: 60 minutes	Religion vs. Spirituality	Wellness Plan **AND** see Journal

Needs, Habits, Healings, Affirmations, & Visualizations

Needs: Creativity/Freedom/Variety

Healing Treatment Eleven

I project a white protective aura of pure God Light around me in all places at all times.

Step & Service Work

Phase 5: Integrate; Steps 10, 11, 12 every day for the rest of your life.

Prayer & Gratitude List

Meetings and Appointments

__00 __30	
__00 __30	
__00 __30	
__00 __30	
__00 __30	
__00 __30	
__00 __30	
__00 __30	
__00 __30	
__00 __30	
__00 __30	
__00 __30	
__00 __30	
__00 __30	
__00 __30	
__00 __30	
__00 __30	

Notes, Numbers, & Future Appointments

Rev. Dr. Robert Hobbs
The Realization of Stainless Souls
www.StainlessSouls.com

Morning Wellness Check		
Physical		
Mental		
Emotional		
Relational		
Spiritual		
Lifestyle		
Immunity		

Evening Wellness Check		
Physical		
Mental		
Emotional		
Relational		
Spiritual		
Lifestyle		
Immunity		

Journaling		
Date:	Sobriety Date:	Number Days Clean & Sober:

Deliverables: DRAFT Version (On separate parchment):

My Definite (Divine, Life's) Purpose (Why I am):

My Values and Beliefs (How I am What I am):

My Eulogy:

What I am Proud of/Happy About Today

What I Want to Improve/Remember

What Did I Learn

What Can I Teach Someone Like Me?

To Discuss with Sponsor, Doctor, Therapist, or Other Professional:

Week 12: Teach Lifestyle Wellness

This week you're going to review your working notes from week 6. The references for this lesson were *Minimalism* and *Essentialism*. Criticize your *wants versus needs* and remember that the less you want and the less you have, the less you need to pay for, and the less you need to take care of. This alone reduces anxiety, stress, and worry. It gets better, because your obligations are lower - your anguish over having a specific job at a certain income is automatically lowered.

Many of us feel stuck in crappy jobs where we are mistreated and our time is abused by the company; Because of our *"perceived"* obligations, we put up with their abuse. We end up miserable all the time - always worrying about our stuff - and then worrying about the job we need to pay for our stuff.

So much pressure can be let out of the balloon by merely minimizing your possessions and then essentializing your work. I think there is no greater freedom than knowing you can always tell your boss where he can stuff his *"side projects."*

> *Be as simple as you can be;*
>
> *you will be astonished at how uncomplicated and happy*
>
> *your life can become!*
>
> *Paramahansa Yogananda-ji, Jai Guru!*

This Week review the following topics, and research and study for even more in-depth knowledge.

- What do I really need to survive?
- What must I really do at work?
- What is real/true happiness?
- How to plan weekly (for max productivity)?
- PMA: Positive Mental Attitude

You will prepare one lesson plan on a topic you are curious about. Lesson plan instructions are provided in the introduction to week 8.

You will also create two plans:

First, your 90-day, 1-year, 3-year, 5-year plans to successfully complete your *lifestyle goals* (again planning instructions are in week eight). Second, you will create and finalize your *"IOP"* plan or discharge plan. If you were getting out of treatment, you would have a *"customized"* discharge plan that would likely include a suggestion for *"IOP"* or *Intensive Outpatient Treatment*.

You're about to complete a program that is 90 days in length and organized in a way that you can copy and use to create a similar plan to get you through the next 90 days. It is up to you to create, write, and commit to how you're going to live in healthy recovery for the next 13 weeks (weeks 14 through 26).

Required Activities

Rev. Dr. Robert Hobbs
The Realization of Stainless Souls
www.StainlessSouls.com

Required activities are the same as the last 2 weeks except your reading assignment is now *The Surrender Experiment* by your now old friend Mickey Singer. I think you will enjoy the experiences Mickey shares in this great follow-on to *The Untethered Soul*.

Needs, Habits, Healings, Affirmations, and Visualizations

Needs

The final need opposes the need for *love and connection*. When one focuses on *significance* - they have less attention to give to relationships. If they focus too much on relationships, they cannot have the focus to obtain significance. We all have, to a varying degree, a need to have significance, or to become significant, to know that our life has meaning or purpose.

There is no escaping this or any need; before you leave your body, you are going to want to have some type of legacy. As you consider the influence this need has on your life, you need to evaluate it relative to your relationships. You will want to know if significance in the material dimension is the *primary* significance you wish to develop.

Does the need for significance outweigh your need for love and connection? It is not *wrong* if your answer is yes. You cannot overcome your dominant needs any more than you could change your fingerprints. The critical thing to realize and address is how to balance these two opposing needs in an optimum way. It is the balance that will determine whether you stay late at the office or make it to your daughter's recital.

If you develop significance through wealth, influence, and power, you may feel fulfilled for a time, but most people don't stay content for long. How can you obtain significance that is going to satisfy your need? You have to struggle with this; the answer lies within you; it's likely related to your *"Divine Purpose."*

Healing Treatments Twelve

Follow the instructions to complete healing treatment 12 three times per day for about 15 minutes.

Affirmations and Visualizations

Follow the instructions to practice the affirmations and visualizations provided.

Steps and Service Work

For this week and next live the life of a person in recovery by practicing Steps 10, 11, and 12, all day every day - and don't forget Step 9 opportunities when they present themselves.

Prayer and Gratitude List

Continue to pray for yourself and others. Try to connect with God first. Always say a prayer for gratitude at the end of every day just before sleeping. Remember what Tony Robbins says,

"When you're grateful you're rich."

Wellness Checks

Continue your two times per day wellness checks and plot the results.

Journaling

Journaling your ideas and inspirations.

And always have at least one thing that you are:

- Happy about or proud of
- You want to improve
- You have learned
- You wish to teach

Notes and Sketches

Rev. Dr. Robert Hobbs
The Realization of Stainless Souls
www.StainlessSouls.com

Day 78 Required Activities
Meditation: 30 Minutes 2 times
Read: Surrender Experiment 25pg
Aerobic: 60 min 1x or 30 min 2x
Flexibility: 10 minutes once
Meeting: 60 minutes

Today's Study Areas
What do I REALLY need to survive
What must I REALLY do at work
What is REAL HAPPINESS?
How to plan weekly
PMA: Positive Mental Attitude

Week 12: This Week's Focus
Teach: Lifestyle
Minimalism & Essentialism
Deliverables
1-Creating a Life:My Lifestyle Plan
2-FINAL IOP PLAN weeks 14-26

Needs, Habits, Healings, Affirmations, & Visualizations
Needs: Purpose/Importance/Significance
Healing Treatment Twelve
I maintain an open mind and all communication channels are continuously open allowing me to receive direction intuitively from the God Presence in the center of my being as to how and where to claim that which will bring me prosperity now.

Step & Service Work
Phase 5: Integrate; Steps 10, 11, 12 every day for the rest of your life.

Prayer & Gratitude List

Meetings and Appointments	
__00 __30	
__00 __30	
__00 __30	
__00 __30	
__00 __30	
__00 __30	
__00 __30	
__00 __30	
__00 __30	
__00 __30	
__00 __30	
__00 __30	
__00 __30	
__00 __30	
__00 __30	
__00 __30	
__00 __30	
__00 __30	

Notes, Numbers, & Future Appointments

Rev. Dr. Robert Hobbs
The Realization of Stainless Souls
www.StainlessSouls.com

Morning Wellness Check		
Physical		
Mental		
Emotional		
Relational		
Spiritual		
Lifestyle		
Immunity		

Evening Wellness Check		
Physical		
Mental		
Emotional		
Relational		
Spiritual		
Lifestyle		
Immunity		

Journaling		
Date:	Sobriety Date:	Number Days Clean & Sober:

What I am Proud of/Happy About Today

What I Want to Improve/Remember

What Did I Learn

What Can I Teach Someone Like Me?

To Discuss with Sponsor, Doctor, Therapist, or Other Professional:

Day 79 Required Activities	Today's Study Areas	Week 12: This Week's Focus
Meditation: 30 Minutes 2 times	What do I REALLY need to survive	Teach: Lifestyle
Read: Surrender Experiment 25pg	What must I REALLY do at work	Minimalism & Essentialism
Aerobic: 60 min 1x or 30 min 2x	What is REAL HAPPINESS?	**Deliverables**
Flexibility: 10 minutes once	How to plan weekly	1-Creating a Life:My Lifestyle Plan
Meeting: 60 minutes	PMA: Positive Mental Attitude	2-FINAL IOP PLAN weeks 14-26

Needs, Habits, Healings, Affirmations, & Visualizations

Needs: Purpose/Importance/Significance

Healing Treatment Twelve

The Higher Mind of God within me makes efficient use of my time and resources ensuring my success and happiness, today and every day.

Meetings and Appointments

Time	
__00 __30	
__00 __30	
__00 __30	
__00 __30	
__00 __30	
__00 __30	
__00 __30	
__00 __30	
__00 __30	
__00 __30	
__00 __30	
__00 __30	
__00 __30	
__00 __30	
__00 __30	
__00 __30	
__00 __30	
__00 __30	

Step & Service Work

Phase 5: Integrate; Steps 10, 11, 12 every day for the rest of your life.

Prayer & Gratitude List

Notes, Numbers, & Future Appointments

Rev. Dr. Robert Hobbs
The Realization of Stainless Souls
www.StainlessSouls.com

Morning Wellness Check	
Physical	
Mental	
Emotional	
Relational	
Spiritual	
Lifestyle	
Immunity	

Evening Wellness Check	
Physical	
Mental	
Emotional	
Relational	
Spiritual	
Lifestyle	
Immunity	

Journaling

Date:	Sobriety Date:	Number Days Clean & Sober:

What I am Proud of/Happy About Today

What I Want to Improve/Remember

What Did I Learn

What Can I Teach Someone Like Me?

To Discuss with Sponsor, Doctor, Therapist, or Other Professional:

Day 80 Required Activities	Today's Study Areas	Week 12: This Week's Focus
Meditation: 30 Minutes 2 times	What do I REALLY need to survive	Teach: Lifestyle
Read: Surrender Experiment 25pg	What must I REALLY do at work	Minimalism & Essentialism
Aerobic: 60 min 1x or 30 min 2x	What is REAL HAPPINESS?	**Deliverables**
Flexibility: 10 minutes once	How to plan weekly	1-Creating a Life:My Lifestyle Plan
Meeting: 60 minutes	PMA: Positive Mental Attitude	2-FINAL IOP PLAN weeks 14-26

Needs, Habits, Healings, Affirmations, & Visualizations

Needs: Purpose/Importance/Significance

Healing Treatment Twelve

My Soul's Purpose was commissioned by God and therefore He already knows my needs and will supply me with all that is necessary for success.

Step & Service Work

Phase 5: Integrate; Steps 10, 11, 12 every day for the rest of your life.

Prayer & Gratitude List

Meetings and Appointments	
__00 __30	
__00 __30	
__00 __30	
__00 __30	
__00 __30	
__00 __30	
__00 __30	
__00 __30	
__00 __30	
__00 __30	
__00 __30	
__00 __30	
__00 __30	
__00 __30	
__00 __30	
__00 __30	
__00 __30	
__00 __30	

Notes, Numbers, & Future Appointments

Rev. Dr. Robert Hobbs
The Realization of Stainless Souls
www.StainlessSouls.com

Morning Wellness Check		
Physical		
Mental		
Emotional		
Relational		
Spiritual		
Lifestyle		
Immunity		

Evening Wellness Check		
Physical		
Mental		
Emotional		
Relational		
Spiritual		
Lifestyle		
Immunity		

Journaling		
Date:	Sobriety Date:	Number Days Clean & Sober:

What I am Proud of/Happy About Today

What I Want to Improve/Remember

What Did I Learn

What Can I Teach Someone Like Me?

To Discuss with Sponsor, Doctor, Therapist, or Other Professional:

Day 81 Required Activities	Today's Study Areas	Week 12: This Week's Focus
Meditation: 30 Minutes 2 times	What do I REALLY need to survive	Teach: Lifestyle
Read: Surrender Experiment 25pg	What must I REALLY do at work	Minimalism & Essentialism
Aerobic: 60 min 1x or 30 min 2x	What is REAL HAPPINESS?	**Deliverables**
Flexibility: 10 minutes once	How to plan weekly	1-Creating a Life:My Lifestyle Plan
Meeting: 60 minutes	PMA: Positive Mental Attitude	2-FINAL IOP PLAN weeks 14-26

Needs, Habits, Healings, Affirmations, & Visualizations

Needs: Purpose/Importance/Significance

Healing Treatment Twelve

Every day live confidently with the knowledge that the source of my prosperity is God working through me and guiding me.

Step & Service Work

Phase 5: Integrate; Steps 10, 11, 12 every day for the rest of your life.

Prayer & Gratitude List

Meetings and Appointments

Time	
__00 __30	
__00 __30	
__00 __30	
__00 __30	
__00 __30	
__00 __30	
__00 __30	
__00 __30	
__00 __30	
__00 __30	
__00 __30	
__00 __30	
__00 __30	
__00 __30	
__00 __30	
__00 __30	
__00 __30	

Notes, Numbers, & Future Appointments

Rev. Dr. Robert Hobbs
The Realization of Stainless Souls
www.StainlessSouls.com

Morning Wellness Check		
Physical		
Mental		
Emotional		
Relational		
Spiritual		
Lifestyle		
Immunity		

Evening Wellness Check		
Physical		
Mental		
Emotional		
Relational		
Spiritual		
Lifestyle		
Immunity		

Journaling		
Date:	Sobriety Date:	Number Days Clean & Sober:

What I am Proud of/Happy About Today

What I Want to Improve/Remember

What Did I Learn

What Can I Teach Someone Like Me?

To Discuss with Sponsor, Doctor, Therapist, or Other Professional:

Day 82 Required Activities	Today's Study Areas	Week 12: This Week's Focus
Meditation: 30 Minutes 2 times	What do I REALLY need to survive	Teach: Lifestyle
Read: Surrender Experiment 25pg	What must I REALLY do at work	Minimalism & Essentialism
Aerobic: 60 min 1x or 30 min 2x	What is REAL HAPPINESS?	**Deliverables**
Flexibility: 10 minutes once	How to plan weekly	1-Creating a Life:My Lifestyle Plan
Meeting: 60 minutes	PMA: Positive Mental Attitude	2-FINAL IOP PLAN weeks 14-26

Needs, Habits, Healings, Affirmations, & Visualizations

Needs: Purpose/Importance/Significance

Healing Treatment Twelve

I am One with the prosperity, abundance, and financial supply of the Universe immediately, today, and every day!

Step & Service Work

Phase 5: Integrate; Steps 10, 11, 12 every day for the rest of your life.

Prayer & Gratitude List

Meetings and Appointments

__00 __30	
__00 __30	
__00 __30	
__00 __30	
__00 __30	
__00 __30	
__00 __30	
__00 __30	
__00 __30	
__00 __30	
__00 __30	
__00 __30	
__00 __30	
__00 __30	
__00 __30	
__00 __30	
__00 __30	
__00 __30	

Notes, Numbers, & Future Appointments

Rev. Dr. Robert Hobbs
The Realization of Stainless Souls
www.StainlessSouls.com

Morning Wellness Check		
Physical		
Mental		
Emotional		
Relational		
Spiritual		
Lifestyle		
Immunity		

Evening Wellness Check		
Physical		
Mental		
Emotional		
Relational		
Spiritual		
Lifestyle		
Immunity		

Journaling		
Date:	Sobriety Date:	Number Days Clean & Sober:

What I am Proud of/Happy About Today

What I Want to Improve/Remember

What Did I Learn

What Can I Teach Someone Like Me?

To Discuss with Sponsor, Doctor, Therapist, or Other Professional:

Day 83 Required Activities
Meditation: 30 Minutes 2 times
Read: Surrender Experiment 25pg
Aerobic: 60 min 1x or 30 min 2x
Flexibility: 10 minutes once
Meeting: 60 minutes

Today's Study Areas
What do I REALLY need to survive
What must I REALLY do at work
What is REAL HAPPINESS?
How to plan weekly
PMA: Positive Mental Attitude

Week 12: This Week's Focus
Teach: Lifestyle
Minimalism & Essentialism
Deliverables
1-Creating a Life:My Lifestyle Plan
2-FINAL IOP PLAN weeks 14-26

Needs, Habits, Healings, Affirmations, & Visualizations

Needs: Purpose/Importance/Significance

Healing Treatment Twelve

I vibrationally project outward thoughts into the Universe that I am already a successful and prosperous person.

Step & Service Work

Phase 5: Integrate; Steps 10, 11, 12 every day for the rest of your life.

Prayer & Gratitude List

Meetings and Appointments	
__00 __30	
__00 __30	
__00 __30	
__00 __30	
__00 __30	
__00 __30	
__00 __30	
__00 __30	
__00 __30	
__00 __30	
__00 __30	
__00 __30	
__00 __30	
__00 __30	
__00 __30	
__00 __30	
__00 __30	
__00 __30	

Notes, Numbers, & Future Appointments

Rev. Dr. Robert Hobbs
The Realization of Stainless Souls
www.StainlessSouls.com

Morning Wellness Check		
Physical		
Mental		
Emotional		
Relational		
Spiritual		
Lifestyle		
Immunity		

Evening Wellness Check		
Physical		
Mental		
Emotional		
Relational		
Spiritual		
Lifestyle		
Immunity		

Journaling		
Date:	Sobriety Date:	Number Days Clean & Sober:

What I am Proud of/Happy About Today

What I Want to Improve/Remember

What Did I Learn

What Can I Teach Someone Like Me?

To Discuss with Sponsor, Doctor, Therapist, or Other Professional:

Day 84 Required Activities
Meditation: 30 Minutes 2 times
Read: Surrender Experiment 25pg
Aerobic: 60 min 1x or 30 min 2x
Flexibility: 10 minutes once
Meeting: 60 minutes

Today's Study Areas
What do I REALLY need to survive
What must I REALLY do at work
What is REAL HAPPINESS?
How to plan weekly
PMA: Positive Mental Attitude

Week 12: This Week's Focus
Teach: Lifestyle
Minimalism & Essentialism
Deliverables
1-Creating a Life:My Lifestyle Plan
2-FINAL IOP PLAN weeks 14-26

Needs, Habits, Healings, Affirmations, & Visualizations

Needs: Purpose/Importance/Significance

Healing Treatment Twelve

I am One with the Creative Expression of God within me.

Step & Service Work

Phase 5: Integrate; Steps 10, 11, 12 every day for the rest of your life.

Prayer & Gratitude List

Meetings and Appointments

__00 / __30	
__00 / __30	
__00 / __30	
__00 / __30	
__00 / __30	
__00 / __30	
__00 / __30	
__00 / __30	
__00 / __30	
__00 / __30	
__00 / __30	
__00 / __30	
__00 / __30	
__00 / __30	
__00 / __30	
__00 / __30	
__00 / __30	

Notes, Numbers, & Future Appointments

Rev. Dr. Robert Hobbs
The Realization of Stainless Souls
www.StainlessSouls.com

Morning Wellness Check		
Physical		
Mental		
Emotional		
Relational		
Spiritual		
Lifestyle		
Immunity		

Evening Wellness Check		
Physical		
Mental		
Emotional		
Relational		
Spiritual		
Lifestyle		
Immunity		

Journaling		
Date:	Sobriety Date:	Number Days Clean & Sober:

What I am Proud of/Happy About Today

What I Want to Improve/Remember

What Did I Learn

What Can I Teach Someone Like Me?

To Discuss with Sponsor, Doctor, Therapist, or Other Professional:

Week 13: Teach Immunity and Relapse Prevention

You've made it! You are finally here at the end. By now, I hope you recognize that this program is not intended to be a *START-STOP* type of experience. From day 1, you have been building skills to help you live a better life daily.

No longer should you be wondering how you're going to fill a day, especially a day without drugs and alcohol. Now you know. You don't need drugs or alcohol, or social media, or TV, or video games, or 24 x 7 cable news, or bars, or pornography, or any of those other dozens of activities that you thought you needed.

Frankly, you need a meditation cushion and a flicker of *Hope or Divine Inspiration*. From there you can fill every day for the rest of this incarnation and any other incarnation. Don't waste this moment; ***don't waste this lifetime***; you are on a path; stay on it. Design how you will spend your time and then live every moment of the rest of your life *with purpose on purpose*. Is up to you; you are not alone. Help is always available; you only have to ask.

> *Suppose the Earth were 100% covered by water.*
> *Suppose in the water floated one floating ring the size of a women's bracelet.*
> *Suppose there lived a blind tortoise in the water and that he surfaced just once every 100 years*
> *What are the odds of that tortoise surfacing exactly where the ring was and—*
>
> *The ring fit around her head perfectly and became a necklace?*
> *These are the same odds our souls have in gaining a human form*
> *And from only the human form we can we find our way back home to Divine Mother-God*
>
> *Human life is precious – you beat the odds to even have one*
>
> *Don't waste one second of what you have*
> *Blood in your veins, breath in your lungs, love in your heart, and God in your Soul!*
> *~Based on the Buddha's Philosophy*

So, this week, we revisit week 7 and the defense of your sober life. We aimed to build a moat around you and your sobriety to defend your well-being. Now, following the instructions given in step 8, you're going to prepare and teach a lesson plan on one of the topics you are most curious about.

You're also going to develop a 90-day, 1-year, 3-year, and 5-year *relapse prevention plan* based on the goals you have set (mostly in week 7). Plan development instructions were given in the intro to week 8. You're going to review and then deepen the knowledge you gained in week 7 by researching and studying the following topics

- Defending sobriety with a moat
- mTriggers: movies, people, media
- eTriggers: media, propaganda, advertisements

Rev. Dr. Robert Hobbs
The Realization of Stainless Souls
www.StainlessSouls.com

- · sTriggers: desires, attachments, obsessions
- · pTriggers: people, places, things

Required Activities

These remain the same except your final reading assignment is *The Tapping Solution*, by Nick Ortner. This incredible technique has been a miracle in my own personal life; it can be in yours as well.

Needs, Habits, Healings, Affirmations, and Visualizations

Needs

Continue this week working through significance and how to balance your desire to be recognized as an individual with an opposing need of having abundant love and connection. Remember the key to contentment and fulfillment from the perspective of my needs is to strike the right balance (*for you*) across all six needs - recognizing that the balance shifts as you age and as you achieve more in each need category.

Healing Treatment Thirteen

Follow the Healing Treatment 13 instructions and practice for 15 minutes 3 times per day. Treat this as an affirmation on steroids and as an advanced form of prayer.

Affirmation and Visualization

Practice affirmations at least three times per day

Step Work

If you have followed the program, you are now entirely in recovery and working steps 10, 11, and 12 simultaneously like we all do. Keep greeting newcomers and make sure they have your phone number.

Prayer and Gratitude list

Every day for the rest of your life, you will be responsible for the gratitude you convey to your higher power. Please don't let this part of your spiritual life fall into the bad habit of reciting from memory some other person's heartfelt prayer. You're a child of God; talk to Him as if you believe you are His child. Naughty or nice it is God's responsibility to care for you as His child. Be grateful and be generous with your prayers for others. Add suffering people you hear about to your prayer list; then sincerely pray for their well-being and for God's will to shape their lives.

Wellness Checks

Record and plot your wellness checks twice daily; hopefully, you notice how things track together, and maybe there is enough information where you can predict a particular mood based on how one of the wellness areas is trending.

Journaling

In the journaling section, you will create the final versions of all of the work you did, most notably the last versions of:

- · Your definite or Divine Purpose
- · Values and beliefs
- · The eulogy you want to be read when you leave your body

Chronic Relapsers:

I strongly suggest that if you are a chronic relapser, that you plan out every minute of every day in your future. Start by planning out your week as instructed in this program and by Dr. Covey in Habit 3. Once the weekly plan takes shape, begin filling in all the white space of the agenda (meetings and appointments) section.

All of your waking hours on your daily appointment or meeting list must be filled in with activities that you've done here and activities that you're going to do along with your IOP plan: reading, researching, studying, walking, meditating, stretching, listening, teaching, leading, mentoring, serving, planning, visualizing, creating.

There is no end to what you can do in a day, so make your sober days - days of endless activity.

Live Your Life! Don't Spend It!

Dilution is the solution to pollution!

Fill your mop bucket with fresh, pure water and drain the dirt out from the bottom.

Finally, complete your day with your happy and proud moments, what you'd like to improve on, what you learned, and what you'd like to teach.

Learning what might work for you in recovery is like panning for gold, you have to sift through the whole riverbed to get one or two nuggets; but the thing is once you have those nuggets, they are pure gold and will last forever.

Don't be afraid to sift, sift, and sift, and know your treasure will be found in the gritty grains of sand of your mind!

With that, we close! Best of luck to you, my dear new friend!!

Godspeed!

Rev. Dr. Robert Hobbs
The Realization of Stainless Souls
www.StainlessSouls.com

Notes and Sketches

Day 85 Required Activities
Meditation: 30 Minutes 2 times
Reading: Tapping Solution 25 Pgs
Aerobic: 60 min 1x or 30 min 2x
Flexibility: 10 minutes once
Meeting: 60 minutes

Today's Study Areas
Defending Sobriety (with a moat)
mTriggers: Movies, People, Media
eTriggers: Media Propaganda, Ads
sTriggers: Desires, Attachments
pTriggers: People, Places, Things

Week 13: This Week's Focus
Teach Immunity: Relapse Prevent
Mind-Body-Spirit-Heart Toxins
Deliverables
Protecting a Life: Relapse
Prevention Plan (A moat for me)

Needs, Habits, Healings, Affirmations, & Visualizations

Needs: Purpose/Importance/Significance

Healing Treatment Thirteen

In the very center of my mind, from the nucleus where I continuously emerge, I recognize that all the so-called difficulties in my life are but a transitional stage leading to greater good in my life.

Step & Service Work

Phase 5: Integrate; Steps 10, 11, 12 every day for the rest of your life.

Prayer & Gratitude List

Meetings and Appointments

Time	
__00 / __30	
__00 / __30	
__00 / __30	
__00 / __30	
__00 / __30	
__00 / __30	
__00 / __30	
__00 / __30	
__00 / __30	
__00 / __30	
__00 / __30	
__00 / __30	
__00 / __30	
__00 / __30	
__00 / __30	
__00 / __30	
__00 / __30	

Notes, Numbers, & Future Appointments

Rev. Dr. Robert Hobbs
The Realization of Stainless Souls
www.StainlessSouls.com

Morning Wellness Check		
Physical		
Mental		
Emotional		
Relational		
Spiritual		
Lifestyle		
Immunity		

Evening Wellness Check		
Physical		
Mental		
Emotional		
Relational		
Spiritual		
Lifestyle		
Immunity		

Journaling		
Date:	Sobriety Date:	Number Days Clean & Sober:

Deliverables: FINAL Version (On separate parchment):

My Definite (Divine, Life's) Purpose (Why I am):

My Values and Beliefs (How I am What I am):

Goals and Objectives and Plans (What I am Going to Do): 90 days, 1 year, 3 years, 5 years, My Eulogy

Suggestion for chronic relapsers: If you made it this far, plan every single day of the next 90 days, NOW, while you are sane. Plan every minute of every day – leave nothing to chance! If you don't have something to do - the active addiction in you will give you something to do. By now, you have plenty of experience on how to fill a meaningful day. Keep on!

What I am Proud of/Happy About Today

What I Want to Improve/Remember

What Did I Learn

What Can I Teach Someone Like Me?

To Discuss with Sponsor, Doctor, Therapist, or Other Professional:

Day 86 Required Activities	Today's Study Areas	Week 13: This Week's Focus
Meditation: 30 Minutes 2 times	Defending Sobriety (with a moat)	Teach Immunity: Relapse Prevent
Reading: Tapping Solution 25 Pgs	mTriggers: Movies, People, Media	Mind-Body-Spirit-Heart Toxins
Aerobic: 60 min 1x or 30 min 2x	eTriggers: Media Propaganda, Ads	**Deliverables**
Flexibility: 10 minutes once	sTriggers: Desires, Attachments	Protecting a Life: Relapse
Meeting: 60 minutes	pTriggers: People, Places, Things	Prevention Plan (A moat for me)

Needs, Habits, Healings, Affirmations, & Visualizations

Needs: Purpose/Importance/Significance

Healing Treatment Thirteen

All so-called good-luck I will have in the future is caused by my positive mental attitude today.

Step & Service Work

Phase 5: Integrate; Steps 10, 11, 12 every day for the rest of your life.

Prayer & Gratitude List

Meetings and Appointments

__00 __30	
__00 __30	
__00 __30	
__00 __30	
__00 __30	
__00 __30	
__00 __30	
__00 __30	
__00 __30	
__00 __30	
__00 __30	
__00 __30	
__00 __30	
__00 __30	
__00 __30	
__00 __30	
__00 __30	
__00 __30	

Notes, Numbers, & Future Appointments

Rev. Dr. Robert Hobbs
The Realization of Stainless Souls
www.StainlessSouls.com

Morning Wellness Check		
Physical		
Mental		
Emotional		
Relational		
Spiritual		
Lifestyle		
Immunity		

Evening Wellness Check		
Physical		
Mental		
Emotional		
Relational		
Spiritual		
Lifestyle		
Immunity		

Journaling		
Date:	Sobriety Date:	Number Days Clean & Sober:

Deliverables: FINAL Version (On separate parchment):

My Definite (Divine, Life's) Purpose (Why I am):

My Values and Beliefs (How I am What I am):

Goals and Objectives and Plans (What I am Going to Do): 90 days, 1 year, 3 years, 5 years, My Eulogy

Suggestion for chronic relapsers: If you made it this far, plan every single day of the next 90 days, NOW, while you are sane. Plan every minute of every day – leave nothing to chance! If you don't have something to do - the active addiction in you will give you something to do. By now, you have plenty of experience on how to fill a meaningful day. Keep on!

What I am Proud of/Happy About Today

What I Want to Improve/Remember

What Did I Learn

What Can I Teach Someone Like Me?

To Discuss with Sponsor, Doctor, Therapist, or Other Professional:

Day 87 Required Activities
Meditation: 30 Minutes 2 times
Reading: Tapping Solution 25 Pgs
Aerobic: 60 min 1x or 30 min 2x
Flexibility: 10 minutes once
Meeting: 60 minutes

Today's Study Areas
Defending Sobriety (with a moat)
mTriggers: Movies, People, Media
eTriggers: Media Propaganda, Ads
sTriggers: Desires, Attachments
pTriggers: People, Places, Things

Week 13: This Week's Focus
Teach Immunity: Relapse Prevent
Mind-Body-Spirit-Heart Toxins
Deliverables
Protecting a Life: Relapse
Prevention Plan (A moat for me)

Needs, Habits, Healings, Affirmations, & Visualizations

Needs: Purpose/Importance/Significance

Healing Treatment Thirteen

The God-Power within me is greater than any temptation of addiction or relapse.

Step & Service Work

Phase 5: Integrate; Steps 10, 11, 12 every day for the rest of your life.

Prayer & Gratitude List

Meetings and Appointments

Time	
__00 __30	
__00 __30	
__00 __30	
__00 __30	
__00 __30	
__00 __30	
__00 __30	
__00 __30	
__00 __30	
__00 __30	
__00 __30	
__00 __30	
__00 __30	
__00 __30	
__00 __30	
__00 __30	
__00 __30	

Notes, Numbers, & Future Appointments

Rev. Dr. Robert Hobbs
The Realization of Stainless Souls
www.StainlessSouls.com

Morning Wellness Check		
Physical		
Mental		
Emotional		
Relational		
Spiritual		
Lifestyle		
Immunity		

Evening Wellness Check		
Physical		
Mental		
Emotional		
Relational		
Spiritual		
Lifestyle		
Immunity		

Journaling		
Date:	Sobriety Date:	Number Days Clean & Sober:

Deliverables: FINAL Version (On separate parchment):

My Definite (Divine, Life's) Purpose (Why I am):

My Values and Beliefs (How I am What I am):

Goals and Objectives and Plans (What I am Going to Do): 90 days, 1 year, 3 years, 5 years, My Eulogy

Suggestion for chronic relapsers: If you made it this far, plan every single day of the next 90 days, NOW, while you are sane. Plan every minute of every day – leave nothing to chance! If you don't have something to do - the active addiction in you will give you something to do. By now, you have plenty of experience on how to fill a meaningful day. Keep on!

What I am Proud of/Happy About Today
What Did I Learn

What I Want to Improve/Remember
What Can I Teach Someone Like Me?

To Discuss with Sponsor, Doctor, Therapist, or Other Professional:

Day 88 Required Activities	Today's Study Areas	Week 13: This Week's Focus
Meditation: 30 Minutes 2 times	Defending Sobriety (with a moat)	Teach Immunity: Relapse Prevent
Reading: Tapping Solution 25 Pgs	mTriggers: Movies, People, Media	Mind-Body-Spirit-Heart Toxins
Aerobic: 60 min 1x or 30 min 2x	eTriggers: Media Propaganda, Ads	**Deliverables**
Flexibility: 10 minutes once	sTriggers: Desires, Attachments	Protecting a Life: Relapse
Meeting: 60 minutes	pTriggers: People, Places, Things	Prevention Plan (A moat for me)

Needs, Habits, Healings, Affirmations, & Visualizations

Needs: Purpose/Importance/Significance

Healing Treatment Thirteen

Every thought, today and every day, is guided by the Mind of God.

Step & Service Work

Phase 5: Integrate; Steps 10, 11, 12 every day for the rest of your life.

Prayer & Gratitude List

Meetings and Appointments

__00 __30	
__00 __30	
__00 __30	
__00 __30	
__00 __30	
__00 __30	
__00 __30	
__00 __30	
__00 __30	
__00 __30	
__00 __30	
__00 __30	
__00 __30	
__00 __30	
__00 __30	
__00 __30	
__00 __30	

Notes, Numbers, & Future Appointments

Rev. Dr. Robert Hobbs
The Realization of Stainless Souls
www.StainlessSouls.com

Morning Wellness Check	
Physical	
Mental	
Emotional	
Relational	
Spiritual	
Lifestyle	
Immunity	

Evening Wellness Check	
Physical	
Mental	
Emotional	
Relational	
Spiritual	
Lifestyle	
Immunity	

Journaling		
Date:	Sobriety Date:	Number Days Clean & Sober:

Deliverables: FINAL Version (On separate parchment):

My Definite (Divine, Life's) Purpose (Why I am):

My Values and Beliefs (How I am What I am):

Goals and Objectives and Plans (What I am Going to Do): 90 days, 1 year, 3 years, 5 years, My Eulogy

Suggestion for chronic relapsers: If you made it this far, plan every single day of the next 90 days, NOW, while you are sane. Plan every minute of every day – leave nothing to chance! If you don't have something to do - the active addiction in you will give you something to do. By now, you have plenty of experience on how to fill a meaningful day. Keep on!

What I am Proud of/Happy About Today

What I Want to Improve/Remember

What Did I Learn

What Can I Teach Someone Like Me?

To Discuss with Sponsor, Doctor, Therapist, or Other Professional:

Day 89 Required Activities
Meditation: 30 Minutes 2 times
Reading: Tapping Solution 25 Pgs
Aerobic: 60 min 1x or 30 min 2x
Flexibility: 10 minutes once
Meeting: 60 minutes

Today's Study Areas
Defending Sobriety (with a moat)
mTriggers: Movies, People, Media
eTriggers: Media Propaganda, Ads
sTriggers: Desires, Attachments
pTriggers: People, Places, Things

Week 13: This Week's Focus
Teach Immunity: Relapse Prevent
Mind-Body-Spirit-Heart Toxins
Deliverables
Protecting a Life: Relapse
Prevention Plan (A moat for me)

Needs, Habits, Healings, Affirmations, & Visualizations

Needs: Purpose/Importance/Significance

Healing Treatment Thirteen

Every time I see a healthy person, I will see myself in my own mind as having the same kind of health today and each moment of each day of my life.

Step & Service Work

Phase 5: Integrate; Steps 10, 11, 12 every day for the rest of your life.

Prayer & Gratitude List

Meetings and Appointments

Time	
__00 __30	
__00 __30	
__00 __30	
__00 __30	
__00 __30	
__00 __30	
__00 __30	
__00 __30	
__00 __30	
__00 __30	
__00 __30	
__00 __30	
__00 __30	
__00 __30	
__00 __30	
__00 __30	
__00 __30	
__00 __30	

Notes, Numbers, & Future Appointments

Rev. Dr. Robert Hobbs
The Realization of Stainless Souls
www.StainlessSouls.com

Morning Wellness Check		
Physical		
Mental		
Emotional		
Relational		
Spiritual		
Lifestyle		
Immunity		

Evening Wellness Check		
Physical		
Mental		
Emotional		
Relational		
Spiritual		
Lifestyle		
Immunity		

Journaling		
Date:	Sobriety Date:	Number Days Clean & Sober:

Deliverables: FINAL Version (On separate parchment):

My Definite (Divine, Life's) Purpose (Why I am):

My Values and Beliefs (How I am What I am):

Goals and Objectives and Plans (What I am Going to Do): 90 days, 1 year, 3 years, 5 years, My Eulogy

Suggestion for chronic relapsers: If you made it this far, plan every single day of the next 90 days, NOW, while you are sane. Plan every minute of every day – leave nothing to chance! If you don't have something to do - the active addiction in you will give you something to do. By now, you have plenty of experience on how to fill a meaningful day. Keep on!

What I am Proud of/Happy About Today

What I Want to Improve/Remember

What Did I Learn

What Can I Teach Someone Like Me?

To Discuss with Sponsor, Doctor, Therapist, or Other Professional:

Day 90 Required Activities	Today's Study Areas	Week 13: This Week's Focus
Meditation: 30 Minutes 2 times	Defending Sobriety (with a moat)	Teach Immunity: Relapse Prevent
Reading: Tapping Solution 25 Pgs	mTriggers: Movies, People, Media	Mind-Body-Spirit-Heart Toxins
Aerobic: 60 min 1x or 30 min 2x	eTriggers: Media Propaganda, Ads	**Deliverables**
Flexibility: 10 minutes once	sTriggers: Desires, Attachments	Protecting a Life: Relapse
Meeting: 60 minutes	pTriggers: People, Places, Things	Prevention Plan (A moat for me)

Needs, Habits, Healings, Affirmations, & Visualizations

Needs: Purpose/Importance/Significance

Healing Treatment Thirteen

I am One with the higher wisdom and awareness of the Universe – immediately, today, and every day!

Step & Service Work

Phase 5: Integrate; Steps 10, 11, 12 every day for the rest of your life.

Prayer & Gratitude List

Meetings and Appointments

__00 __30	
__00 __30	
__00 __30	
__00 __30	
__00 __30	
__00 __30	
__00 __30	
__00 __30	
__00 __30	
__00 __30	
__00 __30	
__00 __30	
__00 __30	
__00 __30	
__00 __30	
__00 __30	
__00 __30	
__00 __30	

Notes, Numbers, & Future Appointments

Rev. Dr. Robert Hobbs
The Realization of Stainless Souls
www.StainlessSouls.com

Morning Wellness Check		
Physical		
Mental		
Emotional		
Relational		
Spiritual		
Lifestyle		
Immunity		

Evening Wellness Check		
Physical		
Mental		
Emotional		
Relational		
Spiritual		
Lifestyle		
Immunity		

Journaling		
Date:	Sobriety Date:	Number Days Clean & Sober:

Deliverables: FINAL Version (On separate parchment):

My Definite (Divine, Life's) Purpose (Why I am):

My Values and Beliefs (How I am What I am):

Goals and Objectives and Plans (What I am Going to Do): 90 days, 1 year, 3 years, 5 years, My Eulogy

Suggestion for chronic relapsers: If you made it this far, plan every single day of the next 90 days, NOW, while you are sane. Plan every minute of every day – leave nothing to chance! If you don't have something to do - the active addiction in you will give you something to do. By now, you have plenty of experience on how to fill a meaningful day. Keep on!

What I am Proud of/Happy About Today

What I Want to Improve/Remember

What Did I Learn

What Can I Teach Someone Like Me?

To Discuss with Sponsor, Doctor, Therapist, or Other Professional:

Day 91 Required Activities
Meditation: 30 Minutes 2 times
Reading: Tapping Solution 25 Pgs
Aerobic: 60 min 1x or 30 min 2x
Flexibility: 10 minutes once
Meeting: 60 minutes

Today's Study Areas
Defending Sobriety (with a moat)
mTriggers: Movies, People, Media
eTriggers: Media Propaganda, Ads
sTriggers: Desires, Attachments
pTriggers: People, Places, Things

Week 13: This Week's Focus
Teach Immunity: Relapse Prevent
Mind-Body-Spirit-Heart Toxins
Deliverables
Protecting a Life: Relapse
Prevention Plan (A moat for me)

Needs, Habits, Healings, Affirmations, & Visualizations

Needs: Purpose/Importance/Significance

Healing Treatment Thirteen

It is not I but the Father that doeth these good works; God is the Doer.

Step & Service Work

Phase 5: Integrate; Steps 10, 11, 12 every day for the rest of your life.

Prayer & Gratitude List

Meetings and Appointments	
__00 __30	
__00 __30	
__00 __30	
__00 __30	
__00 __30	
__00 __30	
__00 __30	
__00 __30	
__00 __30	
__00 __30	
__00 __30	
__00 __30	
__00 __30	
__00 __30	
__00 __30	
__00 __30	
__00 __30	

Notes, Numbers, & Future Appointments

Rev. Dr. Robert Hobbs
The Realization of Stainless Souls
www.StainlessSouls.com

Morning Wellness Check		
Physical		
Mental		
Emotional		
Relational		
Spiritual		
Lifestyle		
Immunity		

Evening Wellness Check		
Physical		
Mental		
Emotional		
Relational		
Spiritual		
Lifestyle		
Immunity		

Journaling		
Date:	Sobriety Date:	Number Days Clean & Sober:

Deliverables: FINAL Version (On separate parchment):

My Definite (Divine, Life's) Purpose (Why I am):

My Values and Beliefs (How I am What I am):

Goals and Objectives and Plans (What I am Going to Do): 90 days, 1 year, 3 years, 5 years, My Eulogy

Suggestion for chronic relapsers: If you made it this far, plan every single day of the next 90 days, NOW, while you are sane. Plan every minute of every day – leave nothing to chance! If you don't have something to do - the active addiction in you will give you something to do. By now, you have plenty of experience on how to fill a meaningful day. Keep on!

What I am Proud of/Happy About Today

What I Want to Improve/Remember

What Did I Learn

What Can I Teach Someone Like Me?

To Discuss with Sponsor, Doctor, Therapist, or Other Professional:

Healing Treatments

{Based on the *Miracle of Metaphysical Healing* by Evelyn M. Monahan, *The Infinite Way by Joel Goldsmith*, my Guru-dev Paramahansa Yogananda, and the work of my professor Dr. Paul Leon Masters.}

You must continuously engage in the battle for positivity in your life because the world is bound to convince you how inadequate and unsuccessful you are. Watch any television commercial.

Biochemically the breath you breathe in contains oxygen and the energy of aerobic processing. The breath you breathe out contains carbon dioxide - the biochemical waste product of aerobics.

Metaphysically, you breathe in the life force of the Universe, or more simply you inhale the Universe itself. Likewise, when you exhale, you breathe out the Universe and your energetic contribution to its never-ending cycle of life. That same contribution is then breathed in by green plants everywhere; they too, take in the Universe and then provide their tribute back to the Universe.

You breathe-in life; you breathe-out life. Trees breathe-in life and breathe-out life. You are surrounded by life; the entire planet is simply a single life. A living breathing planet organized precisely as is necessary for it to live. Consider a honeybee, flower, and hive. Are they not one single unit of life? You and the tree are one single unit of life. There is no separation except as has been formed by generations of thoughts in our ego-based minds.

As you breathe in what happens to your breath inside your body? What's different when you breathe out? What is left inside? What is exhausted to the outside from the inside? Does the inside change? Does the outside change? Does the Universe change?

What is breath relative to the Universe? What are you actually breathing in and exhaling out? Isn't it the Universe? What are you to the Universe? Are you part of the Universe? Or separate? How about your body? Your mind? Your Soul?

The way we label, categorize, and name with thoughts and words drives deeper wedges of separation; yet looking at planet Earth from light-years away you'd see but one single life. That life is no more or less than each of the 50 trillion individually living cells of your body.

Purpose of Prayer

Yes, God does know what we need before we ask - however - ***if we do not ask***, then *no force puts God's power into motion*. Prayer, affirmation, visualization puts the healing power of the Universe into action. Without it, the power sits idle like a battery in a drawer.

Four Different States of Meditation

- A light state of meditation
- A deep state of meditation
- A formal state of mindfulness
- An informal state of mindfulness

A. If asked to enter a "*light state*" *of meditation,* simply perform steps 1 through 4 below, and be open to taking instruction from an outside source. Be able to focus and concentrate on the task at hand - it is essential that you remain available with two-way communication from the physical world.

B. If asked to enter a ***deep state of meditation***, you will perform steps 1 through 4 with the intention of going deeper and deeper inside yourself. Your concentration and focus will be on something specific such as God or your Soul.

C. A ***formal state of mindfulness***. In a formal state of mindfulness, you will complete steps 1 through 4 with the intention of watching what happens with your thoughts as you try to concentrate on something in the present moment such as your breath or an emotion. The exercise is always to notice your thought, let it go without judgment or criticism, and then return gently to your point of focus again commonly your breath sometimes an emotion.

D. ***An informal state of mindfulness*** - you can complete the applicable parts of steps 1 through 4 with any necessary modifications to make your practice safe and practical. For example - you wouldn't need to find a place to sit if you're going to do a walking meditation or brush your teeth or wash the dishes.

Meditative States and Healing Treatments

Entering a State of Meditation - Steps 1-4. Healing Treatments - Steps 1-9.

Substitute the appropriate healing treatment steps 5 and 6 based on your week's assignment or special needs.

1) Find a place that is quiet and physically, emotionally, and spiritually uncluttered. When possible, perform all of your formal spiritual practices in this place. There will be occasions when your practice is urgent, and in those situations, you must make do with what's available. Obviously, your informal practices will be done in a place and time that fits what you are learning.

2) Compose a stable and sturdy sitting position on the edge of a bed, armless chair, or on the floor. Like a mountain, create a firm supported base in a posture that you can maintain comfortably and without distraction for the planned duration of your sit. Keep your back erect and vertical while your chin is level to the floor. Begin to relax your entire body as you gaze slightly upward toward the point between your eyebrows. Keep your hands in a comfortable position on your thighs or on your lap and begin to breathe calmly.

3) Say to yourself,

   a) "I now take a few minutes to turn inward to my innermost self and to the very center and nucleus of my mind, where I can tap into the Universal Intelligence and Source of All Things."

   b) Take notice of your breathing as you inhale and exhale through your nose. Notice the sensation of fresh air on your nose and upper lip on an inhale and the warmer air on your exhale. If necessary, you can draw some air through pursed lips - but most of your breathing should be through your nose. Relax and focus all of your awareness and attention on your breath.

4) When you are ready,

   a) Expel all air from your lungs and slowly and steadily begin to inhale through your nose while visualizing the center and nucleus part of your mind.

   b) Once you have located your center, continue to inhale slowly and deeply while imagining the journey, the life-giving breath of the Universe travels through your lungs, heart, arteries, capillaries, and veins to each of your 50 trillion cells.

   c) Then have the energy of your breath concentrate in the nucleus of your mind.

    d) Then exhale slowly and release all tension in your core muscles.

    e) Repeat this breathing three times, coming to a state of complete but energized relaxation of mind and body.

    f) Realize the energy of your mind.

5) This is interchangeable and focused on healing

6) This is interchangeable based on number five

7) (After completing steps 5 and 6) Breathe deeply

    a) Press out your belly with your diaphragm as you inhale.

    b) Feel the tingling sensations of energy in your body and completely relax your core muscles as you exhale.

    c) Take 3 full slow diaphragmatic breaths and slip into the state of total relaxation of mind-body-soul.

8) Sit for at least one minute enjoying the contentment of sobriety.

9) When you're ready, get up and carry on with your day knowing that all healing has already taken place.

Rev. Dr. Robert Hobbs
The Realization of Stainless Souls
www.StainlessSouls.com

Healing Treatment One and Two

Detox and Physical

Substitute in Step 5 Above

I turn my attention to my innermost self, to that place in my mind where I have just concentrated the energy of the Universe. From this very nucleus of my energized mind where the Infinite Power of my Higher Self and the Universe resides, I command that I be totally, completely, and forever cured of the addiction to narcotics and freed from the evil of active addiction that kidnaps my mind and body.

I direct, with the Presence and Divine Will of the Universe that my mind and body, be restored to a state of perfect health, and that any desires and attachments not in harmony with the perfect health of my mind and body be permanently evicted from my being.

The Presence of God in the center of my being is active now in providing perfect health to me.

The same power that has healed my addiction is working now to eliminate all fears and resentments while restoring to perfect harmony all of my emotions and emotional relationships. I am grateful that not only has the health of my mind and body been restored but the quality of my life and the relationships in it have been reconciled to Perfect Harmony. I give thanks, I let it be so, and so it is.

Substitute In Step 6 Above

Imagine now in your mind's eye, that point between your eyebrows, that you are living free from addiction and the damage it has caused you. Picture what it looks like to prosper without any drug use whatsoever. Picture yourself clean and sober at family events, weddings, and holiday parties. Listen to your friends and family complimenting you on your successes:

"It's so great that you are free of drugs and alcohol. We are also very proud of you."

Feel the emotions of having success in your life as you continue to breathe the power and life-giving energy of the Universe.

Healing Treatment Three

Mental/Intellectual

Substitute In Step 5 Above

Once again say to yourself,

"I now again turn my thoughts inward to my innermost self, to that place that I consider the very center of my mind."

As you continue to breathe normally, begin to imagine that you are surrounded by calm blue or indigo light. Everything around you is a gentle hue of calming blue. As you breathe in, visualize that the air is the power of the Universe, that it contains a pleasing shade of blue, and that that blue light energy is being transported throughout your body.

Every cell begins to calm down and relaxes as the relaxing blue energy of the Universe spreads further and further through your body and mind. You can feel your muscles letting go of all stress and tension as their cells are drenched in the peaceful blue energy of the Universe. The sphere of blue energy takes residence in the very center, the very nucleus of your mind, allowing your entire being to let go. Let go and settle to a place of complete serenity, tranquility, and peace.

Substitute in Step 6 above

Sit with completely stress-free contentment and continue to let all of your tension dissolve into the gentle blue light that you have invited into the center of your mind. After a few moments visualize your friends and family around you complimenting you for your calm and stress-free demeanor:

"You have become so calm and centered and peaceful; you really look happy!"

Acknowledge your new-found peace and show your gratitude,

"I am grateful for the peace and serenity that has entered my life, I let it be so, and so it is."

Healing Treatment Four

Relationships/Emotions

Substitute In Step 5 Above

Say to yourself,

"I once again turn my attention to my innermost self, to the very center of my being, to that place where I continuously emerge from, with every breath I breathe in the healing Grace of the Universe."

Think of each breath as being filled with the healing forgiving Grace of the Universe. Feel Divine forgiveness washing over every cell of your body, cleansing you from all harms you may have caused. Every cell, every thought, every memory, every bone, every muscle, every organ, of your body is completely drenched in the forgiving Grace of the Universe that you breathe in with each and every breath. And now, as you begin to feel fully forgiven by Universal Forgiveness begin to look outward. Begin to collect and then send that same compassionate forgiveness to all who may have harmed you. Visualize each person and their expression as they receive Divine mercy through you as it is channeled through you to them.

Hear yourself saying,

"I have been forgiven by the Absolute Grace of the Universe: I have forgiven myself for all the shame and guilt I carry, and the heavy burdens have been lifted. I now share with you the same power of forgiveness that forgave me. I forgive you for all the activities I perceived as having wronged to me. I share this healing energy with you in the hope your pains will be lifted as my anxieties have been lifted. I am confident this forgiveness is Universal. One day you may find it's powerful enough for you to forgive me for all that I've done that has harmed you. I am deeply sorry for having wronged you. I love you.

Continue breathing in the forgiving energy of the Universe; add *your forgiveness* to that energy and then breathe it outward sharing the combined forgiveness with everyone and everything.

Substitute In Step 6 Above

While continuing to breathe, listen as your friends and loved ones respond to your offer of Universal forgiveness:

"I am impressed with your courage, and I accept your apology. I forgive you for everything, and I'm grateful for your forgiveness. I welcome your friendship and love. I love you too."

Then return to your breathing and gently acknowledge this gift of forgiveness.

"I'm grateful for this Divine gift of forgiveness. I let it be so, and so it is."

Healing Treatment Five

Spiritual Healing

Substitute In Step 5 Above

Once again say to yourself,

"I now turn my concentration toward my innermost self, to the very center of my being."

Breathe the energy of the Universe into your lungs and trace its path as it moves through your body and concentrates at the center or nucleus of your mind. This energy is pure white light. Not white light that you can see with your eyes but the light that was brought into the Universe at the time of the Big Bang - at the beginning of creation when God said out loud,

"Let there be light."

The pure creative light of the Universe you breathe in with every breath and concentrate it at the nucleus of your mind. The pure brilliant light that electrocutes and cauterizes any diseases, dis-eases, impurities, corruptions, contaminations, or other imperfections in the cells of your body as it is continuously absorbed as the force of life.

This pure light is pure life, it is the life of the Universe, and it flows through your body and through each of your 50 trillion cells. Breathe it in along with the pure white light of creation. This pure life carried by the pure white light carries with it, love. The pure love of the Universe that binds all of nature together as one. Inhale, take what you need from the Universe; exhale, contribute what you must as an integral part of the Universal life cycle.

Every cell, on every breath, is bathed in the pure white light of creation, and in the pure life energy and in the pure love of the Universe, and of its Creator. Breathe it in; feel it as it enters your body and travels through every cell. Feel the healing power spread from the nucleus of your mind and outward to all the cells of your body and outward even further so that you are surrounded by a protective aura of Pure White, Loving, Life-Giving Light. Briefly say aloud,

"I feel the light, life, and love the Universe pulsing in all 50 trillion cells of my body.

Consider that light, as you consider the light in yourself, as the same light that is in each and every other human.

"Om, Om, Om, Shanti, Shanti, Shanti, Peace, Amen.

Substitute In Step 6 Above

As you continue to inhale the light, life, and love of the Universe, visualize your interactions with friends and family. When most surrounded by the purity of this aura hear them recognize:

"You look so full of energy and life today; when you are near me, I feel so safe and surrounded by love,"

and then recognize the gift of this energy by saying,

"I am grateful for the realization of the light, life, and love energy in and around me, and I let it be so, and so it is!"

Rev. Dr. Robert Hobbs
The Realization of Stainless Souls
www.StainlessSouls.com

Healing Treatment Six

Lifestyle

Substitute In Step 5 Above

Once again say to yourself aloud,

"I'll turn my attention to my innermost self, the very center of my being, to the nucleus from which I continuously emerge."

and then say the following to yourself

"Through the power of Universal Intelligence coursing through my cells and concentrated in the center nucleus of my mind, the infinite abundance of the Universe is present and available within me now. It is the will of God present within me coupled with the Universal energy of my mind, that I now claim all of the financial resources necessary for my family and me to live comfortably without stress or worry now and forever."

Substitute In Step 6 Above

Visualize you and your family secure in the knowledge that financial stress and worry will never affect your lives again.

Listen to your friends and family as I congratulate you:

"You have really done great for yourself and your family. We are so proud of how well you have tended to your family's financial needs and security."

And then recognize and appreciate your prosperity by saying,

"For the prosperity granted me from the abundance of the Universe I give thanks, I let it be so, and so it is.

Healing Treatment Seven

Healing for Immunity and Defense

Substitute In Step 5 Above

"I now turn to my innermost self and reflect on my spiritual practices that are resulting in lesser exposure to the people, events, thoughts, and triggers that used to excite the formerly active addiction in me. Though I continue to do my best to avoid relapse triggers, I may from time to time encounter temptations. Therefore, with the Divine Presence within me and in coordination with His will for my life, I command my mind, energized with the power of the Universe, to build a defensive moat around my sobriety and serenity, so that never again shall I live in fear of relapse but rather with the light of His love. With the power of this Universal Mind within me, I face all obstacles and adversity with confidence and courage, knowing that I am divinely protected from all that may harm me.

Substitute In Step 6 Above

Visualize yourself in a situation where you can confidently navigate life's challenges without fear of relapse. Listen to your friends, and loved ones express their pride for you -

"I am so happy you could attend this party without fear of losing your sobriety. You really are safe from relapse."

I am grateful, I let it be so, and so it is.

Rev. Dr. Robert Hobbs
The Realization of Stainless Souls
www.StainlessSouls.com

Healing Treatment Eight (Can use as 1 and 2)

Physical and Body

Substitute In Step 5 Above

"I now turn inward once again to the very center and nucleus of my mind. I channel the pure light, the pure life, and the pure love of the Universe to immediately penetrate, energize, and revitalize every cell of my physical body. Any disease, irritation, inflammation, corruption in any part of my body is quickly replaced with new, youthful, and perfect cells. Every bone, muscle, and tissue in my body is in excellent health and perfect harmony with each other. My heart, lungs, and blood vessels are in perfect condition and in perfect synchronicity, distributing the life force of the Universe throughout my body. My organs, brain, and nervous system are in perfect order and are even now organizing and reorganizing themselves to support my Divine Purpose in this body. My body makes perfect use of the air I breathe, the water I drink, and the food I consume, and it is at the ideal weight and physical condition for the purpose it serves.

Substitute In Step 6 Above

Visualize living in perfect physical health in the physical body. Listen to your doctor as he tells you, again and again,

"I am so impressed with the condition of your body. Your physical exam results are perfect. Absolutely perfect," and then with gratitude say,

"I give thanks, I let it be so, and so it is."

Healing Treatment Nine

Mental Well-being

Substitute In Step 5 Above

"I turn inward once again and focus in on the Presence of God and His Will for my life at the very center and nucleus of my mind. With the pure light, life, and love the Universe powering every cell of my body and the cosmic creative sound of Om vibrating through all dimensions of my mind, I now direct that all of my mental capacities, including my personal intelligence, intellect, memory, reading, and listening comprehension, learning faculties, as well as the character traits of resilience, persistence, and loyalty be raised to a maximum and optimum level, so that I may best perform the purpose of this lifetime.

Substitute In Step 6 Above

Visualize yourself walking through your daily life with maximum mental faculties while focused on your life purpose. Hear your friends and loved ones as they express their pride,

"You have become such a dedicated and focused person. You always seem to know what you are doing; we are so proud of you."

And then with gratitude say,

For this I give thanks, I let it be so, and so it is.

Rev. Dr. Robert Hobbs
The Realization of Stainless Souls
www.StainlessSouls.com

Healing Treatment Ten

Emotions and Relationships

Substitute In Step 5 Above

"I now once again turn inward and focus the very center or nucleus of my mind on the health and well-being of my feelings and emotions. Having been freed of all shame and guilt by the compassionate forgiveness of the Universe, I now seek, to finally once and for all, to end the misery caused negative emotions, especially fear and anger.

With the power and presence of the Universal God-mind and my higher self, I replace all negative feelings and emotions, especially anger and fear, with the Universal emotion of love for all, of, and in, this Universe. No longer shall I succumb to my reactions to circumstances that previously caused pain and suffering for myself and those I love.

Further, now that my higher mind is in synch with the higher God-mind in the center of my being, I now permanently remove the negative emotions from my being, while empowered by the forgiveness granted to me and all beings and am ready and willing to fully amend for my past behavior and to restore all relationships to a state of mutual and Divine Universal love.

Substitute In Step 6 Above

Visualize yourself living a life free from the grips of fear and anger. You've already been freed from shame and guilt, and now you can release all fear and anger and walk in confidence as a fully restored member of the Universe. Hear your friends and family as they appreciate you

"We are so impressed with how well you manage your emotions. You seem so stable, so calm. We are so proud of you."

And then with gratitude say, "I give thanks, I let it be so, and so it is.

Healing Treatment Eleven

Spiritual Well-being

Substitute In Step 5 Above

I now once again turn inward to my innermost self into the very nucleus of my mind from which I as a spiritual being continuously emerge from the pure light, pure life, pure love, of the Universe.

Having realized myself to be _a form,_ condensed from the original light and sound energy of the Universe, I now settle and calm the stormy sea of my human thoughts; as the water clears, I realize that I am a perfect reflection of the absolute Creator of the manifested Universe. As I perceive myself in the image of God, I also realize, that each of my human brothers and sisters is also perfectly reflected images of God and therefore are also perfectly reflected images of me. I see myself in all of creation as I see God in all of creation.

Substitute In Step 6 Above

Visualize yourself with a calm and thoughtless mind and as a child of God created in His image. Hear yourself as you speak aloud the words of God's creation:

"Om, Om, Om, Shanti, Shanti, Shanti, Peace, Amen, and

then to yourself say with gratitude,

"I give thanks, I let it be so, and so it is.

Rev. Dr. Robert Hobbs
The Realization of Stainless Souls
www.StainlessSouls.com

Healing Treatment Twelve

Lifestyle, Abundance, Prosperity 2

Substitute In Step 5 Above

I now once again turn inward to the centermost part of my being and recognize now that though all material abundance is available to me as a child of God that I find most peace and tranquility when not desirous or attached to the typical symbols of successful living.

I consciously choose to live my life with only the minimal material items for my happiness and only while performing the essential level of work in order to acquire those minimal items. With the power of my energized mind and the Presence of God within me, I commit to living the rest of my lifetime by the guiding principles of minimalism and essentialism as is appropriate for my true happiness.

Substitute In Step 6 Above

Visualize yourself living a life free of the desire for material items that failed to serve you and free of the attachment to the things you possess. Imagine the freedom you will feel when you can do the work you love without the anxiety of maintaining or keeping the stuff society has convinced you that you need. Hear your friends and loved ones as they express their pride in your lifestyle

"I'm so proud of you; you're doing the work you love, and living the life that is meant for you to live. You seem to be so contented with your life. Keep it up."

And then with gratitude say to yourself,

"I give thanks, I let it be so, and so it is.

Healing Treatment Thirteen

Immunity and Defense

Substitute In Step 5 Above

I turn once more inward to the center nucleus in my mind in this the final week of the 13-week commitment I made myself more than 90 days ago. It is with great gratitude that I have progressed so far and have improved all areas of my life, including:

- My body,
- My mind,
- My spirit,
- My emotions,
- My lifestyle, and
- My immunities,

And that I know how to defend this progress by continuing to improve along these lines each and every day for the rest of my life.

And so, with the energy of light, life, and love of the Universe in me I reinforce and defend the moat I've built around my serenity and sobriety, but now I include all of me because now all of me is worth protecting.

Substitute In Step 6 Above

Again, visualize yourself walking through life wholly composed and confident that you now know who you are and why you're here you're neither angry or fearful about your future you are eternally protected by who and what you are. Be grateful and say to yourself, "For that I give thanks, I let it be so, and so it is."

Rev. Dr. Robert Hobbs
The Realization of Stainless Souls
www.StainlessSouls.com

Notes and Sketches

Affirmations for 30-minute walks

Based on incantations by Tony Robbins as taught in *Get the Edge*.

1. All I need is within me now.
2. All the help I need is within me now.
3. All the love I need is within me now.
4. All the hope I need is within me now.
5. All the joy I need is within me now.
6. All the wealth I need is within me now.
7. All the confidence I need is within me now.

8. All the courage I need is within me now.
9. All the family I need is within me now.
10. All the support I need is within me now.
11. All the faith I need is within me now.
12. All the intelligence I need is within me now.
13. All the serenity I need is within me now.
14. All the energy I need is within me now.

15. All the tranquility I need is within me now.
16. All the strength I need is within me now.
17. All the resolve I need is within me now.
18. All the power I need is within me now.
19. All the pride I need is within me now.
20. All the prosperity I need is within me now.
21. All the creativity I need is within me now.

22. All the peace I need is within me now.
23. All the compassion I need is within me now.
24. All the vitality I need is within me now.
25. All the clarity I need is within me now.
26. All the ingenuity I need is within me now.
27. All the generosity I need is within me now.
28. All the certainty I need is within me now.

29. All the variety I need is within me now.
30. All the security I need is within me now.
31. All the challenge I need is within me now.
32. All the skill I need is within me now.
33. All the wisdom I need is within me now.
34. All the fairness I need is within me now.
35. All the growth I need is within me now.

36. All the connection I need is within me now.
37. All the stability I need is within me now.
38. All the change I need is within me now.
39. All the adversity I need is within me now.
40. All the knowledge I need is within me now.
41. All the justice I need is within me now.
42. All the education I need is within me now.

43. All the significance I need is within me now.
44. All the resources I need are within me now.
45. All the time I need is within me now.
46. All the influence I need is within me now.
47. All the spirituality I need is within me now.
48. All the kindness I need is within me now.
49. All the smiles I need are within me now.

Rev. Dr. Robert Hobbs
The Realization of Stainless Souls
www.StainlessSouls.com

50. All the abundance I need is within me now.
51. All the organization I need is within me now.
52. All the shelter I need is within me now.
53. All the realization I need is within me now.
54. All the empathy I need is within me now.
55. All the bravery I need is within me now.
56. All the inspiration I need is within me now.

57. All the advantage I need is within me now.
58. All the comprehension I need is within me now.
59. All the passion I need is within me now.
60. All the life-energy I need is within me now.
61. All the health I need is within me now.
62. All the talent I need is within me now.
63. All the restraint I need is within me now.

64. All the enthusiasm I need is within me now.
65. All the fundamentals I need are within me now.
66. All the satisfaction I need is within me now.
67. All the belief I need is within me now.
68. All the forgiveness I need is within me now.
69. All the adventure I need is within me now.
70. All the relationships I need are within me now.

71. All the devotion I need is within me now.
72. All the words I need are within me now.
73. All the achievement I need is within me now.
74. All the humility I need is within me now.
75. All the charity I need is within me now.
76. All the prayer I need is within me now.
77. All the recognition I need is within me now.

78. All the sympathy I need is within me now.
79. All the literacy I need is within me now.
80. All the accomplishment I need is within me now.
81. All the surrender I need is within me now.
82. All the harmony I need is within me now.
83. All the relaxation I need is within me now.
84. All the value I need is within me now.

85. All the ability I need is within me now.
86. All the vision I need is within me now.
87. All the persuasion I need is within me now.
88. All the character I need is within me now.
89. All the charm I need is within me now.
90. All the charisma I need is within me now.
91. All the composure I need is within me now.
92. All the poise I need is within me now.

Wellness Check Bubble Chart - Morning

Physical Wellness Scores - Morning

Mental Wellness Scores - Morning

Emotional Wellness Scores - Morning

Relational Wellness Scores - Morning

Spiritual Wellness Scores - Morning

Lifestyle Wellness Scores - Morning

Immunity & Defense Wellness Scores - Morning

Rev. Dr. Robert Hobbs
The Realization of Stainless Souls
www.StainlessSouls.com

Wellness Check Bubble Chart - Evening

Physical Wellness Scores - Evening

Mental Wellness Scores - Evening

Emotional Wellness Scores - Evening

Relational Wellness Scores - Evening

Spiritual Wellness Scores - Evening

Lifestyle Wellness Scores - Evening

Immunity & Defense Wellness Scores - Evening

Meeting Attendance Log

No	Date	Group Name or Location	Signature or Stamp
1			
2			
3			
4			
5			
6			
7			
8			
9			
10			
11			
12			
13			
14			
15			
16			
17			
18			
19			
20			
21			
22			
23			
24			
25			
26			
27			
28			
29			
30			

Rev. Dr. Robert Hobbs
The Realization of Stainless Souls
www.StainlessSouls.com

Meeting Attendance Log

No	Date	Group Name or Location	Signature or Stamp
31			
32			
33			
34			
35			
36			
37			
38			
39			
40			
41			
42			
43			
44			
45			
46			
47			
48			
49			
50			
51			
52			
53			
54			
55			
56			
57			
58			
59			
60			

Meeting Attendence Log

No	Date	Group Name or Location	Signature or Stamp
61			
62			
63			
64			
65			
66			
67			
68			
69			
70			
71			
72			
73			
74			
75			
76			
77			
78			
79			
80			
81			
82			
83			
84			
85			
86			
87			
88			
89			
90			

Rev. Dr. Robert Hobbs
The Realization of Stainless Souls
www.StainlessSouls.com

Service Activity Tracking Bubble Chart

Service Log 1-45	
Other Service	
Other Service	
Other Service	
Teach Topic	
Buy NC Big Book	
Buy NC Coffee	
Meet Newcomers	
Chair Meeting	
Show Meditation	
Listen 100%	
Drive Others	
Tear-Down	
Set-up	
Clean-up	
Greet	
Smile	
Hold Door	
Make B'Fast	
Make Coffee	
Make Bed	

1 2 3 4 5 6 7 8 9 10 11 12 13 14 15 16 17 18 19 20 21 22 23 24 25 26 27 28 29 30 31 32 33 34 35 36 37 38 39 40 41 42 43 44 45

Service Log 46-91	
Other Service	
Other Service	
Other Service	
Teach Topic	
Buy NC Big Book	
Buy NC Coffee	
Meet Newcomers	
Chair Meeting	
Show Meditation	
Listen 100%	
Drive Others	
Tear-Down	
Set-up	
Clean-up	
Greet	
Smile	
Hold Door	
Make B'Fast	
Make Coffee	
Make Bed	

46 47 48 49 50 51 52 53 54 55 56 57 58 59 60 61 62 63 64 65 66 67 68 69 70 71 72 73 74 75 76 77 78 79 80 81 82 83 84 85 86 87 88 89 90 91

Appendix 1

The remainder of this preface is from a paper I wrote on this topic earlier this year.

Adopted from the author's Doctoral Dissertation:

AN INTRODUCTION TO A THEOCENTRIC PSYCHOLOGY SOLUTION TO AMERICA'S MENTAL HEALTH CRISIS

This dissertation claims that current mental health treatment modalities, traditions, and infrastructure, including the number of and skill level of therapists, psychologists, and psychiatrists, are inadequate in addressing the scale and complexity of the multiple mental health crises they are sanctioned to resolve for our society, and therefore proposes that a home-based, Theocentric program of recovery and realization for the millions of souls suffering from afflictions such as: PTSD, Opioid Addiction, Co-dependence, Suicidal Ideation, and Homelessness.

If we make a few underlying assumptions, we can get an idea of how big this problem is. Let us assume there are 60 million people afflicted with at least one of these conditions of PTSD, addiction, codependency, suicidal ideation, and homelessness. Let us assume that to have full remission of these conditions each client would require 50 hours of 1-on-1 therapy with a doctoral-level psychologist or psychiatrist for a total of 3 billion hours of professional care. These 3 billion hours would equate to 1 hour of therapy per week for one calendar year for each client. There are 94,000 practicing psychologists and 28,000 practicing psychiatrists for a rough total of 125,000 combined. Dividing the three billion hours by the 125,000 therapists yields 24,000 hours/doctor. Provided each practicing physician works 40 hours per week for 50 weeks per year and all 40 hours are allocated to 1-on-1 individual therapy, it would take 12 years to bring these 60 million clients into remission. That is assuming 100% success and no relapses. Readers should note that therapists do not see patients 100% of the time; more realistically they see clients 50% of the time. So, it is more likely to take 24 years to bring these 60 million clients into remission assuming a 100% success rate and no relapses.

Readers might suggest that hospitals should be used to lighten the load on these psychologists and psychiatrists. There are 38,000 psychiatric hospital beds in the United States (Becker's Hospital Review n.p.). If the average stay to help one of these afflicted persons enter full remission was just 30 days, it would take 132 years to treat the 60 million patients. Where do 30 days come from readers might ask? The standard duration of residential treatment for substance use disorder clients is 30 days. Further, the standard of care for overeating disorders is 30 days.

Still, readers might suggest that only the addicted require 30 days of inpatient treatment - okay, fine. The number of addicted is 20 million (not including alcoholics). So, we cut 131 years to 43 years and treat only the addicted; we are still left with 40 million non-addicted suffering without any hospitalization at all. I will take this opportunity to point out that current recovery rates for opioid addiction are roughly 13% and most experts tout an overall recovery rate of 40 to 60% for cumulative substance use disorders. This means that in order to heal the 20 million addicted, we are going to have to treat most of them twice. Now the 43 years is 65 to 80 years. We do have the advantage that 72,000 of these potential clients die every year - so maybe something less than 65 years should be the estimate.

Treatment Modalities and Traditions

There are many new treatment modalities that have evidence-based successes.

Regardless of their potential for success, these newer modalities are still steeped in the traditions of psychoanalysis where faulty thoughts, emotions, and behaviors are sought and then modified to fit in with the modern society.

They are still built on talk therapy and require hours and hours of individual one-on-one work.

Rev. Dr. Robert Hobbs
The Realization of Stainless Souls
www.StainlessSouls.com

It does not matter if these modalities are better performing or not, because they all still require professional service hours.

We need new modalities that either work with less than 1-hour sessions weekly or better yet, we need modalities that work instantly! If we cannot find more efficient modalities, then we are going to need far, far more therapists and hospitals.

The afflictions we are concerned with are complex mental and emotional disorders that are generally the result of difficult life circumstances in an unforgiving society. Most of the afflicted were not born this way - they became this way. In nearly all of these cases there are dual and tri-diagnoses where general anxiety disorder and minor depressive disorder are compounded issues supporting the primary diagnosis. These issues require treatment from the best and brightest and most educated and skilled therapists. Run of the mill will not do. While we are focusing on the problems presented by these 5 complex conditions, there are still people who need help with: family and marriage counselling, bi- and multi-personality disorders, schizophrenias, ADD, learning disabilities, general anxiety, minor depressive, and a variety of other mental and emotional health disorders. Readers should begin to realize that we are overwhelmed.

Inadequate Training and Therapist's Skill Level

A recent article from Scientific American references a recent report from the American Association of Suicidology (AAS) that: only 50% of psychology training programs, less than 25% of social work programs, and only 6% of marriage and family therapy programs, teach their students how to spot individuals at risk for suicide and how to prevent them from attempting it (qtd. in Scientific American n.p.). When I first came across these numbers, I was shocked. It seems that the most significant mental health disorder is suicidal ideation and therefore it ought to be taught first and most often to those seeking a career in mental health. Then I recalled my own experiences with PTSD. The first two therapists I visited had no idea what to do with me. I was talking about things that they had no experience dealing with.

A few years later I began working with PTSD afflicted combat vets. Their stories are so horrific they are hard to believe; they are even harder to hear. There are very few human beings equipped to build relationships with and then safely and successfully treat many of the forms of PTSD - especially those that are combat or sexual trauma related.

So even if we had the proper numbers of therapists to deal with the volume of mental health issues we currently face, the skill levels for suicidal ideation and trauma are evidently lacking.

Here are some more statistics:

- 33% of those who commit suicide were in contact with a mental health professional in the 12 months before death - 20% within the month before!

- Further, even though primary care physicians prescribe 50% or more of all psychotropic drugs,

- 77% of those who commit suicide had contact with their primary care physician within the 12 months preceding their death - 45% in the last month (Scientific American n.p.).

These physicians are not responsible for the death of their patients, but perhaps some of the losses could have been prevented if there had been risk identification training and intervention skills.

For the conditions contemplated in this paper, rapport is an essential early element in the healing process. It is challenging for rapport to develop when the patient suspects that not only has the therapist never been in a similar situation as the patient (i.e. combat or rape) - but they have never dealt with a similar patient before. We (the patients) begin to feel as if we are wasting our time talking to people about our difficulties when they possess no understanding of what to do with us. They have little empathy for the fact that talking at all - for us - takes an awful lot of effort - it is tough.

The Psychiatrist Shortage

There are 28,000 psychiatrists in the United States with 60% practicing at 55 years old or older. Part of the problem is that mental health care is not a profitable service line for individuals or hospitals where more defined specialties such as Cardiology and Orthopedics are more profitable. Despite the shortage in psychiatrists, 1 in 6 of all Americans are prescribed antipsychotic drugs (Forbes n.p.).

In an article dated October 23rd, 2017, New American Economy reported that more than 40% of Americans who experience some form of mental illness - 60 million people - will go untreated - primarily due to an understaffing in Psychiatry.

The NAE article also states that 60% of American counties are without a single psychiatrist, and that one-third of all recent positions were filled by doctors from foreign medical schools, and 25% of all psychiatrists are already over the age of 65 (New American Economy n.p.)! In Atlanta, I was initially placed on a long-term waiting list to see a psychiatrist. Waiting likely would have resulted in my death. Fortunately, there was an influential and persuasive intervention on my behalf.

Americans suffering mental or emotional health issues are likely to wait weeks and even months before seeing a psychiatrist. "We are facing a severe shortage at a time our nation is suffering from acute problems such as opioid addiction, depression, and suicide," says Darrell G Kirch, MD, AAMC president. The article references the Journal of American Medical Association that one in five Americans has some sort of mental health condition and that the disease burden of mental health and addiction disorders was higher than for any other condition.

"Our whole society is affected by untreated mental illness." according to Ann Retzlaff, MD. (AAMC News n.p.).

The Psychologist Shortage

Per the American Psychological Association, there are 94,000 active doctoral or professional psychologists working full-time in the United States. Despite a large number of baby boomer retirements, there was – thankfully - a slight increase in the number of practicing psychologists, indicating an interest in the field from recent undergraduates. Although the median and average age of doctors is still too high, the aging trend may be reversing - unlike the psychiatry population (American Psychological Association n.p.).

It is Not All Bad News

Most Americans seem open to counseling according to the Barna Group. 42% of adults have seen a counselor at least once, and 13% are currently active in counseling. Only 25% report that they would never see a counselor. Hopefully, most of them are healthy. Unfortunately, cost and skill level are the two most important factors when electing to see a counselor, and as we have already suggested, even if the number of professionals was adequate, their skill level is not, especially for the complexity of issues facing our population of afflicted. Interestingly 33% of non-Christians seek treatment for a mental illness where only 15% of practicing Christians do (Barna Group n.p.).

For the population we are interested in with this paper - the problems are complex and expensive. Many of those afflicted with these conditions have lost nearly everything and have also lost much of their social support due to their ruinous behavior.

Ability to Pay

The CDC claims that between 2012 and 2013, the number of Americans in all age groups who had insurance and saw a mental health professional was twice as high as the number of Americans who saw a mental health professional without insurance.

This trend indicates a strong propensity for the ability to pay as a factor in willingness to seek treatment. As stated earlier those we are discussing in this paper are less likely to have the financial means, insurance, or the social support necessary to receive the treatment they need.

Therefore, it is essential to make money a non-factor for them, and thus, make money a non-factor for the providers of care. From this information one could conclude that even if there was sufficient infrastructure and adequate training, most Americans would not seek or receive treatment due to cost (CDC n.p.).

Additional Facts and Figures

- · 6 in 10 Americans have mental health issues and receive no treatment. It is estimated to be 44 million people.

- · 4% of Americans seriously consider suicide - estimated to be 9 million people.

- · 10% of 12 to 17-year-old young people suffer from major depression; 64% of those receive no treatment.

- · Of the youth with severe depression, only 37% receive treatment.

- · Cost continues to be a significant barrier to treatment as well as a lack of insurance and the stigma associated with seeking help. Access to treatment usually results in good outcomes (goodtherapy.org n.p.)

New Modalities

Psychology Today contributor, Dr. Stephen Hoffman, Ph.D. writes that progress in psychotherapy research has been slow. Although the cognitive revolution of the 70s and 80s brought new evidence-based treatment, the traditional psychoanalytic methods are still widely used in the United States and remain dominant across the globe. There are many reasons for this including financial issues, the dominance of 'traditional psychiatry,' and a reduced incentive structure to use new modalities (Psychology Today n.p.).

The average cost of residential treatment for eating disorders is $30,000 for a 30-day residential program - $1,000 per day. My experience says that the average cost for a substance use disorder residential treatment is $30,000 for 30 days or $1,000 per day (Saybrook University n.p.).

This paper opened with a statement – the first half of which is shared again here:

This dissertation claims that current mental health treatment modalities, traditions, and infrastructure, including the number of and skill level of therapists, psychologists, and psychiatrists, are inadequate in addressing the scale and complexity of the multiple mental health crises they are sanctioned to resolve for our society.

It should be clear to readers, based on the information provided so far, that our current infrastructure and systems cannot handle the scale and complexities associated with the afflictions contemplated here. Further, it should be evident, that we could not build any meaningful remedy for our situation in a timeframe that would be just for those suffering today and dying tomorrow. Therefore, the afflicted discussed in this paper would be better served by an effective out-patient or home-based recovery program as sufficient residential inpatient facilities do not exist.

It was with this information in mind that we designed the BBBC Recovery Systems and Planners. Here is what to look for from our work:

- · Location Agnostic – you don't have to go anywhere

- · Doctor independent – but you should have a doctor

- · Extended duration 90 days vs. 30

- · Skill Level Agnostic – you don't have to have an advanced degree; but you do have to read – a lot!

- Ability to Pay Agnostic – the price of a book and all revenue goes to fund non-profit services

- Flexibility to work and stay at home – this requires 3-5 hours of commitment per day. Probably the amount of time you were high or drunk.

- Easily Integrated to Existing Residential and Intensive Outpatient Programs

- Flexible Platform that can be easily shared, improved, and re-engineered

- Easily compatible and integrate-able with emerging technology trends

- Distribution Platform for the latest books and multi-media in treatment and spirituality

- All revenues support this non-profit work on an ongoing basis.

Works Cited

Addiction Statistics. AddictionCenters.com. Web.
https://www.addictioncenter.com/addiction/addiction-statistics/

Alcoholics Anonymous. *The Big Book of Alcoholics Anonymous*. New York: Alcoholics Anonymous World Services, Inc. 2013. Kindle Edition.

--- *Twelve Steps and Twelve Traditions*. New York: Alcoholics Anonymous World Services, Inc. 2013. Kindle Edition.

Americans Feel Good About Counseling. Barna Group. February 27th, 2018. Web.

Amid shortage, Number of Psychiatric Beds in US Down 13% from 2010. Becker's Hospital Review. August 2nd, 2016. Web.

Bernstein, Gabrielle. *The Universe Has Your Back: Transform Fear to Faith*. New York: Hay House. 2016. Kindle Edition.

CDC Quick Stats: Percentage of Adults Aged 18 to 64 Years Old Who Have Seen or Talked with a Mental Health Professional in the Past 12 Months. CDC. Centers for Disease Control and Prevention. MMWR. 27 Feb 2015. Web.

Chapman, Gary. *The 5 Love Languages: The Secret to Love that Lasts*. Chicago: Northfield Publishing. 2010. Kindle Edition.

Cost and Duration of Treatment. Saybrook University. Web.
https://www.saybrook.edu/blog/2011/05/22/05-22-11/

Covey, Stephen. *The Seven Habits of Highly Effective People*. Salt Lake City: FranklinCovey. 2015. Ebook.

Dass, Ram. *Polishing the Mirror: How to Live from Your Spiritual Heart*. Boulder, CO.: Sounds True. 2013. Kindle Edition.

Desmond, Matthew. *Evicted*. New York: Crown/Archetype. 2016. Kindle Edition.

Dyer, Wayne. *Change Your Thoughts, Change Your Life: Living the Wisdom of the Tao*. New York: Hay House. 2007. Print.

Goldsmith, Joel, S. *The Infinite Way*. Long Boat Key, FL: Acropolis Books, Inc. 2013. Kindle Edition

Milburn, Joshua Fields and Nicodemus, Ryan. *Minimalism: Live a Meaningful Life*. Missoula, MT: Asymmetrical Press. 2011. Print.

Hill, Napoleon. *Think and Grow Rich*. New Delhi, India: General Press. 2016. Kindle Edition.

Hill, Napoleon, and Stone, W. Clement. *Success Through a Positive Mental Attitude*. New York: Pocket Books. 1977. Print

Hoffman, Stephen G., Ph.D. *Some Differences Between Traditional and New Therapies*. Psychology Today. April 20th, 2017. Web.

Hobbs, Jr. Robert L. *Heroin Living and Dying with an Addict You Love, How to Survive When Everyone Dies*. Atlanta: Paduka Press. 2017. Kindle Edition.

--- *An Introduction To A Theocentric Psychology Solution To America's Mental Health Crisis*. Sedona: University of Sedona. 2019. Print

Jackson, Bruce. *Psychiatrist Shortage Escalates as US Mental Health Needs Grow*. Forbes. February 25th, 2018. Web.

King, Will. *Mental Health Trends in America 2016*. Goodtherapy.org. January 11th, 2016. Web.

Lin, Luona; Stamm, Karen; and Christidis, Peggy. *Demographics of the U.S. psychology workforce: Findings from the 2007-16 American Community Survey*. Washington, DC: American Psychological Association. 2018. Web.

Masters, Dr. Paul Leon. *The Theocentric Way of Life; Doctor of Theocentric Psychology Degree Program*. Sedona: University of Sedona. 2013. PDF

Monahan, Evelyn, M. *The Miracle of Metaphysical Healing,* West Nyack, New York: Parker Publishing Company. 1975. Print.

McKeon, Greg. *Essentialism: The Disciplined Pursuit of Less.* New York: Currency. 2014. Print.

Ortner, Nick. *The Tapping Solution: A Revolutionary System for Stress-Free Living*. New York: Hay House. 2013. Kindle Edition.

National Institute on Drug Abuse

--- Number of Illicit Drug Users. Web. **https://www.drugabuse.gov/publications/drugfacts/nationwide-trends**

--- Number of Overdoses. Web. **https://www.drugabuse.gov/related-topics/trends-statistics/overdose-death-rates**

---*Understanding Drug Abuse and Addiction: What Science Says*. Duration of Treatment. Web. **https://www.drugabuse.gov/publications/teaching-packets/understanding-drug-abuse-addiction/section-iii/6-duration-treatment**

New Study Shows 60% of United States Counties without a Single Psychiatrist. New American Economy. October 23rd, 2017. Web.

NIMH. National Institute on Mental Health. Suicide Statistics. Web. **https://www.nimh.nih.gov/health/statistics/suicide.shtml#part_155143**

PTSD. VA. Veteran's Administration. National Center for PTSD. Web. **https://www.ptsd.va.gov/understand/common/common_adults.asp**

Rath, Tom. *Strengths Finder 2.0*. Omaha, NE: Gallup Press. 2013. Kindle Edition

Robbins, Anthony. *Notes from a Friend A Quick and Simple Guide for Taking Charge of Your Life*. New York: Simon and Schuster. 1995. Print.

--- *Personal Power II*. San Diego: Robbins Research International. 1996. Audio Cassette.

--- *Get The Edge*. San Diego: Robbins Research International. 2001. CD Audio.

Singer, Michael. *The Surrender Experiment: My Journey into Life's Perfection*. New York: Harmony Books, 2015. Kindle Edition.

----*The Untethered Soul: A Journey Beyond Yourself*. Oakland, CA: New Harbinger Publications. 2007. Kindle Edition.

State of Homelessness Report. National Alliance to End Homelessness. Web. **https://endhomelessness.org/homelessness-in-america/homelessness-statistics/state-of-homelessness-report/**

Top Causes of Homelessness. Home Aid America. Annual Homeless Statistics. Web. **http://www.homeaid.org/homeaid-stories/69/top-causes-of-homelessness**

Stanley, Charles. *The Gift of Forgiveness: Put the Past Behind You and Give...* Nashville, TN: Thomas Nelson, Inc. 1991. Kindle Edition.

Tolle, Eckhart *The Power of Now: A Guide to Spiritual Enlightenment.* Novato, CA: New World Library. 2009. E-Book Edition

Weiner, Stacy. AAMCNews. aamc.org. February 13th, 2018. Web.

Why aren't Psychologists Taught How to Prevent Suicides? Scientific American, Mental Health. The Editors. April 1st, 2018. Web.

Yogananda, Paramahansa. *Autobiography of a Yogi.* Los Angeles: Self-Realization Fellowship. 2007. Kindle Edition.

Reading List with Amazon Affiliate Links

Required Reading:

Alcoholics Anonymous. *The Big Book of Alcoholics Anonymous.*

--- *Twelve Steps and Twelve Traditions.*

Bernstein, Gabrielle. *The Universe Has Your Back: Transform Fear to Faith.*

Dass, Ram. *Polishing the Mirror: How to Live from Your Spiritual Heart.*

Milburn, Joshua Fields and Nicodemus, Ryan. *Minimalism: Live a Meaningful Life*

Hobbs, Jr. Robert L. *Heroin Living and Dying with an Addict You Love, How to Survive When Everyone Dies.*

McKeon, Greg. *Essentialism: The Disciplined Pursuit of Less.*

Ortner, Nick. *The Tapping Solution: A Revolutionary System for Stress-Free Living.*

Robbins, Anthony. *Notes from a Friend.* A Quick and Simple Guide for Taking Charge of Your Life

Singer, Michael. *The Surrender Experiment: My Journey into Life's Perfection.*

----*The Untethered Soul: A Journey Beyond Yourself.*

Tolle, Eckhart *The Power of Now: A Guide to Spiritual Enlightenment.* Novato, CA: New World Library. 2009. E-Book Edition

Yogananda, Paramahansa. *Autobiography of a Yogi.*

Optional Reading:

Chapman, Gary. *The 5 Love Languages: The Secret to Love that Lasts.*

Covey, Stephen. *The Seven Habits of Highly Effective People.*

Dyer, Wayne. *Change Your Thoughts, Change Your Life: Living the Wisdom of the Tao.*

Goldsmith, Joel, S. *The Infinite Way.*

Hill, Napoleon. *Think and Grow Rich.*

Hill, Napoleon, and Stone, W. Clement. *Success Through a Positive Mental Attitude.*

Rath, Tom. *Strengths Finder 2.0.*

Monahan, Evelyn, M. *The Miracle of Metaphysical Healing,*

Stanley, Charles. *The Gift of Forgiveness: Put the Past Behind You and Give…*

Rev. Dr. Robert Hobbs
The Realization of Stainless Souls
www.StainlessSouls.com

About

About Robert Hobbs

Robert Hobbs is a person in recovery and a trauma survivor. His practices include theocentric psychology, raja and kriya yoga, Neuro-Linguistic Programming (NLP), Eye Movement Desensitization and Reprocessing (EMDR/EFT), and strategic intervention. He is s a board-certified coach (BCC) number 3769, an ordained minister, and a member of the American Association of Christian Counsellors. He can be reached by email at RHobbs31@gmail.com.

Made in the USA
Monee, IL
07 July 2026

56552270R00181